PINHOK™
LANGUAGES

www.pinhok.com

Introduction

This Book

This vocabulary book contains more than 3000 words and phrases and is organized by topic to make it easier for you to pick what to learn first. On top of that, the second half of the book contains two index sections that can be used as basic dictionaries to look up words in either of the two languages. This book is well suited for learners of all levels who are looking for an extensive resource to improve their vocabulary or are interested in learning vocabularies in one particular area of interest.

Learning Community

If you find this book helpful, do us and other fellow learners a favour and leave a comment wherever you bought this book explaining how you use this book in your learning process. Your thoughts and experiences can help and have a positive impact on numerous other language learners around the world. We are looking forward to your stories and thank you in advance for your insights!

Pinhok Languages

Pinhok Languages strives to create language learning products that support learners around the world in their mission of learning a new language. In doing so, we combine best practice from various fields and industries to come up with innovative products and material.

The Pinhok Team hopes this book can help you with your learning process and gets you to your goal faster. Should you be interested in finding out more about us, please go to our website www.pinhok.com. For feedback, error reports, criticism or simply a quick "hi", please also go to our website and use the contact form.

Disclaimer of Liability

Table of Contents

Topics

Index

Animals

Mammals

English	Japanese	Handwriting
dog	犬 (inu)	いぬ
cat	猫 (neko)	ねこ
rabbit	うさぎ (usagi)	うさぎ
cow	牛 (ushi)	うし
sheep	羊 (hitsuji)	ひつじ
pig	豚 (buta)	ぶた
horse	馬 (uma)	うま
monkey	猿 (saru)	さる
bear	熊 (kuma)	くま
lion	ライオン (raion)	
tiger	虎 (tora)	とら
panda	パンダ (panda)	
giraffe	キリン (kirin)	麒麟
camel	らくだ (rakuda)	駱駝
elephant	象 (zō)	ぞう
wolf	狼 (ōkami)	おおかみ
rat	ラット (ratto)	
mouse (animal)	ねずみ (nezumi)	
zebra	シマウマ (shimauma)	斑馬(しまうま)
hippo	カバ (kaba)	河馬
polar bear	シロクマ (shirokuma)	白熊
rhino 犀牛	サイ (sai)	
kangaroo	カンガルー (kangarū)	
leopard 豹	ヒョウ (hyō)	
cheetah (非洲,印度)猎豹	チーター (chītā)	
donkey	ロバ (roba)	
ant-eater 食蚁兽	アリクイ (arikui)	
buffalo 美国野牛	バッファロー (baffarō)	
deer	鹿 (shika)	しか
squirrel	リス (risu)	栗鼠
elk 麋鹿	ヘラジカ (herajika)	

piglet	子豚 (kobuta)
bat	コウモリ (kōmori)
fox	きつね (kitsune) 狐
hamster	倉鼠 ハムスター (hamusutā)
guinea pig	豚鼠 モルモット (morumotto) marmotte
koala	コアラ (koara)
lemur	狐猴 きつねざる (kitsunezaru) 狐猿
meerkat	猫鼬, 狐獴 ミーアキャット (mīakyatto) あみじま
raccoon	アライグマ (araiguma) 浣熊
tapir	貘 バク (baku)
bison	野牛 バイソン (baison)
goat	ヤギ (yagi) 山羊
llama	羊駝 ラマ (rama)
red panda	レッサーパンダ (ressā panda) lesser panda
bull	雄牛 (oushi) おうし
hedgehog	刺猬 ハリネズミ (harinezumi) 針鼠
otter	水獺 かわうそ (kawauso) 川獺

Birds

pigeon	鳩 (hato) はと
duck	鴨 (kamo) かも
seagull	海鴎 カモメ (kamome) 鴎
chicken (animal)	鶏 (niwatori) にわとり
cockerel	おんどり (ondori) 雄鶏
goose	ガチョウ (gachō)
owl	猫头鷹 フクロウ (fukurō) 梟
swan	白鳥 (hakuchō) はくちょう
penguin	企鵝 ペンギン (pengin)
crow	烏鴉 カラス (karasu)
turkey	七面鳥 (shichimenchō) しちめんちょう
ostrich	駝鳥 ダチョウ (dachō)
stork	鸛 コウノトリ (kōnotori)
chick	雛 (hina) ひな
eagle	雕 鷲 (washi)

raven	カラス (karasu)
peacock	くじゃく (kujaku)
pelican	ペリカン (perikan)
parrot	オウム (ōmu)
magpie	カササギ (kasasagi)
flamingo	フラミンゴ (furamingo)
falcon	ハヤブサ (hayabusa)

Insects

fly	ハエ (hae)
butterfly	蝶 (chō)
bug	虫 (mushi)
bee	蜂 (hachi)
mosquito	蚊 (ka)
ant	アリ (ari)
dragonfly	とんぼ (tonbo)
grasshopper	バッタ (batta)
caterpillar	あおむし (aomushi)
wasp	スズメバチ (suzumebachi)
moth	蛾 (ga)
bumblebee	ミツバチ (mitsubachi)
termite	シロアリ (shiroari)
cricket	キリギリス (kirigirisu)
ladybird	てんとうむし (tentō mushi)
praying mantis	かまきり (kamakiri)

Marine Animals

fish (animal)	魚 (sakana)
whale	鯨 (kujira)
shark	サメ (same)
dolphin	イルカ (iruka)
seal	アザラシ (azarashi)
jellyfish	クラゲ (kurage)
squid	イカ (ika)

9

octopus	たこ (tako)
turtle	亀 (kame)
sea horse	タツノオトシゴ (tatsunootoshigo)
sea lion	アシカ (ashika)
walrus	セイウチ (seiuchi)
shell	貝 (kai)
starfish	ヒトデ (hitode)
killer whale	シャチ (shachi)
crab	カニ (kani)
lobster	ロブスター (robusutā)

Reptiles & More

snail	カタツムリ (katatsumuri)
spider	蜘蛛 (kumo)
frog	カエル (kaeru)
snake	ヘビ (hebi)
crocodile	ワニ (wani)
tortoise	陸亀 (rikugame)
scorpion	サソリ (sasori)
lizard	トカゲ (tokage)
chameleon	カメレオン (kamereon)
tarantula	タランチュラ (taranchura)
gecko	やもり (yamori)
dinosaur	恐竜 (kyōryū)

Sport

Summer

tennis	テニス (tenisu)
badminton	バドミントン (badominton)
boxing	ボクシング (bokushingu)
golf	ゴルフ (gorufu)
running	ランニング (ranningu)
cycling	サイクリング (saikuringu)
gymnastics	体操 (taisō)
table tennis	卓球 (takkyū)
weightlifting	重量挙げ (jūryō age)
long jump	幅跳び (habatobi)
triple jump	三段跳び (san dan tobi)
modern pentathlon	近代五種競技 (kindai go shu kyōgi)
rhythmic gymnastics	新体操 (shin taisō)
hurdles	ハードル競技 (hādoru kyōgi)
marathon	マラソン (marason)
pole vault	棒高跳び (bō takatobi)
high jump	高跳び (takatobi)
shot put	砲丸投げ (hōgan nage)
javelin throw	槍投げ (yarinage)
discus throw	円盤投げ (enban nage)
karate	空手 (karate)
triathlon	トライアスロン (toraiasuron)
taekwondo	テコンドー (tekondō)
sprint	スプリント (supurinto)
show jumping	障害飛越競技 (shōgai tobikoshi kyōgi)
shooting	射撃 (shageki)
wrestling	レスリング (resuringu)
mountain biking	マウンテンバイク (maunten baiku)
judo	柔道 (jūdō)
hammer throw	ハンマー投げ (hanmā nage)
fencing	フェンシング (fenshingu)

archery	アーチェリー (ācherī)
track cycling	トラックレース (torakku rēsu)

Winter

skiing	スキー (sukī)
snowboarding	スノーボーディング (sunō bōdingu)
ice skating	アイススケート (aisu sukēto)
ice hockey	アイスホッケー (aisu hokkē)
figure skating	フィギュアスケート (figyua sukēto)
curling	カーリング (kāringu)
Nordic combined	ノルディックコンバインド (norudikku konbaindo)
biathlon	バイアスロン (baiasuron)
luge	リュージュ (ryūju)
bobsleigh	ボブスレー (bobusurē)
short track	ショートトラック (shōto torakku)
skeleton	スケルトン (sukeruton)
ski jumping	スキージャンプ (sukī janpu)
cross-country skiing	クロスカントリースキー (kurosu kantorī sukī)
ice climbing	アイスクライミング (aisu kuraimingu)
freestyle skiing	フリースタイルスキー (furī sutairu sukī)
speed skating	スピードスケート (supīdo sukēto)

Team

football	サッカー (sakkā)
basketball	バスケットボール (basukettobōru)
volleyball	バレーボール (barēbōru)
cricket	クリケット (kuriketto)
baseball	野球 (yakyū)
rugby	ラグビー (ragubī)
handball	ハンドボール (handobōru)
polo	ポロ (poro)
lacrosse	ラクロス (rakurosu)
field hockey	陸上ホッケー (rikujō hokkē)
beach volleyball	ビーチバレー (bīchi barē)

Australian football	オーストラリアンフットボール (ōsutorarian futtobōru)
American football	アメリカンフットボール (amerikan futtobōru)

Water

swimming	水泳 (suiei)
water polo	水球 (suikyū)
diving (into the water)	飛込競技 (tobikomi kyōgi)
surfing	サーフィン (sāfin)
rowing	ボート競技 (bōto kyōgi)
synchronized swimming	シンクロナイズドスイミング (shinkuronaizudo suimingu)
diving (under the water)	ダイビング (daibingu)
windsurfing	ウインドサーフィン (uindosāfin)
sailing	セーリング (sēringu)
waterskiing	水上スキー (suijō sukī)
rafting	ラフティング (rafutingu)
cliff diving	クリフダイビング (kurifu daibingu)
canoeing	カヌー競技 (kanū kyōgi)

Motor

car racing	カーレース (kā rēsu)
rally racing	ラリー (rarī)
motorcycle racing	オートバイレース (ōtobai rēsu)
motocross	モトクロス (motokurosu)
Formula 1	F1 (F1)
kart	レーシングカート (rēshingu kāto)
jet ski	ジェットスキー (jetto sukī)

Other

hiking	ハイキング (haikingu)
mountaineering	登山 (tozan)
snooker	スヌーカー (sunūkā)
parachuting	パラシューティング (para shūtingu)
poker	ポーカー (pōkā)

dancing	ダンス (dansu)
bowling	ボーリング (bōringu)
skateboarding	スケートボーディング (sukēto bōdingu)
chess	チェス (chesu)
bodybuilding	ボディービルディング (bodībirudingu)
yoga	ヨガ (yoga)
ballet	バレエ (barē)
bungee jumping	バンジージャンプ (banjī janpu)
climbing	クライミング (kuraimingu)
roller skating	ローラースケーティング (rōrā sukētingu)
breakdance	ブレイクダンス (bureiku dansu)
billiards	ビリヤード (biriyādo)

Gym

warm-up	ウオームアップ (uōmu appu)
stretching	ストレッチ (sutorecchi)
sit-ups	シットアップ (shitto appu)
push-up	腕立て伏せ (udetate fuse)
squat	スクワット (sukuwatto)
treadmill	トレッドミル (toreddomiru)
bench press	ベンチプレス (benchi puresu)
exercise bike	フィットネスバイク (fittonesu baiku)
cross trainer	クロストレーナー (kurosu torēnā)
circuit training	サーキットトレーニング (sākitto torēningu)
Pilates	ピラティス (piratisu)
leg press	レッグプレス (reggu puresu)
aerobics	エアロビクス (earobikusu)
dumbbell	ダンベル (danberu)
barbell	バーベル (bāberu)
sauna	サウナ (sauna)

Geography

Europe

United Kingdom	イギリス (Igirisu)
Spain	スペイン (Supein)
Italy	イタリア (Itaria)
France	フランス (Furansu)
Germany	ドイツ (Doitsu)
Switzerland	スイス (Suisu)
Albania	アルバニア (Arubania)
Andorra	アンドラ (Andora)
Austria	オーストリア (Ōsutoria)
Belgium	ベルギー (Berugī)
Bosnia	ボスニア (Bosunia)
Bulgaria	ブルガリア (Burugaria)
Denmark	デンマーク (Denmāku)
Estonia	エストニア (Esutonia)
Faroe Islands	フェロー諸島 (Ferō Shotō)
Finland	フィンランド (Finrando)
Gibraltar	ジブラルタル (Jiburarutaru)
Greece	ギリシャ (Girisha)
Ireland	アイルランド (Airurando)
Iceland	アイスランド (Aisurando)
Kosovo	コソボ (Kosobo)
Croatia	クロアチア (Kuroachia)
Latvia	ラトビア (Ratobia)
Liechtenstein	リヒテンシュタイン (Rihitenshutain)
Lithuania	リトアニア (Ritoania)
Luxembourg	ルクセンブルク (Rukusenburuku)
Malta	マルタ (Maruta)
Macedonia	マケドニア (Makedonia)
Moldova	モルドバ (Morudoba)
Monaco	モナコ (Monako)
Montenegro	モンテネグロ (Monteneguro)

Netherlands	オランダ (Oranda)
Norway	ノルウェー (Noruwē)
Poland	ポーランド (Pōrando)
Portugal	ポルトガル (Porutogaru)
Romania	ルーマニア (Rūmania)
San Marino	サンマリノ (Sanmarino)
Sweden	スウェーデン (Suwēden)
Serbia	セルビア (Serubia)
Slovakia	スロバキア (Surobakia)
Slovenia	スロベニア (Surobenia)
Czech Republic	チェコ共和国 (Cheko Kyōwakoku)
Turkey	トルコ (Toruko)
Ukraine	ウクライナ (Ukuraina)
Hungary	ハンガリー (Hangarī)
Vatican City	バチカン市国 (Bachikan Shikoku)
Belarus	ベラルーシ (Berarūshi)
Cyprus	キプロス (Kipurosu)

Asia

China	中国 (Chūgoku)
Russia	ロシア (Roshia)
India	インド (Indo)
Singapore	シンガポール (Shingapōru)
Japan	日本 (Nihon/Nippon)
South Korea	韓国 (Kankoku)
Afghanistan	アフガニスタン (Afuganisutan)
Armenia	アルメニア (Arumenia)
Azerbaijan	アゼルバイジャン (Azerubaijan)
Bahrain	バーレーン (Bārēn)
Bangladesh	バングラデシュ (Banguradeshu)
Bhutan	ブータン (Būtan)
Brunei	ブルネイ (Burunei)
Georgia	ジョージア (Jōjia)
Hong Kong	香港 (Honkon)

Indonesia	インドネシア	(Indoneshia)
Iraq	イラク	(Iraku)
Iran	イラン	(Iran)
Israel	イスラエル	(Isuraeru)
Yemen	イエメン	(Iemen)
Jordan	ヨルダン	(Yorudan)
Cambodia	カンボジア	(Kanbojia)
Kazakhstan	カザフスタン	(Kazafusutan)
Qatar	カタール	(Katāru)
Kyrgyzstan	キルギスタン	(Kirugisutan)
Kuwait	クウェート	(Kuwēto)
Laos	ラオス	(Raosu)
Lebanon	レバノン	(Rebanon)
Macao	マカオ	(Makao)
Malaysia	マレーシア	(Marēshia)
Maldives	モルディブ	(Morudibu)
Mongolia	モンゴル	(Mongoru)
Burma	ミャンマー	(Myanmā)
Nepal	ネパール	(Nepāru)
North Korea	北朝鮮	(Kitachōsen)
Oman	オマーン	(Omān)
East Timor	東チモール	(Higashichimōru)
Pakistan	パキスタン	(Pakisutan)
Palestine	パレスチナ	(Paresuchina)
Philippines	フィリピン	(Firipin)
Saudi Arabia	サウジアラビア	(Saujiarabia)
Sri Lanka	スリランカ	(Suriranka)
Syria	シリア	(Shiria)
Tajikistan	タジキスタン	(Tajikisutan)
Taiwan	台湾	(Taiwan)
Thailand	タイ	(Tai)
Turkmenistan	トルクメニスタン	(Torukumenisutan)
Uzbekistan	ウズベキスタン	(Uzubekisutan)
United Arab Emirates	アラブ首長国連邦	(Arabu Shuchōkoku Renpō)

Vietnam	ベトナム (Betonamu)

America

The United States of America	アメリカ合衆国 (Amerika Gasshūkoku)
Mexico	メキシコ (Mekishiko)
Canada	カナダ (Kanada)
Brazil	ブラジル (Burajiru)
Argentina	アルゼンチン (Aruzenchin)
Chile	チリ (Chiri)
Antigua and Barbuda	アンティグア・バーブーダ (Antigua Bābūda)
Aruba	アルバ (Aruba)
The Bahamas	バハマ (Bahama)
Barbados	バルバドス (Barubadosu)
Belize	ベリーズ (Berīzu)
Bolivia	ボリビア (Boribia)
Cayman Islands	ケイマン諸島 (Keiman shotō)
Costa Rica	コスタリカ (Kosutarika)
Dominica	ドミニカ (Dominika)
Dominican Republic	ドミニカ共和国 (Dominika Kyōwakoku)
Ecuador	エクアドル (Ekuadoru)
El Salvador	エルサルバドル (Erusarubadoru)
Falkland Islands	フォークランド諸島 (Fōkurando Shotō)
Grenada	グレナダ (Gurenada)
Greenland	グリーンランド (Gurīn Rando)
Guatemala	グアテマラ (Guatemara)
Guyana	ガイアナ (Gaiana)
Haiti	ハイチ (Haichi)
Honduras	ホンジュラス (Honjurasu)
Jamaica	ジャマイカ (Jamaika)
Colombia	コロンビア (Koronbia)
Cuba	キューバ (Kyūba)
Montserrat	モントセラト (Montoserato)
Nicaragua	ニカラグア (Nikaragua)
Panama	パナマ (Panama)

Paraguay	パラグアイ (Paraguai)
Peru	ペルー (Perū)
Puerto Rico	プエルトリコ (Puerutoriko)
Saint Kitts and Nevis	セントキッツ・ネイビス連邦 (Sentokittsu Neibisu Renpō)
Saint Lucia	セントルシア (Sentorushia)
Saint Vincent and the Grenadines	セントビンセント・グレナディーン (Sentobinsento Gurenadīn)
Suriname	スリナム (Surinamu)
Trinidad and Tobago	トリニダードトバゴ (Torinidādotobago)
Uruguay	ウルグアイ (Uruguai)
Venezuela	ベネズエラ (Benezuera)

Africa

South Africa	南アフリカ (Minamiafurika)
Nigeria	ナイジェリア (Naijeria)
Morocco	モロッコ (Morokko)
Libya	リビア (Ribia)
Kenya	ケニア (Kenia)
Algeria	アルジェリア (Arujeria)
Egypt	エジプト (Ejiputo)
Ethiopia	エチオピア (Echiopia)
Angola	アンゴラ (Angora)
Benin	ベニン (Benin)
Botswana	ボツワナ (Botsuwana)
Burkina Faso	ブルキナファソ (Burukinafaso)
Burundi	ブルンジ (Burunji)
Democratic Republic of the Congo	コンゴ民主共和国 (Kongo Minshu Kyōwakoku)
Djibouti	ジブチ (Jibuchi)
Equatorial Guinea	赤道ギニア (Sekidōginia)
Ivory Coast	コートジボワール (Kōtojibowāru)
Eritrea	エリトリア (Eritoria)
Gabon	ガボン (Gabon)
The Gambia	ガンビア (Ganbia)
Ghana	ガーナ (Gāna)

Guinea	ギニア (Ginia)
Guinea-Bissau	ギニアビサウ (Giniabisau)
Cameroon	カメルーン (Kamerūn)
Cape Verde	カーボベルデ (Kābo Berude)
Comoros	コモロ (Komoro)
Lesotho	レソト (Resoto)
Liberia	リベリア (Riberia)
Madagascar	マダガスカル (Madagasukaru)
Malawi	マラウイ (Maraui)
Mali	マリ (Mari)
Mauritania	モーリタニア (Mōritania)
Mauritius	モーリシャス (Mōrishasu)
Mozambique	モザンビーク (Mozanbīku)
Namibia	ナミビア (Namibia)
Niger	ニジェール (Nijēru)
Republic of the Congo	コンゴ共和国 (Kongo Kyōwakoku)
Rwanda	ルワンダ (Ruwanda)
Zambia	ザンビア (Zanbia)
São Tomé and Príncipe	サントメプリンシペ (Santomepurinshipe)
Senegal	セネガル (Senegaru)
Seychelles	セイシェル (Seisheru)
Sierra Leone	シエラレオネ (Shierareone)
Zimbabwe	ジンバブエ (Jinbabue)
Somalia	ソマリア (Somaria)
Sudan	スーダン (Sūdan)
South Sudan	南スーダン (Minami Sūdan)
Swaziland	スワジランド (Suwajirando)
Tanzania	タンザニア (Tanzania)
Togo	トーゴ (Tōgo)
Chad	チャド (Chado)
Tunisia	チュニジア (Chunijia)
Uganda	ウガンダ (Uganda)
Central African Republic	中央アフリカ共和国 (Chūō Afurika Kyōwakoku)

Oceania

Australia	オーストラリア (Ōsutoraria)
New Zealand	ニュージーランド (Nyūjīrando)
Fiji	フィジー (Fijī)
American Samoa	アメリカ領サモア (Amerikaryō Samoa)
Cook Islands	クック諸島 (Kukku Shotō)
French Polynesia	フランス領ポリネシア (Furansuryō Porineshia)
Kiribati	キリバス (Kiribasu)
Marshall Islands	マーシャル諸島 (Māsharu Shotō)
Micronesia	ミクロネシア (Mikuroneshia)
Nauru	ナウル (Nauru)
New Caledonia	ニューカレドニア (Nyūkaredonia)
Niue	ニウエ (Niue)
Palau	パラオ (Parao)
Papua New Guinea	パプアニューギニア (Papuanyūginia)
Solomon Islands	ソロモン諸島 (Soromon Shotō)
Samoa	サモア (Samoa)
Tonga	トンガ (Tonga)
Tuvalu	ツバル (Tsubaru)
Vanuatu	バヌアツ (Banuatsu)

Numbers

0-20

0	零	(rei)
1	一	(ichi)
2	二	(ni)
3	三	(san)
4	四	(yon/shi)
5	五	(go)
6	六	(roku)
7	七	(nana)
8	八	(hachi)
9	九	(kyū)
10	十	(jū)
11	十一	(jū ichi)
12	十二	(jū ni)
13	十三	(jū san)
14	十四	(jū yon)
15	十五	(jū go)
16	十六	(jū roku)
17	十七	(jū nana)
18	十八	(jū hachi)
19	十九	(jū kyū)
20	二十	(nijū)

21-100

21	二十一	(nijū ichi)
22	二十二	(nijū ni)
26	二十六	(nijū roku)
30	三十	(sanjū)
31	三十一	(sanjū ichi)
33	三十三	(sanjū san)
37	三十七	(sanjū nana)
40	四十	(yonjū)

41	四十一 (yonjū ichi)
44	四十四 (yonjū yon)
48	四十八 (yonjū hachi)
50	五十 (gojū)
51	五十一 (gojū ichi)
55	五十五 (gojū go)
59	五十九 (gojū kyū)
60	六十 (rokujū)
61	六十一 (rokujū ichi)
62	六十二 (rokujū ni)
66	六十六 (rokujū roku)
70	七十 (nanajū)
71	七十一 (nanajū ichi)
73	七十三 (nanajū san)
77	七十七 (nanajū nana)
80	八十 (hachijū)
81	八十一 (hachijū ichi)
84	八十四 (hachijū yon)
88	八十八 (hachijū hachi)
90	九十 (kyūjū)
91	九十一 (kyūjū ichi)
95	九十五 (kyūjū go)
99	九十九 (kyūjū kyū)
100	百 (hyaku)

101-1000

101	百一 (hyaku ichi)
105	百五 (hyaku go)
110	百十 (hyaku jū)
151	百五十一 (hyaku gojū ichi)
200	二百 (nihyaku)
202	二百二 (nihyaku ni)
206	二百六 (nihyaku roku)
220	二百二十 (nihyaku nijū)

262	二百六十二 (nihyaku rokujū ni)
300	三百 (sanbyaku)
303	三百三 (sanbyaku san)
307	三百七 (sanbyaku nana)
330	三百三十 (sanbyaku sanjū)
373	三百七十三 (sanbyaku nanajū san)
400	四百 (yonhyaku)
404	四百四 (yonhyaku yon)
408	四百八 (yonhyaku hachi)
440	四百四十 (yonhyaku yonjū)
484	四百八十四 (yonhyaku hachijū yon)
500	五百 (gohyaku)
505	五百五 (gohyaku go)
509	五百九 (gohyaku kyū)
550	五百五十 (gohyaku gojū)
595	五百九十五 (gohyaku kyūjū go)
600	六百 (roppyaku)
601	六百一 (roppyaku ichi)
606	六百六 (roppyaku roku)
616	六百十六 (roppyaku jū roku)
660	六百六十 (roppyaku rokujū)
700	七百 (nanahyaku)
702	七百二 (nanahyaku ni)
707	七百七 (nanahyaku nana)
727	七百二十七 (nanahyaku nijū nana)
770	七百七十 (nanahyaku nanajū)
800	八百 (happyaku)
803	八百三 (happyaku san)
808	八百八 (happyaku hachi)
838	八百三十八 (happyaku sanjū hachi)
880	八百八十 (happyaku hachijū)
900	九百 (kyūhyaku)
904	九百四 (kyūhyaku yon)
909	九百九 (kyūhyaku kyū)

949	九百四十九 (kyūhyaku yonjū kyū)
990	九百九十 (kyūhyaku kyūjū)
1000	千 (sen)

1001-10000

1001	千一 (sen ichi)
1012	千十二 (sen jū ni)
1234	千二百三十四 (sen nihyaku sanjū yon)
2000	二千 (nisen)
2002	二千二 (nisen ni)
2023	二千二十三 (nisen nijū san)
2345	二千三百四十五 (nisen sanbyaku yonjū go)
3000	三千 (sanzen)
3003	三千三 (sanzen san)
3034	三千三十四 (sanzen sanjū yon)
3456	三千四百五十六 (sanzen yonhyaku gojū roku)
4000	四千 (yonsen)
4004	四千四 (yonsen yon)
4045	四千四十五 (yonsen yonjū go)
4567	四千五百六十七 (yonsen gohyaku rokujū nana)
5000	五千 (gosen)
5005	五千五 (gosen go)
5056	五千五十六 (gosen gojū roku)
5678	五千六百七十八 (gosen roppyaku nanajū hachi)
6000	六千 (rokusen)
6006	六千六 (rokusen roku)
6067	六千六十七 (rokusen rokujū nana)
6789	六千七百八十九 (rokusen nanahyaku hachijū kyū)
7000	七千 (nanasen)
7007	七千七 (nanasen nana)
7078	七千七十八 (nanasen nanajū hachi)
7890	七千八百九十 (nanasen happyaku kyūjū)
8000	八千 (hassen)
8008	八千八 (hassen hachi)

8089	八千八十九 (hassen hachijū kyū)
8901	八千九百一 (hassen kyūhyaku ichi)
9000	九千 (kyūsen)
9009	九千九 (kyūsen kyū)
9012	九千十二 (kyūsen jū ni)
9090	九千九十 (kyūsen kyūjū)
10.000	一万 (ichi man)

> 10000

10.001	一万一 (ichi man ichi)
20.020	二万二十 (ni man nijū)
30.300	三万三百 (san man sanbyaku)
44.000	四万四千 (yon man yonsen)
100.000	十万 (jū man)
500.000	五十万 (gojū man)
1.000.000	百万 (hyaku man)
6.000.000	六百万 (roppyaku man)
10.000.000	一千万 (issen man)
70.000.000	七千万 (nanasen man)
100.000.000	一億 (ichi oku)
800.000.000	八億 (hachi oku)
1.000.000.000	十億 (jū oku)
9.000.000.000	九十億 (kyūjū oku)
10.000.000.000	百億 (hyaku oku)
20.000.000.000	二百億 (nihyaku oku)
100.000.000.000	一千億 (issen oku)
300.000.000.000	三千億 (sanzen oku)
1.000.000.000.000	一兆 (ichi chō)

Body

Head

nose	鼻	(hana)
eye	目	(me)
ear	耳	(mimi)
mouth	口	(kuchi)
tooth	歯	(ha)
lip	唇	(kuchibiru)
hair	髪の毛	(kaminoke)
beard	髭	(hige)
forehead	額	(hitai)
eyebrow	眉	(mayu)
eyelashes	睫毛	(matsuge)
pupil	瞳孔	(dōkō)
cheek	頬	(hō)
chin	顎	(ago)
dimple	えくぼ	(ekubo)
wrinkle	皺	(shiwa)
freckles	そばかす	(sobakasu)
tongue	舌	(shita)
nostril	鼻孔	(bikō)
temple	こめかみ	(komekami)

Body Parts

head	頭部	(tōbu)
arm	腕	(ude)
hand	手	(te)
leg	足	(ashi)
knee	膝	(hiza)
foot	脚	(ashi)
belly	腹	(hara)
belly button	臍	(heso)
bosom	胸	(mune)

27

chest	胸部 (kyōbu)
elbow	肘 (hiji)
nipple	乳首 (chikubi)
shoulder	肩 (kata)
neck	首 (kubi)
bottom	尻 (shiri)
nape	項 (kō)
back (part of body)	背中 (senaka)
waist	ウエスト (uesuto)

Hand & Foot

finger	指 (yubi)
thumb	親指 (oyayubi)
fingernail	爪 (tsume)
toe	つま先 (tsumasaki)
heel	かかと (kakato)
palm	手のひら (tenohira)
wrist	手首 (tekubi)
fist	拳 (kobushi)
Achilles tendon	アキレス腱 (Akiresu ken)
index finger	人差し指 (hitosashi yubi)
middle finger	中指 (nakayubi)
ring finger	薬指 (kusuriyubi)
little finger	小指 (koyubi)

Bones & More

bone (part of body)	骨 (hone)
muscle	筋肉 (kinniku)
tendon	腱 (ken)
vertebra	椎骨 (tsuikotsu)
pelvis	骨盤 (kotsuban)
breastbone	胸骨 (kyōkotsu)
rib	肋骨 (rokkotsu)
collarbone	鎖骨 (sakotsu)

skeleton	骸骨 (gaikotsu)
skull	頭蓋骨 (zugaikotsu)
shoulder blade	肩胛骨 (kenkōkotsu)
kneecap	膝頭 (hizagashira)
cartilage	軟骨 (nankotsu)
jawbone	顎骨 (gakkotsu)
nasal bone	鼻骨 (bikotsu)
spine	背骨 (sebone)
ankle	踝 (kurubushi)
bone marrow	骨髄 (kotsuzui)

Organs

heart	心臓 (shinzō)
lung	肺 (hai)
liver	肝臓 (kanzō)
kidney	腎臓 (jinzō)
vein	静脈 (jōmyaku)
artery	動脈 (dōmyaku)
stomach	胃 (i)
intestine	腸 (chō)
bladder	膀胱 (bōkō)
brain	脳 (nō)
anus	肛門 (kōmon)
appendix	盲腸 (mōchō)
spleen	脾臓 (hizō)
oesophagus	食道 (shokudō)
nerve	神経 (shinkei)
spinal cord	脊髄 (sekizui)
pancreas	膵臓 (suizō)
gall bladder	胆嚢 (tannō)
colon	結腸 (kecchō)
small intestine	小腸 (shōchō)
windpipe	気管 (kikan)
diaphragm	横隔膜 (ōkakumaku)

duodenum	十二指腸 (jūnishichō)

Reproduction

testicle	睾丸 (kōgan)
penis	陰茎 (inkei)
prostate	前立腺 (zenritsu sen)
ovary	卵巣 (ransō)
oviduct	卵管 (rankan)
uterus	子宮 (shikyū)
ovum	卵子 (ranshi)
sperm	精子 (seishi)
scrotum	陰嚢 (innō)
clitoris	クリトリス (kuritorisu)
vagina	膣 (chitsu)

Adjective

Colours

white	白 (shiro)
black	黒 (kuro)
grey	灰色 (haiiro)
green	緑 (midori)
blue	青 (ao)
red	赤 (aka)
pink	桃色 (momoiro)
orange (colour)	橙 (daidai)
purple	紫 (murasaki)
yellow	黄色 (kiiro)
brown	茶色 (chairo)
beige	ベージュ (bēju)

Basics

heavy	重い (omoi)
light (weight)	軽い (karui)
correct	正しい (tadashī)
difficult	難しい (muzukashī)
easy	簡単な (kantan na)
wrong	間違った (machigatta)
many	多い (ōi)
few	少ない (sukunai)
new	新しい (atarashī)
old (not new)	古い (furui)
slow	遅い (osoi)
quick	速い (hayai)
poor	貧しい (mazushī)
rich	豊富な (hōfu na)
funny	面白い (omoshiroi)
boring	つまらない (tsumaranai)
fair	公平な (kōhei na)

31

unfair	不公平な (fu kōhei na)

Feelings

good	良い (yoi)
bad	悪い (warui)
weak	弱い (yowai)
happy	嬉しい (ureshī)
sad	悲しい (kanashī)
strong	強い (tsuyoi)
angry	怒り (ikari)
healthy	健康的な (kenkōteki na)
sick	病気の (byōki no)
hungry	腹ペコ (harapeko)
thirsty	渇く (kawaku)
full (from eating)	満腹 (manpuku)
proud	誇り高い (hokori takai)
lonely	寂しい (sabishī)
tired	疲れた (tsukareta)
safe (adjective)	安心な (anshin na)

Space

short (length)	短い (mijikai)
long	長い (nagai)
round	丸い (marui)
small	小さい (chīsai)
big	大きな (ōkina)
square (adjective)	角ばった (kakubatta)
twisting	ねじれた (nejireta)
straight (line)	まっすぐな (massugu na)
high	高い (takai)
low	低い (hikui)
steep	急な (kyū na)
flat	平らな (taira na)
shallow	浅い (asai)

deep	深い (fukai)
broad	幅広い (habahiroi)
narrow	狭い (semai)
huge	広い (hiroi)

Place

right	右 (migi)
left	左 (hidari)
above	上 (ue)
back (position)	後ろ (ushiro)
front	前 (mae)
below	下 (shita)
here	ここ (koko)
there	あそこ (asoko)
close	近い (chikai)
far	遠い (tōi)
inside	中 (naka)
outside	外 (soto)
beside	横 (yoko)
north	北 (kita)
east	東 (higashi)
south	南 (minami)
west	西 (nishi)

Things

cheap	安い (yasui)
expensive	高い (takai)
full (not empty)	満タン (mantan)
hard	固い (katai)
soft	柔らかい (yawarakai)
empty	空っぽ (karappo)
light (colour)	明るい (akarui)
dark	暗い (kurai)
clean	きれい (kirei)

dirty	汚い (kitanai)
boiled	ゆでた (yudeta)
raw	生 (nama)
strange	風変わりな (fūgawari na)
sour	酸っぱい (suppai)
sweet	甘い (amai)
salty	塩辛い (shiokarai)
hot (spicy)	辛い (tsurai)
juicy	ジューシー (jūshī)

People

short (height)	背が低い (se ga hikui)
tall	背が高い (se ga takai)
slim	スリム (surimu)
young	若い (wakai)
old (not young)	年寄り (toshiyori)
plump	豊満 (hōman)
skinny	細身 (hosomi)
chubby	太った (futotta)
cute	可愛い (kawaī)
clever	賢い (kashikoi)
evil	意地悪い (iji warui)
well-behaved	行儀のよい (gyōgi no yoi)
cool	かっこいい (kakko ī)
worried	心配している (shinpai shite iru)
surprised	驚いた (odoroita)
sober	しらふ (shirafu)
drunk	酔っぱらっている (yopparatte iru)
blind	目が見えない (me ga mienai)
mute	口がきけない (kuchi ga kikenai)
deaf	耳が聞こえない (mimi ga kikoenai)
guilty	有罪な (yūzai na)
friendly	フレンドリーな (furendorī na)
busy	忙しい (isogashī)

bloody	血まみれ (chimamire)
pale	青白い (aojiroi)
strict	厳しい (kibishī)
holy	聖なる (sei naru)
beautiful	美しい (utsukushī)
silly	ばかばかしい (bakabakashī)
crazy	狂った (kurutta)
ugly	醜い (minikui)
handsome	ハンサム (hansamu)
greedy	欲深い (yokubukai)
generous	寛大な (kandai na)
brave	勇敢な (yūkan na)
shy	恥ずかしそうな (hazukashi sō na)
lazy	怠惰な (taida na)
sexy	セクシー (sekushī)
stupid	愚かな (oroka na)

Outside

cold (adjective)	寒い (samui)
hot (temperature)	暑い (atsui)
warm	暖かい (atatakai)
silent	静か (shizuka)
quiet	静かな (shizuka na)
loud	うるさい (urusai)
wet	濡れた (nureta)
dry	乾いた (kawaita)
windy	風が強い (kaze ga tsuyoi)
cloudy	曇った (kumotta)
foggy	霧のかかった (kiri no kakatta)
rainy	雨の (ame no)
sunny	晴れ (hare)

Verb

Basics

to open (e.g. a door)	開く (hiraku)
to close	閉める (shimeru)
to sit	座る (suwaru)
to turn on	つける (tsukeru)
to turn off	消す (kesu)
to stand	立つ (tatsu)
to lie	横になる (yoko ni naru)
to come	来る (kuru)
to think	考える (kangaeru)
to know	知る (shiru)
to fail	失敗する (shippai suru)
to win	勝つ (katsu)
to lose	負ける (makeru)
to live	生きる (ikiru)
to die	死ぬ (shinu)

Action

to take	取る (toru)
to put	置く (oku)
to find	見つける (mitsukeru)
to smoke	吸う (sū)
to steal	盗む (nusumu)
to kill	殺す (korosu)
to fly	飛ぶ (tobu)
to carry	運ぶ (hakobu)
to rescue	救う (sukū)
to burn	焼く (yaku)
to injure	怪我をする (kega o suru)
to attack	攻撃する (kōgeki suru)
to defend	守る (mamoru)
to fall	落ちる (ochiru)

to vote	投票する (tōhyō suru)
to choose	選ぶ (erabu)
to gamble	ギャンブルする (gyanburu suru)
to shoot	撃つ (utsu)
to saw	挽く (hiku)
to drill	ドリルする (doriru suru)
to hammer	槌で打つ (tsuchi de utsu)

Body

to eat	食べる (taberu)
to drink	飲む (nomu)
to talk	話す (hanasu)
to laugh	笑う (warau)
to cry	泣く (naku)
to sing	歌う (utau)
to walk	歩く (aruku)
to watch	見る (miru)
to work	働く (hataraku)
to breathe	息をする (iki o suru)
to smell	匂いを嗅ぐ (nioi o kagu)
to listen	聞く (kiku)
to lose weight	痩せる (yaseru)
to gain weight	太る (futoru)
to shrink	収縮する (shūshuku suru)
to grow	成長する (seichō suru)
to smile	笑顔になる (egao ni naru)
to whisper	囁く (sasayaku)
to touch	触る (sawaru)
to shiver	震える (furueru)
to bite	噛む (kamu)
to swallow	飲む (nomu)
to faint	気絶する (kizetsu suru)
to stare	見つめる (mitsumeru)
to kick	蹴る (keru)

to shout	叫ぶ (sakebu)
to spit	唾を吐く (tsuba o haku)
to vomit	吐く (haku)

Interaction

to ask	質問する (shitsumon suru)
to answer	答える (kotaeru)
to help	助ける (tasukeru)
to like	好む (konomu)
to love	愛する (aisuru)
to give (somebody something)	与える (ataeru)
to marry	結婚する (kekkon suru)
to meet	会う (au)
to kiss	キスする (kisu suru)
to argue	喧嘩する (kenka suru)
to share	分け合う (wakeau)
to warn	警告する (keikoku suru)
to follow	従う (shitagau)
to hide	隠す (kakusu)
to bet	賭ける (kakeru)
to feed	食べさせる (tabesaseru)
to threaten	脅す (odosu)
to give a massage	マッサージをする (massāji o suru)

Movements

to run	走る (hashiru)
to swim	泳ぐ (oyogu)
to jump	跳ぶ (tobu)
to lift	持ち上げる (mochiageru)
to pull (... open)	引く (hiku)
to push (... open)	押す (osu)
to press (a button)	押す (osu)
to throw	投げる (nageru)
to crawl	這う (hau)

to fight	戦う (tatakau)
to catch	キャッチする (kyacchi suru)
to hit	叩く (tataku)
to climb	登る (noboru)
to roll	転がる (korogaru)
to dig	掘る (horu)

Business

to buy	買う (kau)
to pay	支払う (shiharau)
to sell	売る (uru)
to study	勉強する (benkyō suru)
to practice	練習する (renshū suru)
to call	電話する (denwa suru)
to read	読む (yomu)
to write	書く (kaku)
to calculate	計算する (keisan suru)
to measure	測る (hakaru)
to earn	得る (uru/eru)
to look for	探す (sagasu)
to cut	切る (kiru)
to count	数える (kazoeru)
to scan	スキャンする (sukyan suru)
to print	印刷する (insatsu suru)
to copy	コピーする (kopī suru)
to fix	修正する (shūsei suru)
to quote	引用する (in yō suru)
to deliver	届ける (todokeru)

Home

to sleep	寝る (neru)
to dream	夢をみる (yume o miru)
to wait	待つ (matsu)
to clean	掃除する (sōji suru)

to wash	洗う (arau)
to cook	料理する (ryōri suru)
to play	遊ぶ (asobu)
to travel	旅行する (ryokō suru)
to enjoy	楽しむ (tanoshimu)
to bake	焼く (yaku)
to fry	炒める (itameru)
to boil	茹でる (yuderu)
to pray	祈る (inoru)
to rest	休憩する (kyūkei suru)
to lock	鍵をかける (kagi o kakeru)
to open (unlock)	開ける (akeru)
to celebrate	祝う (iwau)
to dry	乾かす (kawakasu)
to fish	釣る (tsuru)
to take a shower	シャワーを浴びる (shawā o abiru)
to iron	アイロンをかける (airon o kakeru)
to vacuum	掃除機をかける (sōji ki o kakeru)
to paint	塗る (nuru)

House

Parts

door	ドア (doa)
window (building)	窓 (mado)
wall	壁 (kabe)
roof	屋根 (yane)
elevator	エレベーター (erebētā)
stairs	階段 (kaidan)
toilet (at home)	トイレ (toire)
attic	屋根裏部屋 (yaneura heya)
basement	地下室 (chika shitsu)
solar panel	ソーラーパネル (sōrā paneru)
chimney	煙突 (entotsu)
fifth floor	六階 (roku kai)
first floor	二階 (ni kai)
ground floor	一階 (ikkai)
first basement floor	地下一階 (chika ikkai)
second basement floor	地下二階 (chika ni kai)
living room	リビング (ribingu)
bedroom	寝室 (shinshitsu)
kitchen	キッチン (kicchin)
corridor	廊下 (rōka)
front door	表玄関 (omotegenkan)
bathroom	バスルーム (basurūmu)
workroom	仕事部屋 (shigoto heya)
nursery	子供部屋 (kodomo heya)
floor	床 (yuka)
ceiling	天井 (tenjō)
garage door	車庫のドア (shako no doa)
garage	車庫 (shako)
garden	庭 (niwa)
balcony	ベランダ (beranda)
terrace	テラス (terasu)

Devices

TV set	テレビセット (terebi setto)
remote control	リモコン (rimokon)
security camera	監視カメラ (kanshi kamera)
rice cooker	炊飯器 (suihan ki)
router	ルーター (rūtā)
heating	暖房装置 (danbō sōchi)
washing machine	洗濯機 (sentaku ki)
fridge	冷蔵庫 (reizō ko)
freezer	冷凍庫 (reitō ko)
microwave	電子レンジ (denshi renji)
oven	オーブン (ōbun)
cooker	焜炉 (konro)
cooker hood	レンジフード (renji fūdo)
dishwasher	食器洗い機 (shokki arai ki)
kettle	やかん (yakan)
mixer	ミキサー (mikisā)
electric iron	電気アイロン (denki airon)
toaster	トースター (tōsutā)
hairdryer	ヘアドライヤー (hea doraiyā)
ironing table	アイロン台 (airon dai)
vacuum cleaner	掃除機 (sōji ki)
coffee machine	コーヒーマシン (kōhī mashin)
air conditioner	エアコン (eakon)
satellite dish	テレビ受信用アンテナ (terebi jushin yō antena)
fan	換気扇 (kanki sen)
radiator	ラジエーター (rajiētā)
sewing machine	ミシン (mishin)

Kitchen

spoon	スプーン (supūn)
fork	フォーク (fōku)
knife	ナイフ (naifu)

plate	皿 (sara)
bowl	ボウル (bōru)
glass	グラス (gurasu)
cup (for cold drinks)	コップ (koppu)
garbage bin	ゴミ箱 (gomibako)
chopstick	箸 (hashi)
light bulb	電球 (denkyū)
pan	フライパン (furaipan)
pot	鍋 (nabe)
ladle	しゃもじ (shamoji)
cup (for hot drinks)	カップ (kappu)
teapot	ティーポット (tīpotto)
grater	おろし金 (oroshigane)
cutlery	カトラリー (katorarī)
tap	蛇口 (jaguchi)
sink	シンク (shinku)
wooden spoon	しゃもじ (shamoji)
chopping board	まな板 (manaita)
sponge	スポンジ (suponji)
corkscrew	栓抜き (sennuki)

Bedroom

bed	ベッド (beddo)
alarm clock	目覚まし時計 (mezamashi tokei)
curtain	カーテン (kāten)
bedside lamp	ベッドサイドランプ (beddo saido ranpu)
wardrobe	クローゼット (kurōzetto)
drawer	引き出し (hikidashi)
bunk bed	二段ベッド (ni dan beddo)
desk	机 (tsukue)
cupboard	食器棚 (shokki tana)
shelf	棚 (tana)
blanket	毛布 (mōfu)
pillow	枕 (makura)

mattress	敷布団 (shikifuton)
night table	ナイトテーブル (naitotēburu)
cuddly toy	ぬいぐるみ (nuigurumi)
bookshelf	本棚 (hondana)
lamp	ランプ (ranpu)
safe (for money)	金庫 (kinko)
baby monitor	ベビーモニター (bebī monitā)

Bathroom

broom	箒 (hōki)
shower	シャワー (shawā)
mirror	鏡 (kagami)
scale	体重計 (taijū kei)
bucket	バケツ (baketsu)
toilet paper	トイレットペーパー (toirettopēpā)
basin	洗面器 (senmen ki)
towel	タオル (taoru)
tile	タイル (tairu)
toilet brush	トイレブラシ (toire burashi)
soap	石鹸 (sekken)
bath towel	バスタオル (basu taoru)
bathtub	浴槽 (yokusō)
shower curtain	シャワーカーテン (shawā kāten)
laundry	洗濯物 (sentaku butsu)
laundry basket	洗濯籠 (sentaku kago)
peg	洗濯ばさみ (sentaku basami)
washing powder	洗濯用洗剤 (sentaku yō senzai)

Living room

chair	椅子 (isu)
table	テーブル (tēburu)
clock	時計 (tokei)
calendar	カレンダー (karendā)
picture	写真 (shashin)

carpet	カーペット (kāpetto)
sofa	ソファ (sofa)
power outlet	電源 (dengen)
coffee table	コーヒーテーブル (kōhī tēburu)
houseplant	鉢植え (hachiue)
shoe cabinet	靴箱 (kutsubako)
light switch	照明スイッチ (shōmei suicchi)
stool	スツール (sutsūru)
rocking chair	ロッキングチェア (rokkingu chea)
door handle	ドアノブ (doa nobu)
tablecloth	テーブルクロス (tēburukurosu)
blind	ブラインド (buraindo)
keyhole	鍵穴 (kagiana)
smoke detector	煙感知器 (kemuri kanchi ki)

Garden

neighbour	隣人 (rinjin)
axe	斧 (ono)
saw	鋸 (nokogiri)
ladder	はしご (hashigo)
fence	フェンス (fensu)
swimming pool (garden)	スイミングプール (suimingu pūru)
deck chair	デッキチェア (dekki chea)
mailbox (for letters)	ポスト (posuto)
pond	池 (ike)
shed	小屋 (koya)
flower bed	花壇 (kadan)
lawn mower	芝刈り機 (shibakari ki)
rake	熊手 (kumade)
shovel	シャベル (shaberu)
water can	じょうろ (jōro)
wheelbarrow	手押し車 (teoshi sha)
hose	ホース (hōsu)
pitchfork	ピッチフォーク (picchifōku)

loppers	万能ハサミ (bannō hasami)
flower pot	鉢 (hachi)
hedge	生垣 (ikegaki)
tree house	ツリーハウス (tsurī hausu)
hoe	鍬 (kuwa)
chainsaw	チェーンソー (chēn sō)
kennel	犬小屋 (inugoya)
bell	呼び鈴 (yobirin)
greenhouse	温室 (onshitsu)

Food

Dairy Products

egg	卵 (tamago)
milk	牛乳 (gyūnyū)
cheese	チーズ (chīzu)
butter	バター (batā)
yoghurt	ヨーグルト (yōguruto)
ice cream	アイスクリーム (aisu kurīmu)
cream (food)	クリーム (kurīmu)
sour cream	サワークリーム (sawā kurīmu)
whipped cream	ホイップクリーム (hoippu kurīmu)
egg white	卵白 (ranpaku)
yolk	卵黄 (ranō)
boiled egg	ゆで卵 (yudetamago)
buttermilk	バターミルク (batā miruku)
feta	フェタチーズ (feta chīzu)
mozzarella	モッツァレラ (mottsarera)
parmesan	パルメザン (parumezan)
milk powder	粉ミルク (kona miruku)

Meat & Fish

meat	肉 (niku)
fish (to eat)	魚 (sakana)
steak	ステーキ (sutēki)
sausage	ソーセージ (sōsēji)
bacon	ベーコン (bēkon)
ham	ハム (hamu)
lamb	羊肉 (yōniku)
pork	豚肉 (butaniku)
beef	牛肉 (gyūniku)
chicken (meat)	鶏肉 (keiniku)
turkey	七面鳥肉 (shichimenchō niku)
salami	サラミ (sarami)

game	鹿肉 (shikaniku)
veal	子牛肉 (ko gyūniku)
fat meat	脂身 (aburami)
lean meat	赤身 (akami)
minced meat	挽肉 (hikiniku)
salmon	鮭 (sake)
tuna	マグロ (maguro)
sardine	鰯 (iwashi)
fishbone	魚の骨 (sakana no hone)
bone (food)	骨 (hone)

Vegetables

lettuce	レタス (retasu)
potato	じゃがいも (jagaimo)
mushroom	マッシュルーム (masshurūmu)
garlic	ニンニク (ninniku)
cucumber	キュウリ (kyūri)
onion	タマネギ (tamanegi)
corn	トウモロコシ (tōmorokoshi)
pea	エンドウマメ (endoumame)
bean	豆 (mame)
celery	セロリ (serori)
okra	オクラ (okura)
bamboo (food)	竹 (take)
Brussels sprouts	芽キャベツ (me kyabetsu)
spinach	ほうれん草 (hōren sō)
turnip cabbage	コールラビ (kōrurabi)
broccoli	ブロッコリー (burokkorī)
cabbage	キャベツ (kyabetsu)
artichoke	アーティチョーク (ātichōku)
cauliflower	カリフラワー (karifurawā)
pepper (vegetable)	パプリカ (papurika)
chili	唐辛子 (tōgarashi)
courgette	ズッキーニ (zukkīni)

radish	大根 (daikon)
carrot	人参 (ninjin)
sweet potato	サツマイモ (satsuma imo)
aubergine	茄子 (nasu)
ginger	生姜 (shōga)
spring onion	葱 (negi)
leek	西洋葱 (seiyō negi)
truffle	トリュフ (toryufu)
pumpkin	かぼちゃ (kabocha)
lotus root	れんこん (ren kon)

Fruits & More

apple	リンゴ (ringo)
banana	バナナ (banana)
pear	梨 (nashi)
tomato	トマト (tomato)
orange (food)	オレンジ (orenji)
lemon	レモン (remon)
strawberry	苺 (ichigo)
pineapple	パイナップル (painappuru)
water melon	スイカ (suika)
grapefruit	グレープフルーツ (gurēpufurūtsu)
lime	ライム (raimu)
peach	桃 (momo)
apricot	杏子 (anzu)
plum	梅 (ume)
cherry	サクランボ (sakuranbo)
blackberry	ブラックベリー (burakkuberī)
cranberry	クランベリー (kuranberī)
blueberry	ブルーベリー (burūberī)
raspberry	ラズベリー (razuberī)
currant	スグリ (suguri)
sugar melon	ハニーデューメロン (hanī dyū meron)
grape	ぶどう (budō)

avocado	アボカド (abokado)
kiwi	キウイ (kiui)
lychee	ライチ (raichi)
papaya	パパイヤ (papaiya)
mango	マンゴー (mangō)
pistachio	ピスタチオ (pisutachio)
cashew	カシューナッツ (kashū nattsu)
peanut	ピーナツ (pīnatsu)
hazelnut	ヘーゼルナッツ (hēzerunattsu)
walnut	クルミ (kurumi)
almond	アーモンド (āmondo)
coconut	ココナッツ (kokonattsu)
date (food)	デーツ (dētsu)
fig	イチジク (ichijiku)
raisin	レーズン (rēzun)
olive	オリーブ (orību)
pit	種 (tane)
peel	皮 (kawa)
jackfruit	パラミツ (paramitsu)

Spices

salt	塩 (shio)
pepper (spice)	胡椒 (koshō)
curry	カレー (karē)
vanilla	バニラ (banira)
nutmeg	ナツメグ (natsumegu)
paprika	パプリカ (papurika)
cinnamon	シナモン (shinamon)
lemongrass	レモングラス (remon gurasu)
fennel	フェンネル (fenneru)
thyme	タイム (taimu)
mint	ミント (minto)
chive	チャイブ (chaibu)
marjoram	マジョラム (majoramu)

basil	バジル (bajiru)
rosemary	ローズマリー (rōzumarī)
dill	ディル (diru)
coriander	コリアンダー (koriandā)
oregano	オレガノ (oregano)

Products

flour	小麦粉 (komugiko)
sugar	砂糖 (satō)
rice	米 (kome)
bread	パン (pan)
noodle	麺 (men)
oil	油 (abura)
soy	大豆 (daizu)
wheat	小麦 (komugi)
oat	オート麦 (ōto mugi)
sugar beet	甜菜 (tensai)
sugar cane	サトウキビ (satō kibi)
rapeseed oil	菜種油 (natane abura)
sunflower oil	ひまわり油 (himawariabura)
olive oil	オリーブオイル (orību oiru)
peanut oil	ピーナッツ油 (pīnattsu abura)
soy milk	豆乳 (tōnyū)
corn oil	コーンオイル (kōn oiru)
vinegar	酢 (su)
yeast	イースト (īsuto)
baking powder	ベーキングパウダー (bēkingu paudā)
gluten	グルテン (guruten)
tofu	豆腐 (tōfu)
icing sugar	粉砂糖 (konazatō)
granulated sugar	グラニュー糖 (guranyū tō)
vanilla sugar	バニラシュガー (banira shugā)
tobacco	タバコ (tabako)

Breakfast

honey	蜂蜜 (hachimitsu)
jam	ジャム (jamu)
peanut butter	ピーナッツバター (pīnattsu batā)
nut	ナッツ (nattsu)
oatmeal	オートミール (ōtomīru)
cereal	シリアル (shiriaru)
maple syrup	メープルシロップ (mēpuru shiroppu)
chocolate cream	チョコレートスプレッド (chokorēto supureddo)
porridge	ポリッジ (porijji)
baked beans	ベイクドビーンズ (beikudo bīnzu)
scrambled eggs	スクランブルエッグ (sukuranburu eggu)
muesli	ミューズリー (myūzurī)
fruit salad	フルーツサラダ (furūtsu sarada)
dried fruit	ドライフルーツ (dorai furūtsu)

Sweet Food

cake	ケーキ (kēki)
cookie	クッキー (kukkī)
muffin	マフィン (mafin)
biscuit	ビスケット (bisuketto)
chocolate	チョコレート (chokorēto)
candy	キャンディー (kyandī)
doughnut	ドーナツ (dōnatsu)
brownie	ブラウニー (buraunī)
pudding	プリン (purin)
custard	カスタード (kasutādo)
cheesecake	チーズケーキ (chīzu kēki)
crêpe	クレープ (kurēpu)
croissant	クロワッサン (kurowassan)
pancake	ホットケーキ (hottokēki)
waffle	ワッフル (waffuru)
apple pie	アップルパイ (appuru pai)

marshmallow	マシュマロ (mashumaro)
chewing gum	ガム (gamu)
fruit gum	フルーツガム (furūtsu gamu)
liquorice	リコリス (rikorisu)
caramel	キャラメル (kyarameru)
candy floss	綿菓子 (watagashi)
nougat	ヌガー (nugā)

Drinks

water	水 (mizu)
tea	お茶 (o cha)
coffee	コーヒー (kōhī)
coke	コーラ (kōra)
milkshake	ミルクセーキ (miruku sēki)
orange juice	オレンジジュース (orenji jūsu)
soda	ソーダ (sōda)
tap water	水道水 (suidō sui)
black tea	紅茶 (kōcha)
green tea	緑茶 (ryokucha)
milk tea	ミルクティー (miruku tī)
hot chocolate	ホットチョコレート (hotto chokorēto)
cappuccino	カプチーノ (kapuchīno)
espresso	エスプレッソ (esupuresso)
mocha	モカ (moka)
iced coffee	アイスコーヒー (aisu kōhī)
lemonade	レモネード (remonēdo)
apple juice	リンゴジュース (ringo jūsu)
smoothie	スムージー (sumūjī)
energy drink	栄養ドリンク (eiyō dorinku)

Alcohol

wine	ワイン (wain)
beer	ビール (bīru)
champagne	シャンパン (shanpan)

red wine	赤ワイン (aka wain)
white wine	白ワイン (shiro wain)
gin	ジン (jin)
vodka	ウォッカ (wokka)
whiskey	ウイスキー (uisukī)
rum	ラム酒 (ramu shu)
brandy	ブランデー (burandē)
cider	サイダー (saidā)
tequila	テキーラ (tekīra)
cocktail	カクテル (kakuteru)
martini	マティーニ (Matīni)
liqueur	リキュール (rikyūru)
sake	日本酒 (Nippon shu)
sparkling wine	スパークリングワイン (supākuringu wain)

Meals

soup	スープ (sūpu)
salad	サラダ (sarada)
dessert	デザート (dezāto)
starter	前菜 (zensai)
side dish	副菜 (fukusai)
snack	スナック (sunakku)
breakfast	朝食 (chōshoku)
lunch	ランチ (ranchi)
dinner	ディナー (dinā)
picnic	ピクニック (pikunikku)
seafood	シーフード (shīfūdo)
street food	ストリートフード (sutorīto fūdo)
menu	メニュー (menyū)
tip	チップ (chippu)
buffet	ビュッフェ (byuffe)

Western Food

pizza	ピザ (piza)

spaghetti	スパゲティ (supageti)
potato salad	ポテトサラダ (poteto sarada)
mustard	マスタード (masutādo)
barbecue	バーベキュー (bābekyū)
steak	ステーキ (sutēki)
roast chicken	ローストチキン (rōsuto chikin)
pie	パイ (pai)
meatball	ミートボール (mītobōru)
lasagne	ラザニア (razania)
fried sausage	揚げソーセージ (age sōsēji)
skewer	串もの (kushi mono)
goulash	グーラッシュ (gūrasshu)
roast pork	ローストポーク (rōsuto pōku)
mashed potatoes	マッシュポテト (masshu poteto)

Asian Food

sushi	寿司 (sushi)
spring roll	春巻き (harumaki)
instant noodles	インスタントラーメン (insutanto rāmen)
fried noodles	焼きそば (yakisoba)
fried rice	チャーハン (chāhan)
ramen	ラーメン (rāmen)
dumpling	餃子 (gyōza)
dim sum	点心 (tenshin)
hot pot	鍋料理 (nabe ryōri)
Beijing duck	北京ダック (Pekin dakku)

Fast Food

burger	ハンバーガー (hanbāgā)
French fries	フライドポテト (furaido poteto)
chips	チップス (chippusu)
tomato sauce	トマトソース (tomato sōsu)
mayonnaise	マヨネーズ (mayonēzu)
popcorn	ポップコーン (poppukōn)

hamburger	ハンバーガー (hanbāgā)
cheeseburger	チーズバーガー (chīzubāgā)
hot dog	ホットドック (hotto dokku)
sandwich	サンドイッチ (sandoicchi)
chicken nugget	チキンナゲット (chikin nagetto)
fish and chips	フィッシュアンドチップス (fisshu ando chippusu)
kebab	ケバブ (kebabu)
chicken wings	チキンウイング (chikin uingu)
onion ring	オニオンリング (onion ringu)
potato wedges	ポテトウェッジ (poteto wejji)
nachos	ナチョス (nachosu)

Life

Holiday

luggage	荷物 (nimotsu)
hotel	ホテル (hoteru)
passport	パスポート (pasupōto)
tent	テント (tento)
sleeping bag	寝袋 (nebukuro)
backpack	バックパック (bakkupakku)
room key	ルームキー (rūmu kī)
guest	ゲスト (gesuto)
lobby	ロビー (robī)
room number	ルームナンバー (rūmu nanbā)
single room	シングルルーム (shinguru rūmu)
double room	ダブルルーム (daburu rūmu)
dorm room	相部屋 (aibeya)
room service	ルームサービス (rūmu sābisu)
minibar	ミニバー (mini bā)
reservation	予約 (yoyaku)
membership	メンバーシップ (menbāshippu)
beach	ビーチ (bīchi)
parasol	日傘 (higasa)
camping	キャンプ (kyanpu)
camping site	キャンプ場 (kyanpu jō)
campfire	キャンプファイヤー (kyanpu faiyā)
air mattress	エアマット (ea matto)
postcard	ポストカード (posutokādo)
diary	日記 (nikki)
visa	ビザ (biza)
hostel	ホステル (hosuteru)
booking	予約 (yoyaku)
member	メンバー (menbā)

Time

second (time)	秒 (byō)
minute	分 (bun)
hour	時 (ji)
morning (6:00-9:00)	朝 (asa)
noon	正午 (shōgo)
evening	夕方 (yūgata)
morning (9:00-11:00)	午前 (gozen)
afternoon	午後 (gogo)
night	夜 (yoru)
1:00	一時 (ichi ji)
2:05	二時五分 (ni ji go fun)
3:10	三時十分 (san ji jū fun)
4:15	四時十五分 (yon ji jū go fun)
5:20	五時二十分 (go ji nijū fun)
6:25	六時二十五分 (roku ji nijū go fun)
7:30	七時半 (nana ji han)
8:35	八時三十五分 (hachi ji sanjū go fun)
9:40	九時四十分 (kyū ji yonjū fun)
10:45	十時四十五分 (jū ji yonjū go fun)
11:50	十一時五十分 (jū ichi ji gojū fun)
12:55	十二時五十五分 (jū ni ji gojū go fun)
one o'clock in the morning	午前一時 (gozen ichi ji)
two o'clock in the afternoon	午後二時 (gogo ni ji)
half an hour	三十分 (sanjū fun)
quarter of an hour	十五分 (jū go fun)
three quarters of an hour	四十五分 (yonjū go fun)
midnight	真夜中 (ma yonaka)
now	今 (ima)

Date

the day before yesterday	一昨日 (issakujitsu)
yesterday	昨日 (kinō)
today	今日 (kyō)
tomorrow	明日 (ashita)

the day after tomorrow	明後日 (asatte)
spring	春 (haru)
summer	夏 (natsu)
autumn	秋 (aki)
winter	冬 (fuyu)
Monday	月曜日 (getsuyōbi)
Tuesday	火曜日 (kayōbi)
Wednesday	水曜日 (suiyōbi)
Thursday	木曜日 (mokuyōbi)
Friday	金曜日 (kin yōbi)
Saturday	土曜日 (doyōbi)
Sunday	日曜日 (nichiyōbi)
day	日 (hi)
week	週 (shū)
month	月 (tsuki)
year	年 (toshi)
January	一月 (ichi gatsu)
February	二月 (ni gatsu)
March	三月 (san gatsu)
April	四月 (shi gatsu)
May	五月 (go gatsu)
June	六月 (roku gatsu)
July	七月 (shichi gatsu)
August	八月 (hachi gatsu)
September	九月 (kyū gatsu)
October	十月 (jū gatsu)
November	十一月 (jū ichi gatsu)
December	十二月 (jū ni gatsu)
century	世紀 (seiki)
decade	十年 (jū nen)
millennium	千年紀 (sen nenki)
2014-01-01	２０１４年元日 (ni rei ichi yon nen ganjitsu)
2015-04-03	２０１５年４月３日 (ni rei ichi go nen shi gatsu san nichi)

2016-05-17	２０１６年５月１７日 (ni rei ichi roku nen go gatsu jū nana nichi)
1988-04-12	１９８８年４月１２日 (ichi kyū hachi hachi nen shi gatsu jū ni nichi)
1899-10-13	１８９９年１０月１３日 (ichi hachi kyū kyū nen jū gatsu jū san nichi)
2000-12-12	２０００年１２月１２日 (ni rei rei rei nen jū ni gatsu jū ni nichi)
1900-11-11	１９００年１１月１１日 (ichi kyū rei rei nen jū ichi gatsu jū ichi nichi)
2010-07-14	２０１０年７月１４日 (ni rei ichi rei nen shichi gatsu jū yon nichi)
1907-09-30	１９０７年９月３０日 (ichi kyū rei nana nen kyū gatsu sanjū nichi)
2003-02-25	２００３年２月２５日 (ni rei rei san nen ni gatsu nijū go nichi)
last week	先週 (senshū)
this week	今週 (konshū)
next week	来週 (raishū)
last year	去年 (kyonen)
this year	今年 (kotoshi)
next year	来年 (rainen)
last month	先月 (sengetsu)
this month	今月 (kongetsu)
next month	来月 (raigetsu)
birthday	誕生日 (tanjōbi)
Christmas	クリスマス (kurisumasu)
New Year	新年 (shinnen)
Ramadan	ラマダン (ramadan)
Halloween	ハロウィーン (harowīn)
Thanksgiving	サンクスギビング (sankusugibingu)
Easter	イースター (īsutā)

Relatives

daughter	娘 (musume)
son	息子 (musuko)
mother	母 (haha)

father	父 (chichi)
wife	妻 (tsuma)
husband	夫 (otto)
grandfather (paternal)	祖父 (sofu)
grandfather (maternal)	祖父 (sofu)
grandmother (paternal)	祖母 (sobo)
grandmother (maternal)	祖母 (sobo)
aunt	叔母 (oba)
uncle	叔父 (oji)
cousin (male)	従兄弟 (jūkeitei)
cousin (female)	従姉妹 (jūshimai)
big brother	兄 (ani)
little brother	弟 (otōto)
big sister	姉 (ane)
little sister	妹 (imōto)
niece	姪 (mei)
nephew	甥 (oi)
daughter-in-law	嫁 (yome)
son-in-law	婿 (muko)
grandson	孫 (mago)
granddaughter	孫娘 (magomusume)
brother-in-law	義兄弟 (gi kyōdai)
sister-in-law	義姉妹 (gi shimai)
father-in-law	義父 (gifu)
mother-in-law	義母 (gibo)
parents	両親 (ryōshin)
parents-in-law	舅姑 (kyūko)
siblings	兄弟姉妹 (kyōdai shimai)
grandchild	孫 (mago)
stepfather	継父 (keifu)
stepmother	継母 (mamahaha)
stepdaughter	継娘 (mamamusume)
stepson	継息子 (mamamusuko)
dad	パパ (papa)

mum	ママ (mama)

Life

man	男 (otoko)
woman	女 (onna)
child	子供 (kodomo)
boy	男の子 (otokonoko)
girl	女の子 (onnanoko)
baby	赤ちゃん (akachan)
love	愛 (ai)
job	仕事 (shigoto)
death	死 (shi)
birth	誕生 (tanjō)
infant	幼児 (yōji)
birth certificate	出生証明書 (shusshō shōmei sho)
nursery	保育園 (hoiku en)
kindergarten	幼稚園 (yōchi en)
primary school	小学校 (shō gakkō)
twins	双子 (futago)
triplets	三つ子 (mitsu go)
junior school	中学校 (chū gakkō)
high school	高校 (kōkō)
friend	友達 (tomodachi)
girlfriend	彼女 (kanojo)
boyfriend	彼氏 (kareshi)
university	大学 (daigaku)
vocational training	職業訓練 (shokugyō kunren)
graduation	卒業 (sotsugyō)
engagement	婚約 (kon yaku)
fiancé	婚約者 (kon yaku sha)
fiancée	婚約者 (kon yaku sha)
lovesickness	恋の病 (koi no yamai)
sex	セックス (sekkusu)
engagement ring	婚約指輪 (kon yaku yubiwa)

kiss	キス (kisu)
wedding	結婚式 (kekkon shiki)
divorce	離婚 (rikon)
groom	花婿 (hanamuko)
bride	花嫁 (hanayome)
wedding dress	ウエディングドレス (uedingu doresu)
wedding ring	結婚指輪 (kekkon yubiwa)
wedding cake	ウエディングケーキ (uedingu kēki)
honeymoon	ハネムーン (hanemūn)
funeral	葬式 (sōshiki)
retirement	退職 (taishoku)
coffin	棺桶 (kanoke)
corpse	死体 (shitai)
urn	骨壷 (kotsutsubo)
grave	墓 (haka)
widow	未亡人 (mibōjin)
widower	やもめ (yamome)
orphan	孤児 (koji)
testament	遺言書 (yuigon sho)
heir	跡継ぎ (atotsugi)
heritage	遺産 (isan)
gender	性別 (seibetsu)
cemetery	墓地 (bochi)

Transport

Car

tyre	タイヤ (taiya)
steering wheel	ハンドル (handoru)
throttle	アクセルペダル (akuseru pedaru)
brake	ブレーキ (burēki)
clutch	クラッチ (kuracchi)
horn	クラクション (kurakushon)
windscreen wiper	ワイパー (waipā)
battery	バッテリー (batterī)
rear trunk	トランク (toranku)
wing mirror	サイドミラー (saido mirā)
rear mirror	バックミラー (bakku mirā)
windscreen	フロントガラス (furonto garasu)
bonnet	ボンネット (bonnetto)
side door	サイドドア (saido doa)
front light	フロントライト (furonto raito)
bumper	バンパー (banpā)
seatbelt	シートベルト (shīto beruto)
diesel	ディーゼル (dīzeru)
petrol	ガソリン (gasorin)
back seat	後部座席 (kōbu zaseki)
front seat	フロントシート (furonto shīto)
gear shift	ギアシフト (gia shifuto)
automatic	オートマチック (ōtomachikku)
dashboard	ダッシュボード (dasshubōdo)
airbag	エアバッグ (ea baggu)
GPS	GPS (GPS)
speedometer	メーター (mētā)
gear lever	シフトレバー (shifuto rebā)
motor	モーター (mōtā)
exhaust pipe	排気管 (haiki kan)
hand brake	ハンドブレーキ (hando burēki)

shock absorber	ショックアブソーバ (shokku abusōba)
rear light	テールライト (tēruraito)
brake light	ブレーキライト (burēki raito)

Bus & Train

train	列車 (ressha)
bus	バス (basu)
tram	路面電車 (romen densha)
subway	地下鉄 (chika tetsu)
bus stop	バス停 (basu tei)
train station	駅 (eki)
timetable	時刻表 (jikoku hyō)
fare	運賃 (unchin)
minibus	マイクロバス (maikurobasu)
school bus	スクールバス (sukūru basu)
platform	プラットホーム (purattohōmu)
locomotive	機関車 (kikan sha)
steam train	蒸気機関車 (jōki kikan sha)
high-speed train	快速電車 (kaisoku densha)
monorail	モノレール (monorēru)
freight train	貨物列車 (kamotsu ressha)
ticket office	切符売り場 (kippu uriba)
ticket vending machine	券売機 (kenbai ki)
railtrack	レール (rēru)

Plane

airport	空港 (kūkō)
emergency exit (on plane)	非常口 (hijō guchi)
helicopter	ヘリコプター (herikoputā)
wing	ウイング (uingu)
engine	エンジン (enjin)
life jacket	救命胴衣 (kyūmei dōi)
cockpit	コックピット (kokkupitto)
row	列 (retsu)

window (in plane)	窓側 (madogawa)
aisle	通路側 (tsūro gawa)
glider	グライダー (guraidā)
cargo aircraft	貨物航空機 (kamotsu kōkū ki)
business class	ビジネスクラス (bijinesu kurasu)
economy class	エコノミークラス (ekonomī kurasu)
first class	ファーストクラス (fāsuto kurasu)
carry-on luggage	手荷物 (te nimotsu)
check-in desk	チェックインカウンター (chekku in kauntā)
airline	航空会社 (kōkū kaisha)
control tower	管制塔 (kansei tō)
customs	関税 (kanzei)
arrival	到着 (tōchaku)
departure	出発 (shuppatsu)
runway	滑走路 (kassō ro)

Ship

harbour	港 (minato)
container	コンテナ (kontena)
container ship	コンテナ船 (kontena sen)
yacht	ヨット (yotto)
ferry	フェリー (ferī)
anchor	アンカー (ankā)
rowing boat	ボート (bōto)
rubber boat	ゴムボート (gomu bōto)
mast	マスト (masuto)
life buoy	救命ブイ (kyūmei bui)
sail	帆 (ho)
radar	レーダー (rēdā)
deck	デッキ (dekki)
lifeboat	救命ボート (kyūmei bōto)
bridge	船橋 (funabashi)
engine room	エンジンルーム (enjin rūmu)
cabin	キャビン (kyabin)

sailing boat	帆船 (hansen)
submarine	潜水艦 (sensui kan)
aircraft carrier	空母 (kūbo)
cruise ship	クルーズ船 (kurūzu sen)
fishing boat	漁船 (gyosen)
pier	桟橋 (sanbashi)
lighthouse	灯台 (tōdai)
canoe	カヌー (kanū)

Infrastructure

road	道路 (dōro)
motorway	高速道路 (kōsoku dōro)
petrol station	ガソリンスタンド (gasorin sutando)
traffic light	信号 (shingō)
construction site	工事現場 (kōji genba)
car park	駐車場 (chūsha jō)
traffic jam	交通渋滞 (kōtsū jūtai)
intersection	交差点 (kōsa ten)
toll	通行料金 (tsūkō ryōkin)
overpass	陸橋 (rikkyō)
underpass	地下道 (chika dō)
one-way street	一方通行 (ippō tsūkō)
pedestrian crossing	横断歩道 (ōdan hodō)
speed limit	制限速度 (seigen sokudo)
roundabout	ロータリー (rōtarī)
parking meter	パーキングメーター (pākingu mētā)
car wash	洗車 (sensha)
pavement	歩道 (hodō)
rush hour	ラッシュアワー (rasshu awā)
street light	街灯 (gaitō)

Others

car	車 (kuruma)
ship	船 (fune)

plane	飛行機 (hikō ki)
bicycle	自転車 (jiten sha)
taxi	タクシー (takushī)
lorry	トラック (torakku)
snowmobile	スノーモービル (sunō mōbiru)
cable car	ロープウエー (rōpuuē)
classic car	クラシックカー (kurashikku kā)
limousine	リムジン (rimujin)
motorcycle	バイク (baiku)
motor scooter	スクーター (sukūtā)
tandem	タンデム (tandemu)
racing bicycle	レース用自転車 (rēsu yō jiten sha)
hot-air balloon	熱気球 (netsu kikyū)
caravan	キャラバン (kyaraban)
trailer	トレーラー (torērā)
child seat	チャイルドシート (chairudo shīto)
antifreeze fluid	不凍液 (futō eki)
jack	ジャッキ (jakki)
chain	チェーン (chēn)
air pump	タイヤポンプ (taiya ponpu)
tractor	トラクター (torakutā)
combine harvester	コンバイン (konbain)
excavator	掘削機 (kussaku ki)
road roller	ロードローラー (rōdo rōrā)
crane truck	クレーン車 (kurēn sha)
tank	戦車 (sensha)
concrete mixer	コンクリートミキサー (konkurīto mikisā)
forklift truck	フォークリフト (fōkurifuto)

Culture

Cinema & TV

TV	テレビ (terebi)
cinema	映画 (eiga)
ticket	チケット (chiketto)
comedy	コメディ (komedi)
thriller	スリラー (surirā)
horror movie	ホラー映画 (horā eiga)
western film	西洋映画 (seiyō eiga)
science fiction	サイエンスフィクション (saiensu fikushon)
cartoon	漫画 (manga)
screen (cinema)	スクリーン (sukurīn)
seat	シート (shīto)
news	ニュース (nyūsu)
channel	チャンネル (channeru)
TV series	連続番組 (renzoku bangumi)

Instruments

violin	バイオリン (baiorin)
keyboard (music)	キーボード (kībōdo)
piano	ピアノ (piano)
trumpet	トランペット (toranpetto)
guitar	ギター (gitā)
flute	フルート (furūto)
harp	ハープ (hāpu)
double bass	ダブルベース (daburu bēsu)
viola	ビオラ (biora)
cello	チェロ (chero)
oboe	オーボエ (ōboe)
saxophone	サクソフォン (sakusofon)
bassoon	ファゴット (fagotto)
clarinet	クラリネット (kurarinetto)
tambourine	タンバリン (tanbarin)

cymbals	シンバル (shinbaru)
snare drum	スネアドラム (sunea doramu)
kettledrum	ケトルドラム (ketoru doramu)
triangle	トライアングル (toraianguru)
trombone	トロンボーン (toronbōn)
French horn	フレンチホルン (furenchi horun)
tuba	チューバ (chūba)
bass guitar	ベースギター (bēsu gitā)
electric guitar	エレキギター (ereki gitā)
drums	ドラム (doramu)
organ	オルガン (orugan)
xylophone	木琴 (mokkin)
accordion	アコーディオン (akōdion)
ukulele	ウクレレ (ukurere)
harmonica	ハーモニカ (hāmonika)

Music

opera	オペラ (opera)
orchestra	オーケストラ (ōkesutora)
concert	コンサート (konsāto)
classical music	クラシック音楽 (kurashikku ongaku)
pop	ポップ (poppu)
jazz	ジャズ (jazu)
blues	ブルース (burūsu)
punk	パンク (panku)
rock (music)	ロック (rokku)
folk music	民族音楽 (minzoku ongaku)
heavy metal	ヘビーメタル (hebī metaru)
rap	ラップ (rappu)
reggae	レゲエ (regē)
lyrics	歌詞 (kashi)
melody	メロディ (merodi)
note (music)	音符 (onpu)
clef	音部記号 (on bu kigō)

symphony	シンフォニー (shinfonī)

Arts

theatre	劇場 (gekijō)
stage	ステージ (sutēji)
audience	観客 (kankyaku)
painting	絵画 (kaiga)
drawing	描画 (byōga)
palette	パレット (paretto)
brush (to paint)	ブラシ (burashi)
oil paint	油性塗料 (yusei toryō)
origami	折り紙 (origami)
pottery	陶器 (tōki)
woodwork	木細工 (ki zaiku)
sculpting	彫刻 (chōkoku)
cast	キャスト (kyasuto)
play	演劇 (engeki)
script	台本 (daihon)
portrait	肖像画 (shōzō ga)

Dancing

ballet	バレエ (barē)
Viennese waltz	ウィンナワルツ (winna warutsu)
tango	タンゴ (tango)
Ballroom dance	社交ダンス (shakō dansu)
Latin dance	ラテンダンス (raten dansu)
rock 'n' roll	ロックンロール (rokkunrōru)
waltz	ワルツ (warutsu)
quickstep	クイックステップ (kuikku suteppu)
cha-cha	チャチャチャ (chachacha)
jive	ジャイブ (jaibu)
salsa	サルサ (sarusa)
samba	サンバ (sanba)
rumba	ルンバ (runba)

Writing

newspaper	新聞 (shinbun)
magazine	雑誌 (zasshi)
advertisement	広告 (kōkoku)
letter (like a, b, c)	文字 (moji)
character	文字 (moji)
text	テキスト (tekisuto)
flyer	チラシ (chirashi)
leaflet	リーフレット (rīfuretto)
comic book	漫画本 (manga hon)
article	記事 (kiji)
photo album	フォトアルバム (foto arubamu)
newsletter	ニュースレター (nyūsuretā)
joke	冗談 (jōdan)
Sudoku	数独 (sūdoku)
crosswords	クロスワード (kurosuwādo)
caricature	風刺画 (fūshi ga)
table of contents	目次 (mokuji)
preface	序章 (joshō)
content	内容 (naiyō)
heading	見出し (midashi)
publisher	出版社 (shuppan sha)
novel	小説 (shōsetsu)
textbook	教科書 (kyōka sho)
alphabet	アルファベット (arufabetto)

School

Basics

book	本 (hon)
dictionary	辞書 (jisho)
library	図書館 (tosho kan)
exam	試験 (shiken)
blackboard	黒板 (kokuban)
desk	机 (tsukue)
chalk	チョーク (chōku)
schoolyard	校庭 (kōtei)
school uniform	制服 (seifuku)
schoolbag	通学鞄 (tsūgaku kaban)
notebook	ノート (nōto)
lesson	レッスン (ressun)
homework	宿題 (shukudai)
essay	論文 (ronbun)
term	学期 (gakki)
sports ground	運動場 (undō jō)
reading room	読書室 (dokusho shitsu)

Subjects

history	歴史 (rekishi)
science	科学 (kagaku)
physics	物理学 (butsuri gaku)
chemistry	化学 (kagaku)
art	美術 (bijutsu)
English	英語 (eigo)
Latin	ラテン語 (raten go)
Spanish	スペイン語 (Supein go)
Mandarin	北京語 (Pekin go)
Japanese	日本語 (Nippon go)
French	フランス語 (Furansu go)
German	ドイツ語 (Doitsu go)

Arabic	アラビア語 (Arabia go)
literature	文学 (bungaku)
geography	地理 (chiri)
mathematics	数学 (sūgaku)
biology	生物学 (seibutsu gaku)
physical education	体育 (taiiku)
economics	経済学 (keizai gaku)
philosophy	哲学 (tetsugaku)
politics	政治学 (seiji gaku)
geometry	幾何学 (kika gaku)

Stationery

pen	ペン (pen)
pencil	鉛筆 (enpitsu)
rubber	消しゴム (keshi gomu)
scissors	ハサミ (hasami)
ruler	ものさし (monosashi)
hole puncher	穴あけパンチ (anaake panchi)
paperclip	ペーパークリップ (pēpā kurippu)
ball pen	ボールペン (bōru pen)
glue	のり (nori)
adhesive tape	セロテープ (serotēpu)
stapler	ホッチキス (hocchikisu)
oil pastel	オイルパステル (oiru pasuteru)
ink	インク (inku)
coloured pencil	色鉛筆 (iro enpitsu)
pencil sharpener	鉛筆削り (enpitsu kezuri)
pencil case	筆箱 (fudebako)

Mathematics

result	結果 (kekka)
addition	足し算 (tashizan)
subtraction	引き算 (hikizan)
multiplication	掛け算 (kakezan)

division	割り算 (warizan)
fraction	分数 (bunsū)
numerator	分子 (bunshi)
denominator	分母 (bunbo)
arithmetic	算数 (sansū)
equation	方程式 (hōtei shiki)
first	第一 (dai ichi)
second (2nd)	第二 (dai ni)
third	第三 (dai san)
fourth	第四 (dai yon)
millimeter	ミリメートル (mirimētoru)
centimeter	センチメートル (senchimētoru)
decimeter	デシメートル (deshimētoru)
yard	ヤード (yādo)
meter	メートル (mētoru)
mile	マイル (mairu)
square meter	平方メートル (heihō mētoru)
cubic meter	立方メートル (rippō mētoru)
foot	フィート (fīto)
inch	インチ (inchi)
0%	0パーセント (0 pāsento)
100%	100パーセント (100 pāsento)
3%	3パーセント (3 pāsento)

Geometry

circle	円 (en)
square (shape)	正四角形 (sei shikaku kei)
triangle	三角形 (sankaku kei)
height	高さ (taka sa)
width	横幅 (yokohaba)
vector	ベクトル (bekutoru)
diagonal	対角線 (taikaku sen)
radius	半径 (hankei)
tangent	正接 (seisetsu)

ellipse	楕円 (daen)
rectangle	長方形 (chō hōkei)
rhomboid	平行四辺形 (heikō shihen kei)
octagon	八角形 (hakkaku kei)
hexagon	六角形 (rokkaku kei)
rhombus	菱形 (ryōkei)
trapezoid	台形 (daikei)
cone	円錐形 (ensui kei)
cylinder	円筒 (entō)
cube	立方体 (rippō tai)
pyramid	ピラミッド (piramiddo)
straight line	直線 (chokusen)
right angle	直角 (chokkaku)
angle	角度 (kakudo)
curve	曲線 (kyokusen)
volume	体積 (taiseki)
area	面積 (menseki)
sphere	球体 (kyūtai)

Science

gram	グラム (guramu)
kilogram	キログラム (kiroguramu)
ton	トン (ton)
liter	リッター (rittā)
volt	ヴォルト (boruto)
watt	ワット (watto)
ampere	アンペア (an pea)
laboratory	実験室 (jikken shitsu)
funnel	漏斗 (rōto)
Petri dish	ペトリ皿 (Petori sara)
microscope	顕微鏡 (kenbi kyō)
magnet	磁石 (jishaku)
pipette	ピペット (pipetto)
filter	フィルター (firutā)

pound	ポンド (pondo)
ounce	オンス (onsu)
milliliter	ミリリットル (miririttoru)
force	力 (chikara)
gravity	重力 (jūryoku)
theory of relativity	相対性理論 (sōtai sei riron)

University

lecture	授業 (jugyō)
canteen	カフェテリア (kafeteria)
scholarship	奨学金 (shōgaku kin)
graduation ceremony	卒業式 (sotsugyō shiki)
lecture theatre	講堂 (kōdō)
bachelor	学士 (gakushi)
master	修士 (shūshi)
PhD	博士 (hakase)
diploma	ディプロマ (dipuroma)
degree	学位 (gakui)
thesis	論文 (ronbun)
research	研究 (kenkyū)
business school	ビジネススクール (bijinesu sukūru)

Characters

full stop	句点 (kuten)
question mark	疑問符 (gimon fu)
exclamation mark	感嘆符 (kantan fu)
space	スペース (supēsu)
colon	コロン (koron)
comma	読点 (tōten)
hyphen	ハイフン (haifun)
underscore	アンダースコア (andā sukoa)
apostrophe	アポストロフィ (aposutorofi)
semicolon	セミコロン (semikoron)
()	括弧 (kakko)

/	スラッシュ (surasshu)
&	アンパサンド (anpasando)
...	等 (nado)
1 + 2	一足す二 (ichi tasu ni)
2 x 3	二掛ける三 (ni kakeru san)
3 - 2	三引く二 (san hiku ni)
1 + 1 = 2	一足す一は二 (ichi tasu ichi wa ni)
4 / 2	四割る二 (yon waru ni)
4²	四の二乗 (yon no ni jō)
6³	六の三乗 (roku no san jō)
3 to the power of 5	三の五乗 (san no go jō)
3.4	三・四 (san dotto yon)
www.pinhok.com	ダブリューダブリューダブリュードットピ アイ エヌ エイチ オ ケイ ドットコ (daburyū daburyū daburyū dotto pi ai enu eichi o kei dotto komu)
contact@pinhok.com	コンタクト アト ピ アイ エヌ エイチ オ ケイ ドット コム (kontakuto ato pi ai enu eichi o kei dotto komu)
x < y	XはYよりも小さい (X wa Y yori mo chīsai)
x > y	XはYよりも大きい (X wa Y yori mo ōkī)
x >= y	XはYよりも大きく等しい (X wa Y yori mo ōkiku hitoshī)
x <= y	XはYよりも小さく等しい (X wa Y yori mo chīsaku hitoshī)

Nature

Elements

fire (general)	火 (hi)
soil	土 (tsuchi)
ash	灰 (hai)
sand	砂 (suna)
coal	石炭 (sekitan)
diamond	ダイヤモンド (daiyamondo)
clay	粘土 (nendo)
chalk	チョーク (chōku)
limestone	石灰岩 (sekkai gan)
granite	花崗岩 (kakō gan)
ruby	ルビー (rubī)
opal	オパール (opāru)
jade	翡翠 (hisui)
sapphire	サファイア (safaia)
quartz	石英 (sekiei)
calcite	方解石 (hōkaiseki)
graphite	グラファイト (gurafaito)
lava	溶岩 (yōgan)
magma	マグマ (maguma)

Universe

planet	惑星 (wakusei)
star	星 (hoshi)
sun	太陽 (taiyō)
earth	地球 (chikyū)
moon	月 (tsuki)
rocket	ロケット (roketto)
Mercury	水星 (Sui sei)
Venus	金星 (Kin sei)
Mars	火星 (Ka sei)
Jupiter	木星 (Moku sei)

Saturn	土星 (Do sei)
Neptune	海王星 (Kaiō sei)
Uranus	天王星 (Tennō sei)
Pluto	冥王星 (Meiō sei)
comet	彗星 (suisei)
asteroid	小惑星 (shō wakusei)
galaxy	銀河 (ginga)
Milky Way	天の川 (amanogawa)
lunar eclipse	月食 (gesshoku)
solar eclipse	日食 (nisshoku)
meteorite	隕石 (inseki)
black hole	ブラックホール (burakku hōru)
satellite	衛星 (eisei)
space station	宇宙ステーション (uchū sutēshon)
space shuttle	スペースシャトル (supēsu shatoru)
telescope	望遠鏡 (bōen kyō)

Earth (1)

equator	赤道 (sekidō)
North Pole	北極 (Hokkyoku)
South Pole	南極 (Nankyoku)
tropics	熱帯 (nettai)
northern hemisphere	北半球 (kita hankyū)
southern hemisphere	南半球 (minami hankyū)
longitude	経度 (keido)
latitude	緯度 (ido)
Pacific Ocean	太平洋 (Taihei yō)
Atlantic Ocean	大西洋 (Taisei yō)
Mediterranean Sea	地中海 (Chichū kai)
Black Sea	黒海 (Kokkai)
Sahara	サハラ (Sahara)
Himalayas	ヒマラヤ (Himaraya)
Indian Ocean	インド洋 (Indo yō)
Red Sea	紅海 (Kōkai)

Amazon	アマゾン (Amazon)
Andes	アンデス (Andesu)
continent	大陸 (tairiku)

Earth (2)

sea	海 (umi)
island	島 (shima)
mountain	山 (yama)
river	川 (kawa)
forest	森 (mori)
desert (dry place)	砂漠 (sabaku)
lake	湖 (mizuumi)
volcano	火山 (kazan)
cave	洞窟 (dōkutsu)
pole	極 (kyoku)
ocean	海洋 (kaiyō)
peninsula	半島 (hantō)
atmosphere	大気 (taiki)
earth's crust	地殻 (chikaku)
earth's core	地核 (chikaku)
mountain range	山脈 (sanmyaku)
crater	クレーター (kurētā)
earthquake	地震 (jishin)
tidal wave	津波 (tsunami)
glacier	氷河 (hyōga)
valley	谷 (tani)
slope	坂 (saka)
shore	海岸 (kaigan)
waterfall	滝 (taki)
rock (stone)	岩石 (ganseki)
hill	丘 (oka)
canyon	渓谷 (keikoku)
marsh	沼沢 (shōtaku)
rainforest	雨林 (urin)

stream	川 (kawa)
geyser	間欠泉 (kanketsu sen)
coast	沿岸 (engan)
cliff	崖 (gake)
coral reef	珊瑚礁 (sango shō)
aurora	オーロラ (ōrora)

Weather

rain	雨 (ame)
snow	雪 (yuki)
ice	氷 (kōri)
wind	風 (kaze)
storm	嵐 (arashi)
cloud	雲 (kumo)
thunderstorm	雷雨 (raiu)
lightning	稲妻 (inazuma)
thunder	雷 (kaminari)
sunshine	日光 (nikkō)
hurricane	ハリケーン (harikēn)
typhoon	台風 (taifū)
temperature	気温 (kion)
humidity	湿気 (shikke)
air pressure	気圧 (kiatsu)
rainbow	虹 (niji)
fog	霧 (kiri)
flood	洪水 (kōzui)
monsoon	モンスーン (monsūn)
tornado	竜巻 (tatsumaki)
centigrade	摂氏 (sesshi)
Fahrenheit	華氏 (kashi)
-2 °C	摂氏マイナス２度 (sesshi mainasu ni do)
0 °C	摂氏０度 (sesshi rei do)
12 °C	摂氏１２度 (sesshi ichi ni do)
-4 °F	華氏マイナス４度 (kashi mainasu yon do)

0 °F	華氏０度 (kashi rei do)
30 °F	華氏３０度 (kashi san rei do)

Trees

tree	木 (ki)
trunk	幹 (miki)
root	根 (ne)
leaf	葉 (ha)
branch	枝 (eda)
bamboo (plant)	竹 (take)
oak	柏 (kashiwa)
eucalyptus	ユーカリ (yūkari)
pine	松 (matsu)
birch	樺 (kaba)
larch	カラマツ (karamatsu)
beech	橅 (buna)
palm tree	椰子 (yashi)
maple	楓 (kaede)
willow	柳 (yanagi)

Plants

flower	花 (hana)
grass	草 (kusa)
cactus	サボテン (saboten)
stalk	茎 (kuki)
blossom	花 (hana)
seed	種 (tane)
petal	花びら (hanabira)
nectar	蜜 (mitsu)
sunflower	ひまわり (himawari)
tulip	チューリップ (chūrippu)
rose	薔薇 (bara)
daffodil	水仙 (suisen)
dandelion	タンポポ (tanpopo)

buttercup	金鳳花 (kinpōge)
reed	葦 (ashi)
fern	シダ (shida)
weed	雑草 (zassō)
bush	灌木 (kanboku)
acacia	アカシア (akashia)
daisy	デイジー (deijī)
iris	燕子花 (kakitsubata)
gladiolus	グラジオラス (gurajiorasu)
clover	クローバー (kurōbā)
seaweed	海藻 (kaisō)

Chemistry

gas	ガス (gasu)
fluid	液体 (ekitai)
solid	固体 (kotai)
atom	原子 (genshi)
metal	金属 (kinzoku)
plastic	プラスチック (purasuchikku)
atomic number	原子番号 (genshi bangō)
electron	電子 (denshi)
neutron	中性子 (chūseishi)
proton	プロトン (puroton)
non-metal	非金属 (hi kinzoku)
metalloid	半金属 (han kinzoku)
isotope	アイソトープ (aisotōpu)
molecule	分子 (bunshi)
ion	イオン (ion)
chemical reaction	化学反応 (kagaku hannō)
chemical compound	化合物 (kagō butsu)
chemical structure	化学構造 (kagaku kōzō)
periodic table	周期表 (shūki hyō)
carbon dioxide	二酸化炭素 (ni sanka tanso)
carbon monoxide	一酸化炭素 (issankatanso)

methane メタン (metan)

Periodic Table (1)

hydrogen	水素 (suiso)
helium	ヘリウム (heriumu)
lithium	リチウム (richiumu)
beryllium	ベリリウム (beririumu)
boron	ホウ素 (hōso)
carbon	炭素 (tanso)
nitrogen	窒素 (chisso)
oxygen	酸素 (sanso)
fluorine	フッ素 (fusso)
neon	ネオン (neon)
sodium	ナトリウム (natoriumu)
magnesium	マグネシウム (maguneshiumu)
aluminium	アルミ (arumi)
silicon	シリコン (shirikon)
phosphorus	リン (rin)
sulphur	硫黄 (iō)
chlorine	塩素 (enso)
argon	アルゴン (arugon)
potassium	カリウム (kariumu)
calcium	カルシウム (karushiumu)
scandium	スカンジウム (sukanjiumu)
titanium	チタン (chitan)
vanadium	バナジウム (banajiumu)
chromium	クロム (kuromu)
manganese	マンガン (mangan)
iron	鉄 (tetsu)
cobalt	コバルト (kobaruto)
nickel	ニッケル (nikkeru)
copper	銅 (dō)
zinc	亜鉛 (aen)
gallium	ガリウム (gariumu)

germanium	ゲルマニウム (gerumaniumu)
arsenic	ヒ素 (hiso)
selenium	セレン (seren)
bromine	臭素 (shūso)
krypton	クリプトン (kuriputon)
rubidium	ルビジウム (rubijiumu)
strontium	ストロンチウム (sutoronchiumu)
yttrium	イットリウム (ittoriumu)
zirconium	ジルコニウム (jirukoniumu)

Periodic Table (2)

niobium	ニオブ (niobu)
molybdenum	モリブデン (moribuden)
technetium	テクネチウム (tekunechiumu)
ruthenium	ルテニウム (ruteniumu)
rhodium	ロジウム (rojiumu)
palladium	パラジウム (parajiumu)
silver	銀 (gin)
cadmium	カドミウム (kadomiumu)
indium	インジウム (injiumu)
tin	錫 (suzu)
antimony	アンチモン (anchimon)
tellurium	テルル (teruru)
iodine	ヨウ素 (yōso)
xenon	キセノン (kisenon)
caesium	セシウム (seshiumu)
barium	バリウム (bariumu)
lanthanum	ランタン (rantan)
cerium	セリウム (seriumu)
praseodymium	プラセオジム (puraseojimu)
neodymium	ネオジム (neojimu)
promethium	プロメチウム (puromechiumu)
samarium	サマリウム (samariumu)
europium	ユーロピウム (yūropiumu)

gadolinium	ガドリニウム (gadoriniumu)
terbium	テルビウム (terubiumu)
dysprosium	ジスプロシウム (jisupuroshiumu)
holmium	ホルミウム (horumiumu)
erbium	エルビウム (erubiumu)
thulium	ツリウム (tsuriumu)
ytterbium	イッテルビウム (itterubiumu)
lutetium	ルテチウム (rutechiumu)
hafnium	ハフニウム (hafuniumu)
tantalum	タンタル (tantaru)
tungsten	タングステン (tangusuten)
rhenium	レニウム (reniumu)
osmium	オスミウム (osumiumu)
iridium	イリジウム (irijiumu)
platinum	プラチナ (purachina)
gold	金 (kin)
mercury	水銀 (suigin)

Periodic Table (3)

thallium	タリウム (tariumu)
lead	鉛 (namari)
bismuth	ビスマス (bisumasu)
polonium	ポロニウム (poroniumu)
astatine	アスタチン (asutachin)
radon	ラドン (radon)
francium	フランシウム (furanshiumu)
radium	ラジウム (rajiumu)
actinium	アクチニウム (akuchiniumu)
thorium	トリウム (toriumu)
protactinium	プロトアクチニウム (purotoakuchiniumu)
uranium	ウラン (uran)
neptunium	ネプツニウム (neputsuniumu)
plutonium	プルトニウム (purutoniumu)
americium	アメリシウム (amerishiumu)

curium	キュリウム (kyuriumu)
berkelium	バークリウム (bākuriumu)
californium	カリホルニウム (karihoruniumu)
einsteinium	アインスタイニウム (ainsutainiumu)
fermium	フェルミウム (ferumiumu)
mendelevium	メンデレビウム (menderebiumu)
nobelium	ノーベリウム (nōberiumu)
lawrencium	ローレンシウム (rōrenshiumu)
rutherfordium	ラザホージウム (razahōjiumu)
dubnium	ドブニウム (dobu niumu)
seaborgium	シーボーギウム (shībōgiumu)
bohrium	ボーリウム (bōriumu)
hassium	ハッシウム (hasshiumu)
meitnerium	マイトネリウム (maitoneriumu)
darmstadtium	ダームスタチウム (dāmusutachiumu)
roentgenium	レントゲニウム (rentogeniumu)
copernicium	コペルニシウム (koperunishiumu)
ununtrium	ウンウントリウム (un un toriumu)
flerovium	フレロビウム (furerobiumu)
ununpentium	ウンウンペンチウム (un unpenchiumu)
livermorium	リバモリウム (ribamoriumu)
ununseptium	ウンウンセプチウム (un unsepuchiumu)
ununoctium	ウンウンオクチウム (un un okuchiumu)

Clothes

Shoes

flip-flops	ビーチサンダル (bīchi sandaru)
high heels	ハイヒール (hai hīru)
trainers	スニーカー (sunīkā)
wellington boots	ウェリントンブーツ (Werinton būtsu)
sandals	サンダル (sandaru)
leather shoes	革靴 (kawagutsu)
heel	ヒール (hīru)
sole	ソール (sōru)
lace	靴紐 (kutsuhimo)
slippers	スリッパ (surippa)
bathroom slippers	トイレ用スリッパ (toire yō surippa)
football boots	スパイク (supaiku)
skates	スケート (sukēto)
hiking boots	ハイキングブーツ (haikingu būtsu)
ballet shoes	バレエシューズ (barē shūzu)
dancing shoes	ダンスシューズ (dansu shūzu)

Clothes

T-shirt	Tシャツ (tī shatsu)
shorts	短パン (tanpan)
trousers	ズボン (zubon)
jeans	ジーンズ (jīnzu)
sweater	セーター (sētā)
shirt	シャツ (shatsu)
suit	スーツ (sūtsu)
dress	ドレス (doresu)
skirt	スカート (sukāto)
coat	コート (kōto)
anorak	アノラック (anorakku)
jacket	ジャケット (jaketto)
leggings	レギンス (reginsu)

sweatpants	スエットパンツ (suetto pantsu)
tracksuit	運動着 (undō gi)
polo shirt	ポロシャツ (poro shatsu)
jersey	ジャージ (jāji)
diaper	おむつ (omutsu)
wedding dress	ウエディングドレス (uedingu doresu)
bathrobe	バスローブ (basurōbu)
cardigan	カーディガン (kādigan)
blazer	ブレザー (burezā)
raincoat	レインコート (rein kōto)
evening dress	イブニングドレス (ibuningu doresu)
ski suit	スキーウェア (sukī wea)
space suit	宇宙服 (uchū fuku)

Underwear

bra	ブラジャー (burajā)
thong	Tバック (T bakku)
panties	パンティー (pantī)
underpants	パンツ (pantsu)
undershirt	アンダーシャツ (andāshatsu)
sock	靴下 (kutsushita)
pantyhose	パンスト (pansuto)
stocking	ストッキング (sutokkingu)
thermal underwear	保温インナー (hoon innā)
pyjamas	パジャマ (pajama)
jogging bra	スポーツブラジャー (supōtsu burajā)
negligee	ネグリジェ (negurije)
little black dress	黒いワンピース (kuroi wan pīsu)
nightie	パジャマ (pajama)
lingerie	ランジェリー (ranjerī)

Accessory

| glasses | 眼鏡 (megane) |
| sunglasses | サングラス (sangurasu) |

umbrella	傘 (kasa)
ring	指輪 (yubiwa)
earring	イヤリング (iyaringu)
wallet	財布 (saifu)
watch	腕時計 (ude tokei)
belt	ベルト (beruto)
handbag	ハンドバッグ (handobaggu)
glove	手袋 (tebukuro)
scarf	スカーフ (sukāfu)
hat	帽子 (bōshi)
necklace	ネックレス (nekkuresu)
purse	財布 (saifu)
knit cap	ニット帽 (nitto bō)
tie	ネクタイ (nekutai)
bow tie	蝶ネクタイ (chō nekutai)
baseball cap	ベースボールキャップ (bēsubōru kyappu)
brooch	ブローチ (burōchi)
bracelet	ブレスレット (buresuretto)
pearl necklace	パールネックレス (pāru nekkuresu)
briefcase	ブリーフケース (burīfukēsu)
contact lens	コンタクトレンズ (kontakuto renzu)
sun hat	サンハット (san hatto)
sleeping mask	アイマスク (ai masuku)
earplug	耳栓 (mimisen)
tattoo	刺青 (irezumi)
bib	よだれ掛け (yodare kake)
shower cap	シャワーキャップ (shawā kyappu)
medal	メダル (medaru)
crown	冠 (kanmuri)

Sport

helmet	ヘルメット (herumetto)
boxing glove	ボクシング用グローブ (bokushingu yō gurōbu)
fin	フィン (fin)

swim trunks	水泳パンツ (suiei pantsu)
bikini	ビキニ (bikini)
swimsuit	水着 (mizugi)
shinpad	すね当て (suneate)
sweatband	スエットバンド (suetto bando)
swim goggles	ゴーグル (gōguru)
swim cap	水泳帽 (suiei bō)
wetsuit	ウエットスーツ (uetto sūtsu)
diving mask	ダイビングマスク (daibingu masuku)

Hairstyle

curly	巻き髪 (makigami)
straight (hair)	ストレート (sutorēto)
bald head	はげ頭 (hageatama)
blond	ブロンド (burondo)
brunette	ブルネット (burunetto)
ginger	赤毛の (akage no)
scrunchy	ヘアーゴム (heā gomu)
barrette	バレッタ (baretta)
dreadlocks	ドレッドヘア (doreddo hea)
hair straightener	ストレートヘアアイロン (sutorēto hea airon)
dandruff	フケ (fuke)
dyed	染めた (someta)
wig	かつら (katsura)
ponytail	ポニーテール (ponītēru)

Others

button	ボタン (botan)
zipper	ジッパー (jippā)
pocket	ポケット (poketto)
sleeve	スリーブ (surību)
collar	襟 (eri)
tape measure	巻き尺 (makijaku)
mannequin	マネキン (manekin)

cotton	綿 (men)
fabric	布 (nuno)
silk	シルク (shiruku)
nylon	ナイロン (nairon)
polyester	ポリエステル (poriesuteru)
wool	ウール (ūru)
dress size	洋服サイズ (yōfuku saizu)
changing room	更衣室 (kōi shitsu)

Chemist

Women

perfume	香水 (kōsui)
tampon	タンポン (tanpon)
panty liner	パンティライナー (panti rainā)
face mask	フェイスパック (feisu pakku)
sanitary towel	ナプキン (napukin)
curling iron	ヘアアイロン (hea airon)
antiwrinkle cream	しわ用クリーム (shiwa yō kurīmu)
pedicure	ペディキュア (pedikyua)
manicure	マニキュア (manikyua)

Men

razor	剃刀 (kamisori)
shaving foam	シェービングフォーム (shēbingu fōmu)
shaver	髭剃り器 (higesori ki)
condom	コンドーム (kondōmu)
shower gel	シャワージェル (shawā jeru)
nail clipper	爪切り (tsumekiri)
aftershave	アフターシェーブ (afutā shēbu)
lubricant	ラブローション (rabu rōshon)
hair gel	ヘアジェル (hea jeru)
nail scissors	爪切ハサミ (tsumekire hasami)
lip balm	リップクリーム (rippu kurīmu)
razor blade	かみそりの刃 (kamisori no ha)

Daily Use

toothbrush	歯ブラシ (ha burashi)
toothpaste	歯磨き粉 (hamigakiko)
comb	櫛 (kushi)
tissue	ティッシュペーパー (tisshu pēpā)
cream (pharmaceutical)	クリーム (kurīmu)
shampoo	シャンプー (shanpū)

brush (for cleaning)	ヘアブラシ (hea burashi)
body lotion	ボディーローション (bodī rōshon)
face cream	フェイシャルクリーム (feisharu kurīmu)
sunscreen	日焼け止めクリーム (hiyake tome kurīmu)
insect repellent	虫除け (mushiyoke)

Cosmetics

lipstick	口紅 (kuchibeni)
mascara	マスカラ (masukara)
nail polish	マニキュア (manikyua)
foundation	ファンデーション (fandēshon)
nail file	爪やすり (tsumeyasuri)
eye shadow	アイシャドウ (ai shadō)
eyeliner	アイライナー (airainā)
eyebrow pencil	アイブローペンシル (aiburō penshiru)
facial toner	化粧水 (keshō sui)
nail varnish remover	マニキュア落とし (manikyua otoshi)
tweezers	ピンセット (pinsetto)
lip gloss	リップグロス (rippu gurosu)
concealer	コンシーラー (konshīrā)
face powder	フェイスパウダー (feisu paudā)
powder puff	パフ (pafu)

City

Shopping

bill	請求書 (seikyū sho)
cash register	レジ (reji)
basket	バスケット (basuketto)
market	マーケット (māketto)
supermarket	スーパマーケット (sūpa māketto)
pharmacy	薬局 (yakkyoku)
furniture store	家具屋 (kagu ya)
toy shop	おもちゃ屋 (omochaya)
shopping mall	ショッピングセンター (shoppingu sentā)
sports shop	スポーツ用品店 (supōtsu yōhin ten)
fish market	魚市場 (uoichiba)
fruit merchant	青果店 (seika ten)
bookshop	書店 (shoten)
pet shop	ペットショップ (petto shoppu)
second-hand shop	リサイクルショップ (risaikuru shoppu)
pedestrian area	歩行者天国 (hokō sha tengoku)
square	スクエア (sukuea)
shopping cart	ショッピングカート (shoppingu kāto)
bar code	バーコード (bā kōdo)
bargain	バーゲン (bāgen)
shopping basket	ショッピングバスケット (shoppingu basuketto)
warranty	保証 (hoshō)
bar code scanner	バーコードスキャナー (bā kōdo sukyanā)

Buildings

house	家屋 (kaoku)
apartment	アパート (apāto)
skyscraper	摩天楼 (maten rō)
hospital	病院 (byōin)
farm	農場 (nōjō)
factory	工場 (kōjō)

kindergarten	幼稚園 (yōchi en)
school	学校 (gakkō)
university	大学 (daigaku)
post office	郵便局 (yūbin kyoku)
town hall	市役所 (shi yakusho)
warehouse	倉庫 (sōko)
church	教会 (kyōkai)
mosque	モスク (mosuku)
temple	お寺 (o tera)
synagogue	シナゴーグ (shinagōgu)
embassy	大使館 (taishi kan)
cathedral	大聖堂 (dai seidō)
ruin	廃墟 (haikyo)
castle	城 (shiro)

Leisure

bar	バー (bā)
restaurant	レストラン (resutoran)
gym	スポーツジム (supōtsu jimu)
park	公園 (kōen)
bench	ベンチ (benchi)
fountain	噴水 (funsui)
tennis court	テニスコート (tenisu kōto)
swimming pool (building)	スイミングプール (suimingu pūru)
football stadium	サッカースタジアム (sakkā sutajiamu)
golf course	ゴルフ場 (gorufu jō)
ski resort	スキー場 (sukī ba)
botanic garden	植物園 (shokubutsu en)
ice rink	アイスリンク (aisu rinku)
night club	ナイトクラブ (naitokurabu)

Tourism

museum	博物館 (hakubutsu kan)
casino	カジノ (kajino)

tourist information	観光案内 (kankō annai)
toilet (public)	トイレ (toire)
map	地図 (chizu)
souvenir	お土産 (o miyage)
promenade	プロムナード (puromunādo)
tourist attraction	観光の名所 (kankō no meisho)
tourist guide	ガイドブック (gaidobukku)
monument	記念碑 (kinen hi)
national park	国立公園 (kokuritsu kōen)
art gallery	美術館 (bijutsu kan)

Infrastructure

alley	路地 (roji)
manhole cover	マンホールの蓋 (manhōru no futa)
dam	ダム (damu)
power line	配電線 (haiden sen)
sewage plant	下水処理場 (gesui shori jō)
avenue	大通り (ōdōri)
hydroelectric power station	水力発電所 (suiryoku hatsuden sho)
nuclear power plant	原子力発電所 (genshi ryoku hatsuden sho)
wind farm	風力発電所 (fūryoku hatsuden sho)

Construction

hammer	ハンマー (hanmā)
nail	釘 (kugi)
pincers	釘抜き (kuginuki)
screwdriver	スクリュードライバー (sukuryū doraibā)
drilling machine	ドリル (doriru)
tape measure	巻き尺 (makijaku)
brick	レンガ (renga)
putty	へら (hera)
scaffolding	足場 (ashiba)
spirit level	水平器 (suihei ki)
utility knife	万能ナイフ (bannō naifu)

screw wrench	スパナ (supana)
file	やすり (yasuri)
smoothing plane	かんな (kanna)
safety glasses	保護眼鏡 (hogo megane)
wire	ワイヤー (waiyā)
handsaw	手のこぎり (te nokogiri)
insulating tape	絶縁テープ (zetsuen tēpu)
cement	セメント (semento)
inking roller	インクローラー (inku rōrā)
paint	ペンキ (penki)
pallet	パレット (paretto)
cement mixer	セメントミキサー (semento mikisā)
steel beam	鋼桁 (hagane keta)
roof tile	屋根瓦 (yanegawara)
wooden beam	木造梁 (mokuzō hari)
concrete	コンクリート (konkurīto)
asphalt	アスファルト (asufaruto)
tar	タール (tāru)
crane	クレーン (kurēn)
steel	スチール (suchīru)
varnish	ニス (nisu)

Kids

slide	滑り台 (suberidai)
swing	ブランコ (buranko)
playground	遊び場 (asobiba)
zoo	動物園 (dōbutsu en)
roller coaster	ローラーコースター (rōrā kōsutā)
water slide	ウォータースライダー (wōtā suraidā)
sandbox	砂場 (sunaba)
fairground	遊園地 (yūen chi)
theme park	テーマパーク (tēma pāku)
water park	親水公園 (shinsui kōen)
aquarium	水族館 (suizoku kan)

| carousel | カルーセル (karūseru) |

Ambulance

ambulance	救急車 (kyūkyū sha)
police	警察 (keisatsu)
firefighters	消防組 (shōbō gumi)
helmet	ヘルメット (herumetto)
fire extinguisher	消火器 (shōka ki)
fire (emergency)	火事 (kaji)
emergency exit (in building)	非常口 (hijō guchi)
handcuff	手錠 (tejō)
gun	銃 (jū)
police station	警察署 (keisatsu sho)
hydrant	消火栓 (shōka sen)
fire alarm	火災警報 (kasai keihō)
fire station	消防署 (shōbō sho)
fire truck	消防車 (shōbō sha)
siren	サイレン (sairen)
warning light	警告灯 (keikoku tō)
police car	パトカー (patokā)
uniform	制服 (seifuku)
baton	警棒 (keibō)

More

village	村 (mura)
suburb	郊外 (kōgai)
state	州 (shū)
colony	植民地 (shokumin chi)
region	地域 (chiiki)
district	区 (ku)
territory	領土 (ryōdo)
province	州 (shū)
country	国 (kuni)
capital	首都 (shuto)

metropolis	大都市 (dai toshi)
central business district (CBD)	商業地区 (shōgyō chiku)
industrial district	工場地区 (kōjō chiku)

Health

Hospital

patient	患者 (kanja)
visitor	訪問者 (hōmon sha)
surgery	手術 (shujutsu)
waiting room	待合室 (machiai shitsu)
outpatient	外来患者 (gairai kanja)
clinic	クリニック (kurinikku)
visiting hours	面会時間 (menkai jikan)
intensive care unit	集中治療室 (shūchū chiryō shitsu)
emergency room	救命センター (kyūmei sentā)
appointment	予約 (yoyaku)
operating theatre	手術室 (shujutsu shitsu)
canteen	カフェテリア (kafeteria)

Medicine

pill	錠剤 (jōzai)
capsule	カプセル (kapuseru)
infusion	点滴 (tenteki)
inhaler	吸入器 (kyūnyū ki)
nasal spray	鼻腔用スプレー (bikū yō supurē)
painkiller	鎮痛剤 (chintsū zai)
Chinese medicine	漢方薬 (kanpō yaku)
antibiotics	抗生物質 (kōsei busshitsu)
antiseptic	消毒剤 (shōdoku zai)
vitamin	ビタミン (bitamin)
powder	粉薬 (kogusuri)
insulin	インスリン (insurin)
side effect	副作用 (fuku sayō)
cough syrup	咳止め (sekidome)
dosage	投薬量 (tōyaku ryō)
expiry date	消費期限 (shōhi kigen)
sleeping pill	睡眠薬 (suimin yaku)

aspirin   アスピリン (asupirin)

Disease

virus	ウィルス (wirusu)
bacterium	細菌 (saikin)
flu	インフルエンザ (infuruenza)
diarrhea	下痢 (geri)
heart attack	心臓発作 (shinzō hossa)
asthma	喘息 (zensoku)
rash	湿疹 (shisshin)
chickenpox	水疱瘡 (mizu bōsō)
nausea	吐き気 (hakike)
cancer	癌 (gan)
stroke	脳卒中 (nō socchū)
diabetes	糖尿病 (tōnyō byō)
epilepsy	癲癇 (tenkan)
measles	麻疹 (hashika)
mumps	おたふく風邪 (otafukukaze)
migraine	頭痛 (zutsū)

Discomfort

cough	咳 (seki)
fever	熱 (netsu)
headache	頭痛 (zutsū)
stomach ache	腹痛 (fukutsū)
sunburn	日焼け (hiyake)
cold (sickness)	風邪 (kaze)
nosebleed	鼻血 (hanadi)
cramp	けいれん (keiren)
eczema	アトピー (atopī)
high blood pressure	高血圧症 (kō ketsuatsu shō)
infection	感染症 (kansen shō)
allergy	アレルギー (arerugī)
hay fever	花粉症 (kafun shō)

sore throat	喉の痛み (nodo no itami)
poisoning	中毒 (chūdoku)
toothache	歯痛 (shitsū)
caries	虫歯 (mushiba)
hemorrhoid	イボ痔 (ibo ji)

Tools

needle	針 (hari)
syringe (tool)	シリンジ (shirinji)
bandage	包帯 (hōtai)
plaster	カットバン (katto ban)
cast	ギプス (gipusu)
crutch	松葉杖 (matsuba tsue)
wheelchair	車いす (kuruma isu)
fever thermometer	体温計 (taion kei)
dental brace	矯正具 (kyōsei gu)
neck brace	ネックカラー (nekku karā)
stethoscope	聴診器 (chōshin ki)
CT scanner	CTスキャナー (CT sukyanā)
catheter	カテーテル (katēteru)
scalpel	メス (mesu)
respiratory machine	人工呼吸器 (jinkō kokyū ki)
blood test	血液検査 (ketsueki kensa)
ultrasound machine	超音波検査 (chō onpa kensa)
X-ray photograph	レントゲン写真 (rentogen shashin)
dental prostheses	義歯 (gishi)
dental filling	詰め物 (tsumemono)
spray	スプレー (supurē)
magnetic resonance imaging	磁気共鳴断層撮影装置 (jiki kyōmei dansō satsuei sōchi)

Accident

injury	怪我 (kega)
accident	事故 (jiko)

wound	傷口 (kizuguchi)
pulse	脈拍 (myakuhaku)
fracture	骨折 (kossetsu)
bruise	打撲 (daboku)
burn	火傷 (yakedo)
bite	歯型 (hagata)
electric shock	電気ショック (denki shokku)
suture	縫合 (hōgō)
concussion	脳震盪 (nō shintō)
head injury	頭部外傷 (tōbu gaishō)
emergency	緊急 (kinkyū)

Departments

cardiology	心臓病学 (shinzō byō gaku)
orthopaedics	整形外科 (seikei geka)
gynaecology	婦人科 (fujin ka)
radiology	放射線科 (hōsha sen ka)
dermatology	皮膚科 (hifu ka)
paediatrics	小児科 (shōni ka)
psychiatry	精神科 (seishin ka)
surgery	外科 (geka)
urology	泌尿器科 (hinyō ki ka)
neurology	神経科 (shinkei ka)
endocrinology	内分泌学 (nai bunpitsu gaku)
pathology	病理学 (byōri gaku)
oncology	腫瘍学 (shuyō gaku)

Therapy

massage	マッサージ (massāji)
meditation	瞑想 (meisō)
acupuncture	鍼治療 (hari chiryō)
physiotherapy	理学療法 (rigaku ryōhō)
hypnosis	催眠 (saimin)
homoeopathy	ホメオパシー (homeopashī)

aromatherapy	アロマセラピー (aromaserapī)
group therapy	グループセラピー (gurūpu serapī)
psychotherapy	心理療法 (shinri ryōhō)
feng shui	風水 (fūsui)
hydrotherapy	水治療法 (suichi ryōhō)
behaviour therapy	行動療法 (kōdō ryōhō)
psychoanalysis	精神分析 (seishin bunseki)
family therapy	家族療法 (kazoku ryōhō)

Pregnancy

birth control pill	避妊用ピル (hinin yō piru)
pregnancy test	妊娠検査 (ninshin kensa)
foetus	胎児 (taiji)
embryo	胎児 (taiji)
womb	子宮 (shikyū)
delivery	出産 (shussan)
miscarriage	流産 (ryūzan)
cesarean	帝王切開 (teiō sekkai)
episiotomy	会陰切開術 (kaiinsekkai jutsu)

Business

Company

office	オフィス (ofisu)
meeting room	会議室 (kaigi shitsu)
business card	名刺 (meishi)
employee	従業員 (jūgyō in)
employer	雇用主 (koyō shu)
colleague	同僚 (dōryō)
staff	スタッフ (sutaffu)
salary	給料 (kyūryō)
insurance	保険 (hoken)
department	部門 (bumon)
sales	営業 (eigyō)
marketing	マーケティング (māketingu)
accounting	経理 (keiri)
legal department	法務部 (hōmu bu)
human resources	人事 (jinji)
IT	IT (IT)
stress	ストレス (sutoresu)
business dinner	ビジネスディナー (bijinesu dinā)
business trip	出張 (shucchō)
tax	税金 (zeikin)

Office

letter (post)	手紙 (tegami)
envelope	封筒 (fūtō)
stamp	切手 (kitte)
address	住所 (jūsho)
zip code	郵便番号 (yūbin bangō)
parcel	小包 (kozutsumi)
fax	ファックス (fakkusu)
text message	テキストメッセージ (tekisuto messēji)
voice message	音声メール (onsei mēru)

bulletin board	掲示板 (keiji ban)
flip chart	フリップチャート (furippu chāto)
projector	プロジェクター (purojekutā)
rubber stamp	スタンプ (sutanpu)
clipboard	クリップボード (kurippu bōdo)
folder (physical)	フォルダー (forudā)
lecturer	講演者 (kōen sha)
presentation	プレゼンテーション (purezentēshon)
note (information)	メモ (memo)

Jobs (1)

doctor	医者 (isha)
policeman	警察官 (keisatsu kan)
firefighter	消防士 (shōbō shi)
nurse	看護婦 (kango fu)
pilot	パイロット (pairotto)
stewardess	客室乗務員 (kyakushitsu jōmu in)
architect	建築家 (kenchiku ka)
manager	マネージャー (manējā)
secretary	秘書 (hisho)
general manager	総支配人 (sō shihai nin)
director	ディレクター (direkutā)
chairman	会長 (kaichō)
judge	裁判官 (saiban kan)
assistant	アシスタント (ashisutanto)
prosecutor	検察官 (kensatsu kan)
lawyer	弁護士 (bengo shi)
consultant	コンサルタント (konsarutanto)
accountant	会計士 (kaikei shi)
stockbroker	株式仲買人 (kabushiki nakagai nin)
librarian	司書 (shisho)
teacher	教師 (kyōshi)
kindergarten teacher	保育士 (hoiku shi)
scientist	科学者 (kagaku sha)

professor	教授 (kyōju)
physicist	物理学者 (butsuri gakusha)
programmer	プログラマー (puroguramā)
politician	政治家 (seiji ka)
intern	研修員 (kenshū in)
captain	キャプテン (kyaputen)
entrepreneur	起業家 (kigyō ka)
chemist	化学者 (kagaku sha)
dentist	歯医者 (ha isha)
chiropractor	カイロプラクター (kairopurakutā)
detective	探偵 (tantei)
pharmacist	薬剤師 (yakuzai shi)
vet	獣医 (jūi)
midwife	助産婦 (jo sanpu)
surgeon	外科医 (geka i)
physician	内科医 (naika i)
prime minister	総理大臣 (sōri daijin)
minister	大臣 (daijin)
president (of a state)	大統領 (daitōryō)

Jobs (2)

cook	コック (kokku)
waiter	ウェイター (weitā)
barkeeper	バーテンダー (bātendā)
farmer	農家 (nōka)
lorry driver	トラックの運転手 (torakku no unten shu)
train driver	電車の運転手 (densha no unten shu)
hairdresser	ヘアドレッサー (hea doressā)
butcher	肉屋 (nikuya)
travel agent	旅行代理店 (ryokō dairi ten)
real-estate agent	不動産業者 (fu dōsan gyōsha)
jeweller	宝石商人 (hōseki shōnin)
tailor	テーラー (tērā)
cashier	レジ係 (reji kakari)

postman	郵便配達人 (yūbin haitatsu nin)
receptionist	受付係 (uketsuke kakari)
construction worker	土木作業員 (doboku sagyō in)
carpenter	大工 (daiku)
electrician	電気技師 (denki gishi)
plumber	水道屋 (suidō ya)
mechanic	整備士 (seibi shi)
cleaner	清掃員 (seisō in)
gardener	庭師 (niwashi)
fisherman	漁師 (ryōshi)
florist	花屋 (hanaya)
shop assistant	店員 (ten in)
optician	眼鏡商人 (megane shōnin)
soldier	兵士 (heishi)
security guard	警備員 (keibi in)
bus driver	バスの運転手 (basu no unten shu)
taxi driver	タクシーの運転手 (takushī no unten shu)
conductor	車掌 (shashō)
apprentice	見習い (minarai)
landlord	大家 (ooya)
bodyguard	ボディーガード (bodīgādo)

Jobs (3)

priest	神父 (shinpu)
nun	修道女 (shūdō onna)
monk	僧侶 (sōryo)
photographer	写真家 (shashin ka)
coach (sport)	コーチ (kōchi)
cheerleader	チアリーダー (chiarīdā)
referee	審判員 (shinpan in)
reporter	レポーター (repōtā)
actor	俳優 (haiyū)
musician	ミュージシャン (myūjishan)
conductor	指揮者 (shiki sha)

singer	歌手 (kashu)
artist	アーティスト (ātisuto)
designer	デザイナー (dezainā)
model	モデル (moderu)
DJ	DJ (DJ)
tour guide	ツアーガイド (tsuā gaido)
lifeguard	ライフガード (raifu gādo)
physiotherapist	理学療法士 (rigaku ryōhō shi)
masseur	マッサージ師 (massāji shi)
anchor	ニュースキャスター (nyūsukyasutā)
host	ホスト (hosuto)
commentator	コメンテーター (komentētā)
camera operator	カメラマン (kameraman)
engineer	エンジニア (enjinia)
thief	泥棒 (dorobō)
criminal	犯罪者 (hanzai sha)
dancer	ダンサー (dansā)
journalist	ジャーナリスト (jānarisuto)
prostitute	売春婦 (baishun fu)
author	作家 (sakka)
air traffic controller	航空交通管制官 (kōkū kōtsū kansei kan)
director	ディレクター (direkutā)
mufti	ムフティー (mufu tī)
rabbi	ラビ (rabi)

Technology

e-mail	電子メール (denshi mēru)
telephone	電話 (denwa)
smartphone	スマートフォン (sumāto fon)
e-mail address	メールアドレス (mēru adoresu)
website	ウェブサイト (webusaito)
telephone number	電話番号 (denwa bangō)
file	ファイル (fairu)
folder (computer)	フォルダー (forudā)

app	アプリ (apuri)
laptop	ノートパソコン (nōto pasokon)
screen (computer)	ディスプレイ (disupurei)
printer	プリンター (purintā)
scanner	スキャナー (sukyanā)
USB stick	USBメモリー (USB memorī)
hard drive	ハードディスク (hādodisuku)
central processing unit (CPU)	CPU (CPU)
random access memory (RAM)	RAM (RAM)
keyboard (computer)	キーボード (kībōdo)
mouse (computer)	マウス (mausu)
earphone	イヤフォン (iyafon)
mobile phone	携帯 (keitai)
webcam	ウェブカム (webu kamu)
server	サーバー (sābā)
network	ネットワーク (nettowāku)
browser	ブラウザ (burauza)
inbox	受信ボックス (jushin bokkusu)
url	URL (URL)
icon	アイコン (aikon)
scrollbar	スクロールバー (sukurōru bā)
recycle bin	ゴミ箱 (gomibako)
chat	チャット (chatto)
social media	ソーシャルメディア (sōsharu media)
signal (of phone)	信号 (shingō)
database	データベース (dētabēsu)

Law

law	法律 (hōritsu)
fine	罰金 (bakkin)
prison	刑務所 (keimu sho)
court	裁判所 (saiban sho)
jury	陪審 (baishin)
witness	証人 (shōnin)

defendant	被告人 (hikoku nin)
case	事件 (jiken)
evidence	証拠 (shōko)
suspect	容疑者 (yōgi sha)
fingerprint	指紋 (shimon)
paragraph	段落 (danraku)

Bank

money	お金 (o kane)
coin	貨幣 (kahei)
note (money)	紙幣 (shihei)
credit card	クレジットカード (kurejitto kādo)
cash machine	ATM (ATM)
signature	署名 (shomei)
dollar	ドル (doru)
euro	ユーロ (yūro)
pound	ポンド (pondo)
bank account	銀行口座 (ginkō kōza)
password	パスワード (pasuwādo)
account number	口座番号 (kōza bangō)
amount	金額 (kingaku)
cheque	小切手 (kogitte)
customer	顧客 (kokyaku)
savings	積み立て (tsumitate)
loan	ローン (rōn)
interest	利子 (rishi)
bank transfer	銀行振込 (ginkō furikomi)
yuan	元 (moto)
yen	円 (en)
krone	クローネ (kurōne)
dividend	配当 (haitō)
share	株 (kabu)
share price	株価 (kabuka)
stock exchange	証券取引所 (shōken torihiki sho)

investment	投資 (tōshi)
portfolio	ポートフォリオ (pōtoforio)
profit	利益 (rieki)
loss	損失 (sonshitsu)

Things

Sport

basketball	バスケットボール (basukettobōru)
football	サッカーボール (sakkā bōru)
goal	ゴール (gōru)
tennis racket	テニスラケット (tenisu raketto)
tennis ball	テニスボール (tenisu bōru)
net	ネット (netto)
cup (trophy)	カップ (kappu)
medal	メダル (medaru)
swimming pool (competition)	スイミングプール (suimingu pūru)
football	フットボール (futtobōru)
bat	バット (batto)
mitt	ミット (mitto)
gold medal	金メダル (kin medaru)
silver medal	銀メダル (gin medaru)
bronze medal	銅メダル (dō medaru)
shuttlecock	シャトルコック (shatoru kokku)
golf club	ゴルフクラブ (gorufu kurabu)
golf ball	ゴルフボール (gorufu bōru)
stopwatch	ストップウオッチ (sutoppuuocchi)
trampoline	トランポリン (toranporin)
boxing ring	ボクシングリング (bokushingu ringu)
mouthguard	マウスピース (mausupīsu)
surfboard	サーフボード (sāfubōdo)
ski	スキー (sukī)
ski pole	スキーストック (sukī sutokku)
sledge	そり (sori)
parachute	パラシュート (parashūto)
cue	キュー (kyū)
bowling ball	ボーリングボール (bōringu bōru)
snooker table	ビリヤード台 (biriyādo dai)
saddle	サドル (sadoru)

whip	鞭 (muchi)
hockey stick	ホッケースティック (hokkē sutikku)
basket	バスケット (basuketto)
world record	世界記録 (sekai kiroku)
table tennis table	卓球台 (takkyū dai)
puck	パック (pakku)

Technology

robot	ロボット (robotto)
radio	ラジオ (rajio)
loudspeaker	スピーカー (supīkā)
cable	ケーブル (keiburu)
plug	プラグ (puragu)
camera	カメラ (kamera)
MP3 player	MP3プレーヤー (MP3 purēyā)
CD player	CDプレーヤー (CD purēyā)
DVD player	DVDプレーヤー (DVD purēyā)
record player	レコードプレーヤー (rekōdo purēyā)
camcorder	ビデオカメラ (bideo kamera)
power	電気 (denki)
flat screen	薄型テレビ (usugata terebi)
flash	フラッシュ (furasshu)
tripod	三脚 (sankyaku)
instant camera	インスタントカメラ (insutanto kamera)
generator	発電機 (hatsuden ki)
digital camera	デジカメ (dejikame)
walkie-talkie	トランシーバー (toranshībā)

Home

key	鍵 (kagi)
torch	懐中電灯 (kaichū dentō)
candle	蝋燭 (rōsoku)
bottle	ボトル (botoru)
tin	缶 (kan)

vase	花瓶 (kabin)
present (gift)	プレゼント (purezento)
match	マッチ棒 (macchi bō)
lighter	ライター (raitā)
key chain	キーチェーン (kī chēn)
water bottle	水筒 (suitō)
thermos jug	魔法瓶 (mahō bin)
rubber band	輪ゴム (wa gomu)
birthday party	誕生日会 (tanjōbikai)
birthday cake	バースデーケーキ (bāsudē kēki)
pushchair	ベビーカー (bebī kā)
soother	おしゃぶり (oshaburi)
baby bottle	哺乳瓶 (honyū bin)
hot-water bottle	湯たんぽ (yu tanpo)
rattle	ガラガラ (garagara)
family picture	家族写真 (kazoku shashin)
jar	瓶 (bin)
bag	バッグ (baggu)
package	パッケージ (pakkēji)
plastic bag	ビニール袋 (binīru bukuro)
picture frame	額縁 (gakubuchi)

Games

doll	人形 (ningyō)
dollhouse	ドールハウス (dōru hausu)
puzzle	パズル (pazuru)
dominoes	ドミノ (domino)
Monopoly	モノポリー (monoporī)
Tetris	テトリス (tetorisu)
bridge	ブリッジ (burijj i)
darts	ダーツ (dātsu)
card game	カードゲーム (kādo gēmu)
board game	ボードゲーム (bōdo gēmu)
backgammon	バックギャモン (bakkugyamon)

117

draughts	チェッカー (chekkā)

Others

cigarette	たばこ (tabako)
cigar	葉巻 (hamaki)
compass	コンパス (konpasu)
angel	天使 (tenshi)

Phrases

Personal

I	私 (watashi)
you (singular)	あなた (anata)
he	彼 (kare)
she	彼女 (kanojo)
we	私達 (watashi tachi)
you (plural)	あなた達 (anata tachi)
they	彼ら (kare ra)
my dog	私の犬 (watashi no inu)
your cat	あなたの猫 (anata no neko)
her dress	彼女のドレス (kanojo no doresu)
his car	彼の車 (kare no kuruma)
our home	私達の家 (watashitachi no ie)
your team	あなたのチーム (anata no chīmu)
their company	彼らの会社 (kare ra no kaisha)
everybody	みんな (minna)
together	一緒に (issho ni)
other	他人 (tanin)

Common

and	と (to)
or	又は (mata wa)
very	とっても (tottemo)
all	全て (subete)
none	何もない (nanimonai)
that	あれ (are)
this	これ (kore)
not	ではない (de wa nai)
more	もっと (motto)
most	ほとんど (hotondo)
less	よりも少ない (yori mo sukunai)
because	だから (da kara)

but	でも (de mo)
already	既に (sudeni)
again	再度 (saido)
really	本当に (hontō ni)
if	もし (moshi)
although	それでも (sore de mo)
suddenly	突然 (totsuzen)
then	そして (soshite)
actually	実は (jitsu wa)
immediately	すぐに (sugu ni)
often	たいてい (taitei)
always	いつも (itsu mo)
every	ごと (goto)

Phrases

hi	やあ (yā)
hello	こんにちは (konnichiwa)
good day	今日は (kyō wa)
bye bye	またね (mata ne)
good bye	さようなら (sayōnara)
see you later	行って来ます (itte kimasu)
please	お願いします (o negaishimasu)
thank you	ありがとうございます (arigatō gozaimasu)
sorry	ごめんなさい (gomen nasai)
no worries	大丈夫 (daijōbu)
don't worry	気にしないで (ki ni shinaide)
take care	気を付けて (ki o tsukete)
ok	はい (hai)
cheers	乾杯 (kanpai)
welcome	ようこそ (yō koso)
excuse me	すみません (sumimasen)
of course	もちろん (mochiron)
I agree	賛成です (sansei desu)
relax	楽にして (raku ni shite)

doesn't matter	関係ない (kankei nai)
I want this	これが欲しいです (kore ga hoshī desu)
Come with me	一緒においで (issho ni o ide)
go straight	真っすぐ行く (massugu iku)
turn left	左に曲がる (hidari ni magaru)
turn right	右に曲がる (migi ni magaru)

Questions

who	誰 (dare)
where	どこ (doko)
what	何 (nani)
why	なぜ (naze)
how	どのように (dono yō ni)
which	どれ (dore)
when	いつ (itsu)
how many?	いくつですか？ (iku tsu desu ka)
how much?	いくら？ (ikura)
How much is this?	これはいくらですか？ (kore wa ikura desu ka)
Do you have a phone?	電話はありますか？ (denwa wa arimasu ka)
Where is the toilet?	トイレはどこですか？ (toire wa doko desu ka)
What's your name?	名前はなんですか？ (namae wa nan desu ka)
Do you love me?	私のことが好きですか？ (watakushi no koto ga suki desu ka)
How are you?	元気ですか？ (genki desu ka)
Are you ok?	大丈夫ですか？ (daijōbu desu ka)
Can you help me?	手伝ってくれますか？ (tetsudatte kuremasu ka)

Sentences

I like you	あなたが好きです (anata ga suki desu)
I love you	愛しています (aishite imasu)
I miss you	恋しいです (koishī desu)
I don't like this	これは好きではありません (kore wa suki de wa arimasen)
I have a dog	犬を飼っています (inu o katte imasu)

I know	知っています (shitte imasu)
I don't know	知りません (shirimasen)
I don't understand	分かりません (wakarimasen)
I want more	もっと欲しいです (motto hoshī desu)
I want a cold coke	冷たいコーラが欲しいです (tsumetai kōra ga hoshī desu)
I need this	これが必要です (kore ga hitsuyō desu)
I want to go to the cinema	映画を見に行きたいです (eiga o mi ni ikitaidesu)
I am looking forward to seeing you	会えるのを楽しみにしています (aeru no o tanoshimi ni shite imasu)
Usually I don't eat fish	私は普段魚を食べません (watashi wa fudan sakana o tabemasen)
You definitely have to come	絶対に来ないといけません (zettai ni konai to ikemasen)
This is quite expensive	これはかなり高価です (kore wa kanari kōka desu)
Sorry, I'm a little late	遅くなってすみません (osoku natte sumimasen)
My name is David	私の名前はデイビッドです (watashi no namae wa Deibiddo desu)
I'm David, nice to meet you	デイビッドです、よろしくお願いします (deibiddo desu, yoroshiku o negaishimasu)
I'm 22 years old	22歳です (22 sai desu)
This is my girlfriend Anna	これは私のガールフレンドアンナです (kore wa watashi no gārufurendo Anna desu)
Let's watch a film	映画を見ましょう (eiga o mimashō)
Let's go home	帰りましょう (kaerimashō)
My telephone number is one four three two eight seven five four three	私の電話番号は143287543です (watashi no denwa bangō wa 143287543 desu)
My email address is david at pinhok dot com	私のメールアドレスはディ エイ ヴィ アイ ディ アットマーク ピー アイ エヌ エイチ オー ケイ ドット コムです (watashi no mēruadoresu wa di ei vui ai di attomāku pi ai enu eichi o kei dotto komu)
Tomorrow is Saturday	明日は土曜日です (ashita wa doyō hi desu)
Silver is cheaper than gold	銀は金よりも安いです (gin wa kin yori mo yasui desu)
Gold is more expensive than silver	金は銀よりも高いです (kin wa gin yori mo takai desu)

English - Japanese

A

above: 上 上(ue)

acacia: アカシア アカシア(akashia)

accident: 事故 事故(jiko)

accordion: アコーディオン アコーディオン(akōdion)

accountant: 会計士 会計士(kaikei shi)

accounting: 経理 経理(keiri)

account number: 口座番号 口座番号(kōza bangō)

Achilles tendon: アキレス腱 アキレス腱(Akiresu ken)

actinium: アクチニウム アクチニウム(akuchiniumu)

actor: 俳優 俳優(haiyū)

actually: 実は 実は(jitsu wa)

acupuncture: 鍼治療 鍼治療(hari chiryō)

addition: 足し算 足し算(tashizan)

address: 住所 住所(jūsho)

adhesive tape: セロテープ セロテープ(serotēpu)

advertisement: 広告 広告(kōkoku)

aerobics: エアロビクス エアロビクス(earobikusu)

Afghanistan: アフガニスタン アフガニスタン(Afuganisutan)

afternoon: 午後 午後(gogo)

aftershave: アフターシェーブ アフターシェーブ(afutā shēbu)

again: 再度 再度(saido)

airbag: エアバッグ エアバッグ(ea baggu)

air conditioner: エアコン エアコン(eakon)

aircraft carrier: 空母 空母(kūbo)

airline: 航空会社 航空会社(kōkū kaisha)

air mattress: エアマット エアマット(ea matto)

airport: 空港 空港(kūkō)

air pressure: 気圧 気圧(kiatsu)

air pump: タイヤポンプ タイヤポンプ(taiya ponpu)

air traffic controller: 航空交通管制官 航空交通管制官(kōkū kōtsū kansei kan)

aisle: 通路側 通路側(tsūro gawa)

alarm clock: 目覚まし時計 目覚まし時計(mezamashi tokei)

Albania: アルバニア アルバニア(Arubania)

Algeria: アルジェリア アルジェリア(Arujeria)

all: 全て 全て(subete)

allergy: アレルギー アレルギー(arerugī)

alley: 路地 路地(roji)

almond: アーモンド アーモンド(āmondo)

alphabet: アルファベット アルファベット(arufabetto)

already: 既に 既に(sudeni)

although: それでも それでも(sore de mo)

aluminium: アルミ アルミ(arumi)

always: いつも いつも(itsu mo)

Amazon: アマゾン アマゾン(Amazon)

ambulance: 救急車 救急車(kyūkyū sha)

American football: アメリカンフットボール アメリカンフットボール(amerikan futtobōru)

American Samoa: アメリカ領サモア アメリカ領サモア(Amerikaryō Samoa)

americium: アメリシウム アメリシウム(amerishiumu)

amount: 金額 金額(kingaku)

ampere: アンペア アンペア(an pea)

anchor: アンカー アンカー(ankā), ニュースキャスター ニュースキャスター(nyūsukyasutā)

and: と と(to)

Andes: アンデス アンデス(Andesu)

Andorra: アンドラ アンドラ(Andora)

angel: 天使 天使(tenshi)

angle: 角度 角度(kakudo)

Angola: アンゴラ アンゴラ(Angora)

angry: 怒り 怒り(ikari)

ankle: 踝 踝(kurubushi)

anorak: アノラック アノラック(anorakku)

answer: 答える 答える(kotaeru)

ant: アリ アリ(ari)

ant-eater: アリクイ アリクイ(arikui)

antibiotics: 抗生物質 抗生物質(kōsei busshitsu)

antifreeze fluid: 不凍液 不凍液(futō eki)

Antigua and Barbuda: アンティグア・バーブーダ アンティグア・バーブーダ(Antigua Bābūda)

antimony: アンチモン アンチモン(anchimon)

antiseptic: 消毒剤 消毒剤(shōdoku zai)

antiwrinkle cream: しわ用クリーム しわ用クリーム(shiwa yō kurīmu)

anus: 肛門 肛門(kōmon)

apartment: アパート アパート(apāto)

apostrophe: アポストロフィ アポストロフィ(aposutorofi)

app: アプリ アプリ(apuri)

appendix: 盲腸 盲腸(mōchō)

apple: リンゴ リンゴ(ringo)

apple juice: リンゴジュース リンゴジュース(ringo jūsu)

apple pie: アップルパイ アップルパイ(appuru pai)

appointment: 予約 予約(yoyaku)

apprentice: 見習い 見習い(minarai)

apricot: 杏子 杏子(anzu)

April: 四月 四月(shi gatsu)

aquarium: 水族館 水族館(suizoku kan)

Arabic: アラビア語 アラビア語(Arabia go)

archery: アーチェリー アーチェリー(ācherī)

architect: 建築家 建築家(kenchiku ka)

area: 面積 面積(menseki)

Are you ok?: 大丈夫ですか？ 大丈夫ですか？(daijōbu desu ka)

Argentina: アルゼンチン アルゼンチン(Aruzenchin)

argon: アルゴン アルゴン(arugon)

argue: 喧嘩する 喧嘩する(kenka suru)

arithmetic: 算数 算数(sansū)

arm: 腕 腕(ude)

Armenia: アルメニア アルメニア(Arumenia)

aromatherapy: アロマセラピー アロマセラピー(aromaserapī)

arrival: 到着 到着(tōchaku)

arsenic: ヒ素 ヒ素(hiso)

art: 美術 美術(bijutsu)

artery: 動脈 動脈(dōmyaku)

art gallery: 美術館 美術館(bijutsu kan)

artichoke: アーティチョーク アーティチョーク(ātichōku)

article: 記事 記事(kiji)

artist: アーティスト アーティスト(ātisuto)

Aruba: アルバ アルバ(Aruba)

ash: 灰 灰(hai)

ask: 質問する 質問する(shitsumon suru)

asphalt: アスファルト アスファルト(asufaruto)

aspirin: アスピリン アスピリン(asupirin)

assistant: アシスタント アシスタント(ashisutanto)

astatine: アスタチン アスタチン(asutachin)

asteroid: 小惑星 小惑星(shō wakusei)

asthma: 喘息 喘息(zensoku)

Atlantic Ocean: 大西洋 大西洋(Taisei yō)

atmosphere: 大気 大気(taiki)

atom: 原子 原子(genshi)

atomic number: 原子番号 原子番号(genshi bangō)

attack: 攻撃する 攻撃する(kōgeki suru)

attic: 屋根裏部屋 屋根裏部屋(yaneura heya)

aubergine: 茄子 茄子(nasu)

audience: 観客 観客(kankyaku)

August: 八月 八月(hachi gatsu)

aunt: 叔母 叔母(oba)

aurora: オーロラ オーロラ(ōrora)

Australia: オーストラリア オーストラリア(Ōsutoraria)

Australian football: オーストラリアンフットボール オーストラリアンフットボール(ōsutorarian futtobōru)

Austria: オーストリア オーストリア(Ōsutoria)

author: 作家 作家(sakka)

automatic: オートマチック オートマチック(ōtomachikku)

autumn: 秋 秋(aki)

avenue: 大通り 大通り(ōdōri)

avocado: アボカド アボカド(abokado)

axe: 斧 斧(ono)

Azerbaijan: アゼルバイジャン アゼルバイジャン(Azerubaijan)

B

baby: 赤ちゃん 赤ちゃん(akachan)

baby bottle: 哺乳瓶 哺乳瓶(honyū bin)

baby monitor: ベビーモニター ベビーモニター(bebī monitā)

bachelor: 学士 学士(gakushi)

back: 背中 背中(senaka), 後ろ 後ろ(ushiro)

backgammon: バックギャモン バックギャモン(bakkugyamon)

backpack: バックパック バックパック(bakkupakku)

back seat: 後部座席 後部座席(kōbu zaseki)

bacon: ベーコン ベーコン(bēkon)

bacterium: 細菌 細菌(saikin)

bad: 悪い 悪い(warui)

badminton: バドミントン バドミントン(badominton)

bag: バッグ バッグ(baggu)

Bahrain: バーレーン バーレーン(Bārēn)

bake: 焼く 焼く(yaku)

baked beans: ベイクドビーンズ ベイクドビーンズ(beikudo bīnzu)

baking powder: ベーキングパウダー ベーキングパウダー(bēkingu paudā)

balcony: ベランダ ベランダ(beranda)

bald head: はげ頭 はげ頭(hageatama)

ballet: バレエ バレエ(barē)

ballet shoes: バレエシューズ バレエシューズ(barē shūzu)

ball pen: ボールペン ボールペン(bōru pen)

Ballroom dance: 社交ダンス 社交ダンス(shakō dansu)

bamboo: 竹 竹(take)

banana: バナナ バナナ(banana)

bandage: 包帯 包帯(hōtai)

Bangladesh: バングラデシュ バングラデシュ(Banguradeshu)

bank account: 銀行口座 銀行口座(ginkō kōza)

bank transfer: 銀行振込 銀行振込(ginkō furikomi)

bar: バー バー(bā)

Barbados: バルバドス バルバドス(Barubadosu)

barbecue: バーベキュー バーベキュー(bābekyū)

barbell: バーベル バーベル(bāberu)

bar code: バーコード バーコード(bā kōdo)

bar code scanner: バーコードスキャナー バーコードスキャナー(bā kōdo sukyanā)

bargain: バーゲン バーゲン(bāgen)

barium: バリウム バリウム(bariumu)

barkeeper: バーテンダー バーテンダー(bātendā)

barrette: バレッタ バレッタ(baretta)

baseball: 野球 野球(yakyū)

baseball cap: ベースボールキャップ ベースボールキャップ(bēsubōru kyappu)

basement: 地下室 地下室(chika shitsu)

basil: バジル バジル(bajiru)

basin: 洗面器 洗面器(senmen ki)

basket: バスケット バスケット(basuketto)

basketball: バスケットボール バスケットボール(basukettobōru)

bass guitar: ベースギター ベースギター(bēsu gitā)

bassoon: ファゴット ファゴット(fagotto)

bat: コウモリ コウモリ(kōmori), バット バット(batto)

bathrobe: バスローブ バスローブ(basurōbu)

bathroom: バスルーム バスルーム(basurūmu)

bathroom slippers: トイレ用スリッパ トイレ用スリッパ(toire yō surippa)

bath towel: バスタオル バスタオル(basu taoru)

bathtub: 浴槽 浴槽(yokusō)

baton: 警棒 警棒(keibō)

battery: バッテリー バッテリー(batterī)

beach: ビーチ ビーチ(bīchi)

beach volleyball: ビーチバレー ビーチバレー(bīchi barē)

bean: 豆 豆(mame)

bear: 熊 熊(kuma)

beard: 髭 髭(hige)

beautiful: 美しい 美しい(utsukushī)

because: だから だから(da kara)

bed: ベッド ベッド(beddo)

bedroom: 寝室 寝室(shinshitsu)

bedside lamp: ベッドサイドランプ ベッドサイドランプ(beddo saido ranpu)

bee: 蜂 蜂(hachi)

beech: 橅 橅(buna)

beef: 牛肉 牛肉(gyūniku)

beer: ビール ビール(bīru)

behaviour therapy: 行動療法 行動療法(kōdō ryōhō)

beige: ベージュ ベージュ(bēju)

Beijing duck: 北京ダック 北京ダック(Pekin dakku)

Belarus: ベラルーシ ベラルーシ(Berarūshi)

Belgium: ベルギー ベルギー(Berugī)

Belize: ベリーズ ベリーズ(Berīzu)

bell: 呼び鈴 呼び鈴(yobirin)

belly: 腹 腹(hara)

belly button: 臍 臍(heso)

below: 下 下(shita)

belt: ベルト ベルト(beruto)

bench: ベンチ ベンチ(benchi)

bench press: ベンチプレス ベンチプレス(benchi puresu)

Benin: ベニン ベニン(Benin)

berkelium: バークリウム バークリウム(bākuriumu)

beryllium: ベリリウム ベリリウム(beririumu)

beside: 横 横(yoko)

bet: 賭ける 賭ける(kakeru)

Bhutan: ブータン ブータン(Būtan)

biathlon: バイアスロン バイアスロン(baiasuron)

bib: よだれ掛け よだれ掛け(yodare kake)

bicycle: 自転車 自転車(jiten sha)

big: 大きな 大きな(ōkina)

big brother: 兄 兄(ani)

big sister: 姉 姉(ane)

bikini: ビキニ ビキニ(bikini)

bill: 請求書 請求書(seikyū sho)

billiards: ビリヤード ビリヤード(biriyādo)

biology: 生物学 生物学(seibutsu gaku)

birch: 樺 樺(kaba)

birth: 誕生 誕生(tanjō)

birth certificate: 出生証明書 出生証明書(shusshō shōmei sho)

birth control pill: 避妊用ピル 避妊用ピル(hinin yō piru)

birthday: 誕生日 誕生日(tanjōbi)

birthday cake: バースデーケーキ バースデーケーキ(bāsudē kēki)

birthday party: 誕生日会 誕生日会(tanjōbikai)

biscuit: ビスケット ビスケット(bisuketto)

bismuth: ビスマス ビスマス(bisumasu)

bison: バイソン バイソン(baison)

bite: 噛む 噛む(kamu), 歯型 歯型(hagata)

black: 黒 黒(kuro)

blackberry: ブラックベリー ブラックベリー(burakkuberī)

blackboard: 黒板 黒板(kokuban)

black hole: ブラックホール ブラックホール(burakku hōru)

Black Sea: 黒海 黒海(Kokkai)

black tea: 紅茶 紅茶(kōcha)

bladder: 膀胱 膀胱(bōkō)

blanket: 毛布 毛布(mōfu)

blazer: ブレザー ブレザー(burezā)

blind: 目が見えない 目が見えない(me ga mienai), ブラインド ブラインド(buraindo)

blond: ブロンド ブロンド(burondo)

blood test: 血液検査 血液検査(ketsueki kensa)

bloody: 血まみれ 血まみれ(chimamire)

blossom: 花 花(hana)

blue: 青 青(ao)

blueberry: ブルーベリー ブルーベリー(burūberī)

blues: ブルース ブルース(burūsu)

board game: ボードゲーム ボードゲーム(bōdo gēmu)

bobsleigh: ボブスレー ボブスレー(bobusurē)

bodybuilding: ボディービルディング ボディービルディング(bodībirudingu)

bodyguard: ボディーガード ボディーガード(bodīgādo)

body lotion: ボディーローション ボディーローション(bodī rōshon)

bohrium: ボーリウム ボーリウム(bōriumu)

boil: 茹でる 茹でる(yuderu)

boiled: ゆでた ゆでた(yudeta)

boiled egg: ゆで卵 ゆで卵(yudetamago)

Bolivia: ボリビア ボリビア(Boribia)

bone: 骨 骨(hone)

bone marrow: 骨髄 骨髄(kotsuzui)

bonnet: ボンネット ボンネット(bonnetto)

book: 本 本(hon)

booking: 予約 予約(yoyaku)

bookshelf: 本棚 本棚(hondana)

bookshop: 書店 書店(shoten)

boring: つまらない つまらない(tsumaranai)

boron: ホウ素 ホウ素(hōso)

Bosnia: ボスニア ボスニア(Bosunia)

bosom: 胸 胸(mune)

botanic garden: 植物園 植物園(shokubutsu en)

Botswana: ボツワナ ボツワナ(Botsuwana)

bottle: ボトル ボトル(botoru)

bottom: 尻 尻(shiri)

bowl: ボウル ボウル(bōru)

bowling: ボーリング ボーリング(bōringu)

bowling ball: ボーリングボール ボーリングボール(bōringu bōru)

bow tie: 蝶ネクタイ 蝶ネクタイ(chō nekutai)

boxing: ボクシング ボクシング(bokushingu)

boxing glove: ボクシング用グローブ ボクシング用グローブ(bokushingu yō gurōbu)

boxing ring: ボクシングリング ボクシングリング(bokushingu ringu)

boy: 男の子 男の子(otokonoko)

boyfriend: 彼氏 彼氏(kareshi)

bra: ブラジャー ブラジャー(burajā)

bracelet: ブレスレット ブレスレット(buresuretto)

brain: 脳 脳(nō)

brake: ブレーキ ブレーキ(burēki)

brake light: ブレーキライト ブレーキライト(burēki raito)

branch: 枝 枝(eda)
brandy: ブランデー ブランデー(burandē)
brave: 勇敢な 勇敢な(yūkan na)
Brazil: ブラジル ブラジル(Burajiru)
bread: パン パン(pan)
breakdance: ブレイクダンス ブレイクダンス(bureiku dansu)
breakfast: 朝食 朝食(chōshoku)
breastbone: 胸骨 胸骨(kyōkotsu)
breathe: 息をする 息をする(iki o suru)
brick: レンガ レンガ(renga)
bride: 花嫁 花嫁(hanayome)
bridge: 船橋 船橋(funabashi), ブリッジ ブリッジ(burijj i)
briefcase: ブリーフケース ブリーフケース(burīfukēsu)
broad: 幅広い 幅広い(habahiroi)
broccoli: ブロッコリー ブロッコリー(burokkorī)
bromine: 臭素 臭素(shūso)
bronze medal: 銅メダル 銅メダル(dō medaru)
brooch: ブローチ ブローチ(burōchi)
broom: 箒 箒(hōki)
brother-in-law: 義兄弟 義兄弟(gi kyōdai)
brown: 茶色 茶色(chairo)
brownie: ブラウニー ブラウニー(buraunī)
browser: ブラウザ ブラウザ(burauza)
bruise: 打撲 打撲(daboku)
Brunei: ブルネイ ブルネイ(Burunei)
brunette: ブルネット ブルネット(burunetto)
brush: ブラシ ブラシ(burashi), ヘアブラシ ヘアブラシ(hea burashi)
Brussels sprouts: 芽キャベツ 芽キャベツ(me kyabetsu)
bucket: バケツ バケツ(baketsu)
buffalo: バッファロー バッファロー(baffarō)
buffet: ビュッフェ ビュッフェ(byuffe)
bug: 虫 虫(mushi)
Bulgaria: ブルガリア ブルガリア(Burugaria)
bull: 雄牛 雄牛(oushi)
bulletin board: 掲示板 掲示板(keiji ban)
bumblebee: ミツバチ ミツバチ(mitsubachi)
bumper: バンパー バンパー(banpā)
bungee jumping: バンジージャンプ バンジージャンプ(banjī janpu)
bunk bed: 二段ベッド 二段ベッド(ni dan beddo)
burger: ハンバーガー ハンバーガー(hanbāgā)
Burkina Faso: ブルキナファソ ブルキナファソ(Burukinafaso)
Burma: ミャンマー ミャンマー(Myanmā)
burn: 焼く 焼く(yaku), 火傷 火傷(yakedo)
Burundi: ブルンジ ブルンジ(Burunji)
bus: バス バス(basu)
bus driver: バスの運転手 バスの運転手(basu no unten shu)
bush: 灌木 灌木(kanboku)
business card: 名刺 名刺(meishi)
business class: ビジネスクラス ビジネスクラス(bijinesu kurasu)
business dinner: ビジネスディナー ビジネスディナー(bijinesu dinā)
business school: ビジネススクール ビジネススクール(bijinesu sukūru)

business trip: 出張 出張(shucchō)

bus stop: バス停 バス停(basu tei)

busy: 忙しい 忙しい(isogashī)

but: でも でも(de mo)

butcher: 肉屋 肉屋(nikuya)

butter: バター バター(batā)

buttercup: 金鳳花 金鳳花(kinpōge)

butterfly: 蝶 蝶(chō)

buttermilk: バターミルク バターミルク(batā miruku)

button: ボタン ボタン(botan)

buy: 買う 買う(kau)

bye bye: またね またね(mata ne)

C

cabbage: キャベツ キャベツ(kyabetsu)

cabin: キャビン キャビン(kyabin)

cable: ケーブル ケーブル(keiburu)

cable car: ロープウエー ロープウエー(rōpuuē)

cactus: サボテン サボテン(saboten)

cadmium: カドミウム カドミウム(kadomiumu)

caesium: セシウム セシウム(seshiumu)

cake: ケーキ ケーキ(kēki)

calcite: 方解石 方解石(hōkaiseki)

calcium: カルシウム カルシウム(karushiumu)

calculate: 計算する 計算する(keisan suru)

calendar: カレンダー カレンダー(karendā)

californium: カリホルニウム カリホルニウム(karihoruniumu)

call: 電話する 電話する(denwa suru)

Cambodia: カンボジア カンボジア(Kanbojia)

camcorder: ビデオカメラ ビデオカメラ(bideo kamera)

camel: らくだ らくだ(rakuda)

camera: カメラ カメラ(kamera)

camera operator: カメラマン カメラマン(kameraman)

Cameroon: カメルーン カメルーン(Kamerūn)

campfire: キャンプファイヤー キャンプファイヤー(kyanpu faiyā)

camping: キャンプ キャンプ(kyanpu)

camping site: キャンプ場 キャンプ場(kyanpu jō)

Canada: カナダ カナダ(Kanada)

cancer: 癌 癌(gan)

candle: 蝋燭 蝋燭(rōsoku)

candy: キャンディー キャンディー(kyandī)

candy floss: 綿菓子 綿菓子(watagashi)

canoe: カヌー カヌー(kanū)

canoeing: カヌー競技 カヌー競技(kanū kyōgi)

canteen: カフェテリア カフェテリア(kafeteria)

canyon: 渓谷 渓谷(keikoku)

Can you help me?: 手伝ってくれますか？ 手伝ってくれますか？(tetsudatte kuremasu ka)

Cape Verde: カーボベルデ カーボベルデ(Kābo Berude)

capital: 首都 首都(shuto)

cappuccino: カプチーノ カプチーノ(kapuchīno)

capsule: カプセル カプセル(kapuseru)

captain: キャプテン キャプテン(kyaputen)

car: 車 車(kuruma)

caramel: キャラメル キャラメル(kyarameru)

caravan: キャラバン キャラバン(kyaraban)

carbon: 炭素 炭素(tanso)

carbon dioxide: 二酸化炭素 二酸化炭素(ni sanka tanso)

carbon monoxide: 一酸化炭素 一酸化炭素(issankatanso)

card game: カードゲーム カードゲーム(kādo gēmu)

cardigan: カーディガン カーディガン(kādigan)

cardiology: 心臓病学 心臓病学(shinzō byō gaku)

cargo aircraft: 貨物航空機 貨物航空機(kamotsu kōkū ki)

caricature: 風刺画 風刺画(fūshi ga)

caries: 虫歯 虫歯(mushiba)

carousel: カルーセル カルーセル(karūseru)

car park: 駐車場 駐車場(chūsha jō)

carpenter: 大工 大工(daiku)

carpet: カーペット カーペット(kāpetto)

car racing: カーレース カーレース(kā rēsu)

carrot: 人参 人参(ninjin)

carry: 運ぶ 運ぶ(hakobu)

carry-on luggage: 手荷物 手荷物(te nimotsu)

cartilage: 軟骨 軟骨(nankotsu)

cartoon: 漫画 漫画(manga)

car wash: 洗車 洗車(sensha)

case: 事件 事件(jiken)

cashew: カシューナッツ カシューナッツ(kashū nattsu)

cashier: レジ係 レジ係(reji kakari)

cash machine: ATM ATM(ATM)

cash register: レジ レジ(reji)

casino: カジノ カジノ(kajino)

cast: キャスト キャスト(kyasuto), ギプス ギプス(gipusu)

castle: 城 城(shiro)

cat: 猫 猫(neko)

catch: キャッチする キャッチする(kyacchi suru)

caterpillar: あおむし あおむし(aomushi)

cathedral: 大聖堂 大聖堂(dai seidō)

catheter: カテーテル カテーテル(katēteru)

cauliflower: カリフラワー カリフラワー(karifurawā)

cave: 洞窟 洞窟(dōkutsu)

Cayman Islands: ケイマン諸島 ケイマン諸島(Keiman shotō)

CD player: CDプレーヤー CDプレーヤー(CD purēyā)

ceiling: 天井 天井(tenjō)

celebrate: 祝う 祝う(iwau)

celery: セロリ セロリ(serori)

cello: チェロ チェロ(chero)

cement: セメント セメント(semento)

cement mixer: セメントミキサー セメントミキサー(semento mikisā)

cemetery: 墓地 墓地(bochi)

centigrade: 摂氏 摂氏(sesshi)

centimeter: センチメートル センチメートル(senchimētoru)

Central African Republic: 中央アフリカ共和国 中央アフリカ共和国(Chūō Afurika Kyōwakoku)

central business district (CBD): 商業地区 商業地区(shōgyō chiku)

central processing unit (CPU): CPU CPU(CPU)

century: 世紀 世紀(seiki)

cereal: シリアル シリアル(shiriaru)

cerium: セリウム セリウム (seriumu)

cesarean: 帝王切開 帝王切開(teiō sekkai)

cha-cha: チャチャチャ チャチャチャ(chachacha)

Chad: チャド チャド(Chado)

chain: チェーン チェーン(chēn)

chainsaw: チェーンソー チェーンソー(chēn sō)

chair: 椅子 椅子(isu)

chairman: 会長 会長(kaichō)

chalk: チョーク チョーク(chōku)

chameleon: カメレオン カメレオン(kamereon)

champagne: シャンパン シャンパン(shanpan)

changing room: 更衣室 更衣室(kōi shitsu)

channel: チャンネル チャンネル(channeru)

character: 文字 文字(moji)

chat: チャット チャット(chatto)

cheap: 安い 安い(yasui)

check-in desk: チェックインカウンター チェックインカウンター(chekku in kauntā)

cheek: 頬 頬(hō)

cheerleader: チアリーダー チアリーダー(chiarīdā)

cheers: 乾杯 乾杯(kanpai)

cheese: チーズ チーズ(chīzu)

cheeseburger: チーズバーガー チーズバーガー(chīzubāgā)

cheesecake: チーズケーキ チーズケーキ(chīzu kēki)

cheetah: チーター チーター(chītā)

chemical compound: 化合物 化合物(kagō butsu)

chemical reaction: 化学反応 化学反応(kagaku hannō)

chemical structure: 化学構造 化学構造(kagaku kōzō)

chemist: 化学者 化学者(kagaku sha)

chemistry: 化学 化学(kagaku)

cheque: 小切手 小切手(kogitte)

cherry: サクランボ サクランボ(sakuranbo)

chess: チェス チェス(chesu)

chest: 胸部 胸部(kyōbu)

chewing gum: ガム ガム(gamu)

chick: 雛 雛(hina)

chicken: 鶏 鶏(niwatori), 鶏肉 鶏肉(keiniku)

chicken nugget: チキンナゲット チキンナゲット (chikin nagetto)

chickenpox: 水疱瘡 水疱瘡(mizu bōsō)

chicken wings: チキンウイング チキンウイング(chikin uingu)

child: 子供 子供(kodomo)

child seat: チャイルドシート チャイルドシート(chairudo shīto)

Chile: チリ チリ(Chiri)

chili: 唐辛子 唐辛子(tōgarashi)

chimney: 煙突 煙突(entotsu)

chin: 顎 顎(ago)

China: 中国 中国(Chūgoku)

Chinese medicine: 漢方薬 漢方薬(kanpō yaku)

chips: チップス チップス(chippusu)

chiropractor: カイロプラクター カイロプラクター(kairopurakutā)

chive: チャイブ チャイブ(chaibu)

chlorine: 塩素 塩素(enso)

chocolate: チョコレート チョコレート(chokorēto)

chocolate cream: チョコレートスプレッド チョコレートスプレッド (chokorēto supureddo)

choose: 選ぶ 選ぶ(erabu)

chopping board: まな板 まな板(manaita)

chopstick: 箸 箸(hashi)

Christmas: クリスマス クリスマス(kurisumasu)

chromium: クロム クロム(kuromu)

chubby: 太った 太った(futotta)

church: 教会 教会(kyōkai)

cider: サイダー サイダー(saidā)

cigar: 葉巻 葉巻(hamaki)

cigarette: たばこ たばこ(tabako)

cinema: 映画 映画(eiga)

cinnamon: シナモン シナモン(shinamon)

circle: 円 円(en)

circuit training: サーキットトレーニング サーキットトレーニング(sākitto torēningu)

clarinet: クラリネット クラリネット(kurarinetto)

classical music: クラシック音楽 クラシック音楽(kurashikku ongaku)

classic car: クラシックカー クラシックカー(kurashikku kā)

clay: 粘土 粘土(nendo)

clean: きれい きれい(kirei), 掃除する 掃除する(sōji suru)

cleaner: 清掃員 清掃員(seisō in)

clef: 音部記号 音部記号(on bu kigō)

clever: 賢い 賢い(kashikoi)

cliff: 崖 崖(gake)

cliff diving: クリフダイビング クリフダイビング(kurifu daibingu)

climb: 登る 登る(noboru)

climbing: クライミング クライミング(kuraimingu)

clinic: クリニック クリニック(kurinikku)

clipboard: クリップボード クリップボード(kurippu bōdo)

clitoris: クリトリス クリトリス(kuritorisu)

clock: 時計 時計(tokei)

close: 近い 近い(chikai), 閉める 閉める(shimeru)

cloud: 雲 雲(kumo)

cloudy: 曇った 曇った(kumotta)

clover: クローバー クローバー(kurōbā)

clutch: クラッチ クラッチ(kuracchi)

coach: コーチ コーチ(kōchi)

coal: 石炭 石炭(sekitan)

coast: 沿岸 沿岸(engan)

coat: コート コート(kōto)

cobalt: コバルト コバルト(kobaruto)

cockerel: おんどり おんどり(ondori)

cockpit: コックピット コックピット(kokkupitto)

cocktail: カクテル カクテル(kakuteru)

coconut: ココナッツ ココナッツ(kokonattsu)

coffee: コーヒー コーヒー(kōhī)

coffee machine: コーヒーマシン コーヒーマシン(kōhī mashin)

coffee table: コーヒーテーブル コーヒーテーブル(kōhī tēburu)

coffin: 棺桶 棺桶(kanoke)

coin: 貨幣 貨幣(kahei)

coke: コーラ コーラ(kōra)

cold: 寒い 寒い(samui), 風邪 風邪(kaze)

collar: 襟 襟(eri)

collarbone: 鎖骨 鎖骨(sakotsu)

colleague: 同僚 同僚(dōryō)

Colombia: コロンビア コロンビア(Koronbia)

colon: 結腸 結腸(kecchō), コロン コロン(koron)

colony: 植民地 植民地(shokumin chi)

coloured pencil: 色鉛筆 色鉛筆(iro enpitsu)

comb: 櫛 櫛(kushi)

combine harvester: コンバイン コンバイン(konbain)

come: 来る 来る(kuru)

comedy: コメディ コメディ (komedi)

comet: 彗星 彗星(suisei)

Come with me: 一緒においで 一緒においで(issho ni o ide)

comic book: 漫画本 漫画本(manga hon)

comma: 読点 読点(tōten)

commentator: コメンテーター コメンテーター(komentētā)

Comoros: コモロ コモロ(Komoro)

compass: コンパス コンパス(konpasu)

concealer: コンシーラー コンシーラー(konshīrā)

concert: コンサート コンサート(konsāto)

concrete: コンクリート コンクリート(konkurīto)

concrete mixer: コンクリートミキサー コンクリートミキサー(konkurīto mikisā)

concussion: 脳震盪 脳震盪(nō shintō)

condom: コンドーム コンドーム(kondōmu)

conductor: 車掌 車掌(shashō), 指揮者 指揮者(shiki sha)

cone: 円錐形 円錐形(ensui kei)

construction site: 工事現場 工事現場(kōji genba)

construction worker: 土木作業員 土木作業員(doboku sagyō in)

consultant: コンサルタント コンサルタント(konsarutanto)

contact lens: コンタクトレンズ コンタクトレンズ(kontakuto renzu)

container: コンテナ コンテナ(kontena)

container ship: コンテナ船 コンテナ船(kontena sen)

content: 内容 内容(naiyō)

continent: 大陸 大陸(tairiku)

control tower: 管制塔 管制塔(kansei tō)

cook: 料理する 料理する(ryōri suru), コック コック(kokku)

cooker: 焜炉 焜炉(konro)

cooker hood: レンジフード レンジフード(renji fūdo)

cookie: クッキー クッキー(kukkī)

Cook Islands: クック諸島 クック諸島(Kukku Shotō)

cool: かっこいい かっこいい(kakko ī)

copernicium: コペルニシウム コペルニシウム(koperunishiumu)

copper: 銅 銅(dō)

copy: コピーする コピーする(kopī suru)

coral reef: 珊瑚礁 珊瑚礁(sango shō)

coriander: コリアンダー コリアンダー(koriandā)

corkscrew: 栓抜き 栓抜き(sennuki)

corn: トウモロコシ トウモロコシ(tōmorokoshi)

corn oil: コーンオイル コーンオイル(kōn oiru)

corpse: 死体 死体(shitai)

correct: 正しい 正しい(tadashī)

corridor: 廊下 廊下(rōka)

Costa Rica: コスタリカ コスタリカ(Kosutarika)

cotton: 綿 綿(men)

cough: 咳 咳(seki)

cough syrup: 咳止め 咳止め(sekidome)

count: 数える 数える(kazoeru)

country: 国 国(kuni)

courgette: ズッキーニ ズッキーニ(zukkīni)

court: 裁判所 裁判所(saiban sho)

cousin: 従兄弟 従兄弟(jūkeitei), 従姉妹 従姉妹(jūshimai)

cow: 牛 牛(ushi)

crab: カニ カニ(kani)

cramp: けいれん けいれん(keiren)

cranberry: クランベリー クランベリー(kuranberī)

crane: クレーン クレーン(kurēn)

crane truck: クレーン車 クレーン車(kurēn sha)

crater: クレーター クレーター(kurētā)

crawl: 這う 這う(hau)

crazy: 狂った 狂った(kurutta)

cream: クリーム クリーム(kurīmu)

credit card: クレジットカード クレジットカード(kurejitto kādo)

cricket: キリギリス キリギリス(kirigirisu), クリケット クリケット(kuriketto)

criminal: 犯罪者 犯罪者(hanzai sha)

Croatia: クロアチア クロアチア(Kuroachia)

crocodile: ワニ ワニ(wani)

croissant: クロワッサン クロワッサン(kurowassan)

cross-country skiing: クロスカントリースキー クロスカントリースキー(kurosu kantorī sukī)

cross trainer: クロストレーナー クロストレーナー(kurosu torēnā)

crosswords: クロスワード クロスワード(kurosuwādo)

crow: カラス カラス(karasu)

crown: 冠 冠(kanmuri)

cruise ship: クルーズ船 クルーズ船(kurūzu sen)

crutch: 松葉杖 松葉杖(matsuba tsue)

cry: 泣く 泣く(naku)

crêpe: クレープ クレープ(kurēpu)

CT scanner: CTスキャナー CTスキャナー(CT sukyanā)

Cuba: キューバ キューバ(Kyūba)

cube: 立方体 立方体(rippō tai)

cubic meter: 立方メートル 立方メートル(rippō mētoru)

cucumber: キュウリ キュウリ(kyūri)

cuddly toy: ぬいぐるみ ぬいぐるみ(nuigurumi)

cue: キュー キュー(kyū)

cup: コップ コップ(koppu), カップ カップ(kappu)

cupboard: 食器棚 食器棚(shokki tana)

curium: キュリウム キュリウム(kyuriumu)

curling: カーリング カーリング(kāringu)

curling iron: ヘアアイロン ヘアアイロン(hea airon)

curly: 巻き髪 巻き髪(makigami)

currant: スグリ スグリ(suguri)

curry: カレー カレー(karē)

curtain: カーテン カーテン(kāten)

curve: 曲線 曲線(kyokusen)

custard: カスタード カスタード(kasutādo)

customer: 顧客 顧客(kokyaku)

customs: 関税 関税(kanzei)

cut: 切る 切る(kiru)

cute: 可愛い 可愛い(kawaī)

cutlery: カトラリー カトラリー(katorarī)

cycling: サイクリング サイクリング(saikuringu)

cylinder: 円筒 円筒(entō)

cymbals: シンバル シンバル(shinbaru)

Cyprus: キプロス キプロス(Kipurosu)

Czech Republic: チェコ共和国 チェコ共和国(Cheko Kyōwakoku)

D

dad: パパ パパ(papa)

daffodil: 水仙 水仙(suisen)

daisy: デイジー デイジー(deijī)

dam: ダム ダム(damu)

dancer: ダンサー ダンサー(dansā)

dancing: ダンス ダンス(dansu)

dancing shoes: ダンスシューズ ダンスシューズ(dansu shūzu)

dandelion: タンポポ タンポポ(tanpopo)

dandruff: フケ フケ(fuke)

dark: 暗い 暗い(kurai)

darmstadtium: ダームスタチウム ダームスタチウム(dāmusutachiumu)

darts: ダーツ ダーツ(dātsu)

dashboard: ダッシュボード ダッシュボード(dasshubōdo)

database: データベース データベース(dētabēsu)

date: デーツ デーツ(dētsu)

daughter: 娘 娘(musume)

daughter-in-law: 嫁 嫁(yome)

day: 日 日(hi)

deaf: 耳が聞こえない 耳が聞こえない(mimi ga kikoenai)

death: 死 死(shi)

decade: 十年 十年(jū nen)

December: 十二月 十二月(jū ni gatsu)

decimeter: デシメートル デシメートル(deshimētoru)

deck: デッキ デッキ(dekki)

deck chair: デッキチェア デッキチェア(dekki chea)

deep: 深い 深い(fukai)

deer: 鹿 鹿(shika)

defend: 守る 守る(mamoru)

defendant: 被告人 被告人(hikoku nin)

degree: 学位 学位(gakui)

deliver: 届ける 届ける(todokeru)

delivery: 出産 出産(shussan)

Democratic Republic of the Congo: コンゴ民主共和国 コンゴ民主共和国(Kongo Minshu Kyōwakoku)

Denmark: デンマーク デンマーク(Denmāku)

denominator: 分母 分母(bunbo)

dental brace: 矯正具 矯正具(kyōsei gu)

dental filling: 詰め物 詰め物(tsumemono)

dental prostheses: 義歯 義歯(gishi)

dentist: 歯医者 歯医者(ha isha)

department: 部門 部門(bumon)

departure: 出発 出発(shuppatsu)

dermatology: 皮膚科 皮膚科(hifu ka)

desert: 砂漠 砂漠(sabaku)

designer: デザイナー デザイナー(dezainā)

desk: 机 机(tsukue)

dessert: デザート デザート(dezāto)

detective: 探偵 探偵(tantei)

diabetes: 糖尿病 糖尿病(tōnyō byō)

diagonal: 対角線 対角線(taikaku sen)

diamond: ダイヤモンド ダイヤモンド(daiyamondo)

diaper: おむつ おむつ(omutsu)

diaphragm: 横隔膜 横隔膜(ōkakumaku)

diarrhea: 下痢 下痢(geri)

diary: 日記 日記(nikki)

dictionary: 辞書 辞書(jisho)

die: 死ぬ 死ぬ(shinu)

diesel: ディーゼル ディーゼル(dīzeru)

difficult: 難しい 難しい(muzukashī)

dig: 掘る 掘る(horu)

digital camera: デジカメ デジカメ(dejikame)

dill: ディル ディル(diru)

dimple: えくぼ えくぼ(ekubo)

dim sum: 点心 点心(tenshin)

dinner: ディナー ディナー(dinā)

dinosaur: 恐竜 恐竜(kyōryū)

diploma: ディプロマ ディプロマ(dipuroma)

director: ディレクター ディレクター(direkutā)

dirty: 汚い 汚い(kitanai)

discus throw: 円盤投げ 円盤投げ(enban nage)

dishwasher: 食器洗い機 食器洗い機(shokki arai ki)

district: 区 区(ku)

dividend: 配当 配当(haitō)

diving: 飛込競技 飛込競技(tobikomi kyōgi), ダイビング ダイビング(daibingu)

diving mask: ダイビングマスク ダイビングマスク(daibingu masuku)

division: 割り算 割り算(warizan)

divorce: 離婚 離婚(rikon)

DJ: DJ DJ(DJ)

Djibouti: ジブチ ジブチ(Jibuchi)

doctor: 医者 医者(isha)

doesn't matter: 関係ない 関係ない(kankei nai)

dog: 犬 犬(inu)

doll: 人形 人形(ningyō)

dollar: ドル ドル(doru)

dollhouse: ドールハウス ドールハウス(dōru hausu)

dolphin: イルカ イルカ(iruka)

Dominica: ドミニカ ドミニカ(Dominika)

Dominican Republic: ドミニカ共和国 ドミニカ共和国(Dominika Kyōwakoku)

dominoes: ドミノ ドミノ(domino)

don't worry: 気にしないで 気にしないで(ki ni shinaide)

donkey: ロバ ロバ(roba)

door: ドア ドア(doa)

door handle: ドアノブ ドアノブ(doa nobu)

dorm room: 相部屋 相部屋(aibeya)

dosage: 投薬量 投薬量(tōyaku ryō)

double bass: ダブルベース ダブルベース(daburu bēsu)

double room: ダブルルーム ダブルルーム(daburu rūmu)

doughnut: ドーナツ ドーナツ(dōnatsu)

Do you love me?: 私のことが好きですか？ 私のことが好きですか？(watakushi no koto ga suki desu ka)

dragonfly: とんぼ とんぼ(tonbo)

draughts: チェッカー チェッカー(chekkā)

drawer: 引き出し 引き出し(hikidashi)

drawing: 描画 描画(byōga)

dreadlocks: ドレッドヘア ドレッドヘア(doreddo hea)

dream: 夢をみる 夢をみる(yume o miru)

dress: ドレス ドレス(doresu)

dress size: 洋服サイズ 洋服サイズ(yōfuku saizu)

dried fruit: ドライフルーツ ドライフルーツ(dorai furūtsu)

drill: ドリルする ドリルする(doriru suru)

drilling machine: ドリル ドリル(doriru)

drink: 飲む 飲む(nomu)

drums: ドラム ドラム(doramu)

drunk: 酔っぱらっている 酔っぱらっている(yopparatte iru)

dry: 乾いた 乾いた(kawaita), 乾かす 乾かす(kawakasu)

dubnium: ドブニウム ドブニウム(dobu niumu)

duck: 鴨 鴨(kamo)

dumbbell: ダンベル ダンベル(danberu)

dumpling: 餃子 餃子(gyōza)

duodenum: 十二指腸 十二指腸(jūnishichō)

DVD player: DVDプレーヤー DVDプレーヤー(DVD purēyā)

dyed: 染めた 染めた(someta)

dysprosium: ジスプロシウム ジスプロシウム(jisupuroshiumu)

E

e-mail: 電子メール 電子メール(denshi mēru)

e-mail address: メールアドレス メールアドレス(mēru adoresu)

eagle: 鷲 鷲(washi)

ear: 耳 耳(mimi)

earn: 得る 得る(uru/eru)

earphone: イヤフォン イヤフォン(iyafon)

earplug: 耳栓 耳栓(mimisen)

earring: イヤリング イヤリング(iyaringu)

earth: 地球 地球(chikyū)

earth's core: 地核 地核(chikaku)

earth's crust: 地殻 地殻(chikaku)

earthquake: 地震 地震(jishin)

east: 東 東(higashi)

Easter: イースター イースター(īsutā)

East Timor: 東チモール 東チモール(Higashichimōru)

easy: 簡単な 簡単な(kantan na)

eat: 食べる 食べる(taberu)

economics: 経済学 経済学(keizai gaku)

economy class: エコノミークラス エコノミークラス(ekonomī kurasu)

Ecuador: エクアドル エクアドル(Ekuadoru)

eczema: アトピー アトピー(atopī)

egg: 卵 卵(tamago)

egg white: 卵白 卵白(ranpaku)

Egypt: エジプト エジプト(Ejiputo)

einsteinium: アインスタイニウム アインスタイニウム(ainsutainiumu)

elbow: 肘 肘(hiji)

electric guitar: エレキギター エレキギター(ereki gitā)

electrician: 電気技師 電気技師(denki gishi)

electric iron: 電気アイロン 電気アイロン(denki airon)

electric shock: 電気ショック 電気ショック(denki shokku)

electron: 電子 電子(denshi)

elephant: 象 象(zō)

elevator: エレベーター エレベーター(erebētā)

elk: ヘラジカ ヘラジカ(herajika)

ellipse: 楕円 楕円(daen)

El Salvador: エルサルバドル エルサルバドル(Erusarubadoru)

embassy: 大使館 大使館(taishi kan)

embryo: 胎児 胎児(taiji)

emergency: 緊急 緊急(kinkyū)

emergency exit: 非常口 非常口(hijō guchi)

emergency room: 救命センター 救命センター(kyūmei sentā)

employee: 従業員 従業員(jūgyō in)

employer: 雇用主 雇用主(koyō shu)

empty: 空っぽ 空っぽ(karappo)

endocrinology: 内分泌学 内分泌学(nai bunpitsu gaku)

energy drink: 栄養ドリンク 栄養ドリンク(eiyō dorinku)

engagement: 婚約 婚約(kon yaku)

engagement ring: 婚約指輪 婚約指輪(kon yaku yubiwa)

engine: エンジン エンジン(enjin)

engineer: エンジニア エンジニア(enjinia)

engine room: エンジンルーム エンジンルーム(enjin rūmu)

English: 英語 英語(eigo)

enjoy: 楽しむ 楽しむ(tanoshimu)

entrepreneur: 起業家 起業家(kigyō ka)

envelope: 封筒 封筒(fūtō)

epilepsy: 癲癇 癲癇(tenkan)

episiotomy: 会陰切開術 会陰切開術(kaiinsekkai jutsu)

equation: 方程式 方程式(hōtei shiki)

equator: 赤道 赤道(sekidō)

Equatorial Guinea: 赤道ギニア 赤道ギニア(Sekidōginia)

erbium: エルビウム エルビウム(erubiumu)

Eritrea: エリトリア エリトリア(Eritoria)

espresso: エスプレッソ エスプレッソ(esupuresso)

essay: 論文 論文(ronbun)

Estonia: エストニア エストニア(Esutonia)

Ethiopia: エチオピア エチオピア(Echiopia)

eucalyptus: ユーカリ ユーカリ(yūkari)

euro: ユーロ ユーロ(yūro)

europium: ユーロピウム ユーロピウム(yūropiumu)

evening: 夕方 夕方(yūgata)

evening dress: イブニングドレス イブニングドレス(ibuningu doresu)

every: ごと ごと(goto)

everybody: みんな みんな(minna)

evidence: 証拠 証拠(shōko)

evil: 意地悪い 意地悪い(iji warui)

exam: 試験 試験(shiken)

excavator: 掘削機 掘削機(kussaku ki)

exclamation mark: 感嘆符 感嘆符(kantan fu)

excuse me: すみません すみません(sumimasen)

exercise bike: フィットネスバイク フィットネスバイク(fittonesu baiku)

exhaust pipe: 排気管 排気管(haiki kan)

expensive: 高い 高い(takai)

expiry date: 消費期限 消費期限(shōhi kigen)

eye: 目 目(me)

eyebrow: 眉 眉(mayu)

eyebrow pencil: アイブローペンシル アイブローペンシル(aiburō penshiru)

eyelashes: 睫毛 睫毛(matsuge)

eyeliner: アイライナー アイライナー(airainā)

eye shadow: アイシャドウ アイシャドウ(ai shadō)

F

fabric: 布 布(nuno)

face cream: フェイシャルクリーム フェイシャルクリーム(feisharu kurīmu)

face mask: フェイスパック フェイスパック(feisu pakku)

face powder: フェイスパウダー フェイスパウダー(feisu paudā)

facial toner: 化粧水 化粧水(keshō sui)

factory: 工場 工場(kōjō)

Fahrenheit: 華氏 華氏(kashi)

fail: 失敗する 失敗する(shippai suru)

faint: 気絶する 気絶する(kizetsu suru)

fair: 公平な 公平な(kōhei na)

fairground: 遊園地 遊園地(yūen chi)

falcon: ハヤブサ ハヤブサ(hayabusa)

Falkland Islands: フォークランド諸島 フォークランド諸島(Fōkurando Shotō)

fall: 落ちる 落ちる(ochiru)

family picture: 家族写真 家族写真(kazoku shashin)

family therapy: 家族療法 家族療法(kazoku ryōhō)

fan: 換気扇 換気扇(kanki sen)

far: 遠い 遠い(tōi)

fare: 運賃 運賃(unchin)

farm: 農場 農場(nōjō)

farmer: 農家 農家(nōka)

Faroe Islands: フェロー諸島 フェロー諸島(Ferō Shotō)

father: 父 父(chichi)

father-in-law: 義父 義父(gifu)

fat meat: 脂身 脂身(aburami)

fax: ファックス ファックス(fakkusu)

February: 二月 二月(ni gatsu)

feed: 食べさせる 食べさせる(tabesaseru)

fence: フェンス フェンス(fensu)

fencing: フェンシング フェンシング(fenshingu)

feng shui: 風水 風水(fūsui)

fennel: フェンネル フェンネル(fenneru)

fermium: フェルミウム フェルミウム(ferumiumu)

fern: シダ シダ(shida)

ferry: フェリー フェリー(ferī)

feta: フェタチーズ フェタチーズ(feta chīzu)

fever: 熱 熱(netsu)

fever thermometer: 体温計 体温計(taion kei)

few: 少ない 少ない(sukunai)

fiancé: 婚約者 婚約者(kon yaku sha)

fiancée: 婚約者 婚約者(kon yaku sha)

field hockey: 陸上ホッケー 陸上ホッケー(rikujō hokkē)

fifth floor: 六階 六階(roku kai)

fig: イチジク イチジク(ichijiku)

fight: 戦う 戦う(tatakau)

figure skating: フィギュアスケート フィギュアスケート(figyua sukēto)

Fiji: フィジー フィジー(Fijī)

file: やすり やすり(yasuri), ファイル ファイル(fairu)

filter: フィルター フィルター(firutā)

fin: フィン フィン(fin)

find: 見つける 見つける(mitsukeru)

fine: 罰金 罰金(bakkin)

finger: 指 指(yubi)

fingernail: 爪 爪(tsume)

fingerprint: 指紋 指紋(shimon)

Finland: フィンランド フィンランド(Finrando)

fire: 火 火(hi), 火事 火事(kaji)

fire alarm: 火災警報 火災警報(kasai keihō)

fire extinguisher: 消火器 消火器(shōka ki)

firefighter: 消防士 消防士(shōbō shi)

firefighters: 消防組 消防組(shōbō gumi)

fire station: 消防署 消防署(shōbō sho)

fire truck: 消防車 消防車(shōbō sha)

first: 第一 第一(dai ichi)

first basement floor: 地下一階 地下一階(chika ikkai)

first class: ファーストクラス ファーストクラス(fāsuto kurasu)

first floor: 二階 二階(ni kai)

fish: 魚 魚(sakana), 釣る 釣る(tsuru)

fish and chips: フィッシュアンドチップス フィッシュアンドチップス (fisshu ando chippusu)

fishbone: 魚の骨 魚の骨 (sakana no hone)

fisherman: 漁師 漁師 (ryōshi)

fishing boat: 漁船 漁船 (gyosen)

fish market: 魚市場 魚市場 (uoichiba)

fist: 拳 拳 (kobushi)

fix: 修正する 修正する (shūsei suru)

flamingo: フラミンゴ フラミンゴ (furamingo)

flash: フラッシュ フラッシュ (furasshu)

flat: 平らな 平らな (taira na)

flat screen: 薄型テレビ 薄型テレビ (usugata terebi)

flerovium: フレロビウム フレロビウム (furerobiumu)

flip-flops: ビーチサンダル ビーチサンダル (bīchi sandaru)

flip chart: フリップチャート フリップチャート (furippu chāto)

flood: 洪水 洪水 (kōzui)

floor: 床 床 (yuka)

florist: 花屋 花屋 (hanaya)

flour: 小麦粉 小麦粉 (komugiko)

flower: 花 花 (hana)

flower bed: 花壇 花壇 (kadan)

flower pot: 鉢 鉢 (hachi)

flu: インフルエンザ インフルエンザ (infuruenza)

fluid: 液体 液体 (ekitai)

fluorine: フッ素 フッ素 (fusso)

flute: フルート フルート (furūto)

fly: ハエ ハエ (hae), 飛ぶ 飛ぶ (tobu)

flyer: チラシ チラシ (chirashi)

foetus: 胎児 胎児 (taiji)

fog: 霧 霧 (kiri)

foggy: 霧のかかった 霧のかかった (kiri no kakatta)

folder: フォルダー フォルダー (forudā)

folk music: 民族音楽 民族音楽 (minzoku ongaku)

follow: 従う 従う (shitagau)

foot: 脚 脚 (ashi), フィート フィート (fīto)

football: サッカー サッカー (sakkā), サッカーボール サッカーボール (sakkā bōru), フットボール フットボール (futtobōru)

football boots: スパイク スパイク (supaiku)

football stadium: サッカースタジアム サッカースタジアム (sakkā sutajiamu)

force: 力 力 (chikara)

forehead: 額 額 (hitai)

forest: 森 森 (mori)

fork: フォーク フォーク (fōku)

forklift truck: フォークリフト フォークリフト (fōkurifuto)

Formula 1: F1 F1 (F1)

foundation: ファンデーション ファンデーション (fandēshon)

fountain: 噴水 噴水 (funsui)

fourth: 第四 第四 (dai yon)

fox: きつね きつね (kitsune)

fraction: 分数 分数 (bunsū)

fracture: 骨折 骨折 (kossetsu)

France: フランス フランス (Furansu)

francium: フランシウム フランシウム(furanshiumu)

freckles: そばかす そばかす(sobakasu)

freestyle skiing: フリースタイルスキー フリースタイルスキー(furī sutairu sukī)

freezer: 冷凍庫 冷凍庫(reitō ko)

freight train: 貨物列車 貨物列車(kamotsu ressha)

French: フランス語 フランス語(Furansu go)

French fries: フライドポテト フライドポテト(furaido poteto)

French horn: フレンチホルン フレンチホルン(furenchi horun)

French Polynesia: フランス領ポリネシア フランス領ポリネシア(Furansuryō Porineshia)

Friday: 金曜日 金曜日(kin yōbi)

fridge: 冷蔵庫 冷蔵庫(reizō ko)

fried noodles: 焼きそば 焼きそば(yakisoba)

fried rice: チャーハン チャーハン(chāhan)

fried sausage: 揚げソーセージ 揚げソーセージ(age sōsēji)

friend: 友達 友達(tomodachi)

friendly: フレンドリーな フレンドリーな(furendorī na)

frog: カエル カエル(kaeru)

front: 前 前(mae)

front door: 表玄関 表玄関(omotegenkan)

front light: フロントライト フロントライト(furonto raito)

front seat: フロントシート フロントシート(furonto shīto)

fruit gum: フルーツガム フルーツガム(furūtsu gamu)

fruit merchant: 青果店 青果店(seika ten)

fruit salad: フルーツサラダ フルーツサラダ(furūtsu sarada)

fry: 炒める 炒める(itameru)

full: 満腹 満腹(manpuku), 満タン 満タン(mantan)

full stop: 句点 句点(kuten)

funeral: 葬式 葬式(sōshiki)

funnel: 漏斗 漏斗(rōto)

funny: 面白い 面白い(omoshiroi)

furniture store: 家具屋 家具屋(kagu ya)

G

Gabon: ガボン ガボン(Gabon)

gadolinium: ガドリニウム ガドリニウム(gadoriniumu)

gain weight: 太る 太る(futoru)

galaxy: 銀河 銀河(ginga)

gall bladder: 胆嚢 胆嚢(tannō)

gallium: ガリウム ガリウム(gariumu)

gamble: ギャンブルする ギャンブルする (gyanburu suru)

game: 鹿肉 鹿肉(shikaniku)

garage: 車庫 車庫(shako)

garage door: 車庫のドア 車庫のドア(shako no doa)

garbage bin: ゴミ箱 ゴミ箱(gomibako)

garden: 庭 庭(niwa)

gardener: 庭師 庭師(niwashi)

garlic: ニンニク ニンニク(ninniku)

gas: ガス ガス(gasu)

gear lever: シフトレバー シフトレバー(shifuto rebā)

gear shift: ギアシフト ギアシフト(gia shifuto)

gecko: やもり やもり (yamori)

gender: 性別 性別 (seibetsu)

general manager: 総支配人 総支配人 (sō shihai nin)

generator: 発電機 発電機 (hatsuden ki)

generous: 寛大な 寛大な (kandai na)

geography: 地理 地理 (chiri)

geometry: 幾何学 幾何学 (kika gaku)

Georgia: ジョージア ジョージア (Jōjia)

German: ドイツ語 ドイツ語 (Doitsu go)

germanium: ゲルマニウム ゲルマニウム (gerumaniumu)

Germany: ドイツ ドイツ (Doitsu)

geyser: 間欠泉 間欠泉 (kanketsu sen)

Ghana: ガーナ ガーナ (Gāna)

Gibraltar: ジブラルタル ジブラルタル (Jiburarutaru)

gin: ジン ジン (jin)

ginger: 生姜 生姜 (shōga), 赤毛の 赤毛の (akage no)

giraffe: キリン キリン (kirin)

girl: 女の子 女の子 (onnanoko)

girlfriend: 彼女 彼女 (kanojo)

give: 与える 与える (ataeru)

give a massage: マッサージをする マッサージをする (massāji o suru)

glacier: 氷河 氷河 (hyōga)

gladiolus: グラジオラス グラジオラス (gurajiorasu)

glass: グラス グラス (gurasu)

glasses: 眼鏡 眼鏡 (megane)

glider: グライダー グライダー (guraidā)

glove: 手袋 手袋 (tebukuro)

glue: のり のり (nori)

gluten: グルテン グルテン (guruten)

goal: ゴール ゴール (gōru)

goat: ヤギ ヤギ (yagi)

gold: 金 金 (kin)

Gold is more expensive than silver: 金は銀よりも高いです 金は銀よりも高いです (kin wa gin yori mo takai desu)

gold medal: 金メダル 金メダル (kin medaru)

golf: ゴルフ ゴルフ (gorufu)

golf ball: ゴルフボール ゴルフボール (gorufu bōru)

golf club: ゴルフクラブ ゴルフクラブ (gorufu kurabu)

golf course: ゴルフ場 ゴルフ場 (gorufu jō)

good: 良い 良い (yoi)

good bye: さようなら さようなら (sayōnara)

good day: 今日は 今日は (kyō wa)

goose: ガチョウ ガチョウ (gachō)

go straight: 真っすぐ行く 真っすぐ行く (massugu iku)

goulash: グーラッシュ グーラッシュ (gūrasshu)

GPS: GPS GPS (GPS)

graduation: 卒業 卒業 (sotsugyō)

graduation ceremony: 卒業式 卒業式 (sotsugyō shiki)

gram: グラム グラム (guramu)

grandchild: 孫 孫 (mago)

granddaughter: 孫娘 孫娘 (magomusume)

grandfather: 祖父 祖父(sofu)

grandmother: 祖母 祖母(sobo)

grandson: 孫 孫(mago)

granite: 花崗岩 花崗岩(kakō gan)

granulated sugar: グラニュー糖 グラニュー糖(guranyū tō)

grape: ぶどう ぶどう(budō)

grapefruit: グレープフルーツ グレープフルーツ(gurēpufurūtsu)

graphite: グラファイト グラファイト(gurafaito)

grass: 草 草(kusa)

grasshopper: バッタ バッタ(batta)

grater: おろし金 おろし金(oroshigane)

grave: 墓 墓(haka)

gravity: 重力 重力(jūryoku)

Greece: ギリシャ ギリシャ(Girisha)

greedy: 欲深い 欲深い(yokubukai)

green: 緑 緑(midori)

greenhouse: 温室 温室(onshitsu)

Greenland: グリーンランド グリーンランド(Gurīn Rando)

green tea: 緑茶 緑茶(ryokucha)

Grenada: グレナダ グレナダ(Gurenada)

grey: 灰色 灰色(haiiro)

groom: 花婿 花婿(hanamuko)

ground floor: 一階 一階(ikkai)

group therapy: グループセラピー グループセラピー(gurūpu serapī)

grow: 成長する 成長する(seichō suru)

Guatemala: グアテマラ グアテマラ(Guatemara)

guest: ゲスト ゲスト(gesuto)

guilty: 有罪な 有罪な(yūzai na)

Guinea: ギニア ギニア(Ginia)

Guinea-Bissau: ギニアビサウ ギニアビサウ(Giniabisau)

guinea pig: モルモット モルモット(morumotto)

guitar: ギター ギター(gitā)

gun: 銃 銃(jū)

Guyana: ガイアナ ガイアナ(Gaiana)

gym: スポーツジム スポーツジム(supōtsu jimu)

gymnastics: 体操 体操(taisō)

gynaecology: 婦人科 婦人科(fujin ka)

H

hafnium: ハフニウム ハフニウム(hafuniumu)

hair: 髪の毛 髪の毛(kaminoke)

hairdresser: ヘアドレッサー ヘアドレッサー(hea doressā)

hairdryer: ヘアドライヤー ヘアドライヤー(hea doraiyā)

hair gel: ヘアジェル ヘアジェル(hea jeru)

hair straightener: ストレートヘアアイロン ストレートヘアアイロン(sutorēto hea airon)

Haiti: ハイチ ハイチ(Haichi)

half an hour: 三十分 三十分(sanjū fun)

Halloween: ハロウィーン ハロウィーン(harowīn)

ham: ハム ハム(hamu)

hamburger: ハンバーガー ハンバーガー(hanbāgā)

hammer: 槌で打つ 槌で打つ(tsuchi de utsu), ハンマー ハンマー(hanmā)
hammer throw: ハンマー投げ ハンマー投げ(hanmā nage)
hamster: ハムスター ハムスター(hamusutā)
hand: 手 手(te)
handbag: ハンドバッグ ハンドバッグ(handobaggu)
handball: ハンドボール ハンドボール(handobōru)
hand brake: ハンドブレーキ ハンドブレーキ(hando burēki)
handcuff: 手錠 手錠(tejō)
handsaw: 手のこぎり 手のこぎり(te nokogiri)
handsome: ハンサム ハンサム(hansamu)
happy: 嬉しい 嬉しい(ureshī)
harbour: 港 港(minato)
hard: 固い 固い(katai)
hard drive: ハードディスク ハードディスク(hādodisuku)
harmonica: ハーモニカ ハーモニカ(hāmonika)
harp: ハープ ハープ(hāpu)
hassium: ハッシウム ハッシウム(hasshiumu)
hat: 帽子 帽子(bōshi)
hay fever: 花粉症 花粉症(kafun shō)
hazelnut: ヘーゼルナッツ ヘーゼルナッツ(hēzerunattsu)
he: 彼 彼(kare)
head: 頭部 頭部(tōbu)
headache: 頭痛 頭痛(zutsū)
heading: 見出し 見出し(midashi)
head injury: 頭部外傷 頭部外傷(tōbu gaishō)
healthy: 健康的な 健康的な(kenkōteki na)
heart: 心臓 心臓(shinzō)
heart attack: 心臓発作 心臓発作(shinzō hossa)
heating: 暖房装置 暖房装置(danbō sōchi)
heavy: 重い 重い(omoi)
heavy metal: ヘビーメタル ヘビーメタル(hebī metaru)
hedge: 生垣 生垣(ikegaki)
hedgehog: ハリネズミ ハリネズミ(harinezumi)
heel: かかと かかと(kakato), ヒール ヒール(hīru)
height: 高さ 高さ(taka sa)
heir: 跡継ぎ 跡継ぎ(atotsugi)
helicopter: ヘリコプター ヘリコプター(herikoputā)
helium: ヘリウム ヘリウム(heriumu)
hello: こんにちは こんにちは(konnichiwa)
helmet: ヘルメット ヘルメット(herumetto)
help: 助ける 助ける(tasukeru)
hemorrhoid: イボ痔 イボ痔(ibo ji)
her dress: 彼女のドレス 彼女のドレス(kanojo no doresu)
here: ここ ここ(koko)
heritage: 遺産 遺産(isan)
hexagon: 六角形 六角形(rokkaku kei)
hi: やあ やあ(yā)
hide: 隠す 隠す(kakusu)
high: 高い 高い(takai)
high-speed train: 快速電車 快速電車(kaisoku densha)
high blood pressure: 高血圧症 高血圧症(kō ketsuatsu shō)

high heels: ハイヒール ハイヒール(hai hīru)

high jump: 高跳び 高跳び(takatobi)

high school: 高校 高校(kōkō)

hiking: ハイキング ハイキング(haikingu)

hiking boots: ハイキングブーツ ハイキングブーツ (haikingu būtsu)

hill: 丘 丘(oka)

Himalayas: ヒマラヤ ヒマラヤ(Himaraya)

hippo: カバ カバ(kaba)

his car: 彼の車 彼の車(kare no kuruma)

history: 歴史 歴史(rekishi)

hit: 叩く 叩く(tataku)

hockey stick: ホッケースティック ホッケースティック (hokkē sutikku)

hoe: 鍬 鍬(kuwa)

hole puncher: 穴あけパンチ 穴あけパンチ(anaake panchi)

holmium: ホルミウム ホルミウム(horumiumu)

holy: 聖なる 聖なる(sei naru)

homework: 宿題 宿題(shukudai)

homoeopathy: ホメオパシー ホメオパシー(homeopashī)

Honduras: ホンジュラス ホンジュラス(Honjurasu)

honey: 蜂蜜 蜂蜜(hachimitsu)

honeymoon: ハネムーン ハネムーン(hanemūn)

Hong Kong: 香港 香港(Honkon)

horn: クラクション クラクション(kurakushon)

horror movie: ホラー映画 ホラー映画(horā eiga)

horse: 馬 馬(uma)

hose: ホース ホース(hōsu)

hospital: 病院 病院(byōin)

host: ホスト ホスト(hosuto)

hostel: ホステル ホステル(hosuteru)

hot: 辛い 辛い(tsurai), 暑い 暑い(atsui)

hot-air balloon: 熱気球 熱気球(netsu kikyū)

hot-water bottle: 湯たんぽ 湯たんぽ(yu tanpo)

hot chocolate: ホットチョコレート ホットチョコレート (hotto chokorēto)

hot dog: ホットドック ホットドック(hotto dokku)

hotel: ホテル ホテル(hoteru)

hot pot: 鍋料理 鍋料理(nabe ryōri)

hour: 時 時(ji)

house: 家屋 家屋(kaoku)

houseplant: 鉢植え 鉢植え(hachiue)

how: どのように どのように(dono yō ni)

How are you?: 元気ですか？ 元気ですか？ (genki desu ka)

how many?: いくつですか？ いくつですか？ (iku tsu desu ka)

how much?: いくら？ いくら？(ikura)

How much is this?: これはいくらですか？ これはいくらですか？ (kore wa ikura desu ka)

huge: 広い 広い(hiroi)

human resources: 人事 人事(jinji)

humidity: 湿気 湿気(shikke)

Hungary: ハンガリー ハンガリー(Hangarī)

hungry: 腹ペコ 腹ペコ(harapeko)

hurdles: ハードル競技 ハードル競技(hādoru kyōgi)

hurricane: ハリケーン ハリケーン(harikēn)

husband: 夫 夫(otto)

hydrant: 消火栓 消火栓(shōka sen)

hydroelectric power station: 水力発電所 水力発電所(suiryoku hatsuden sho)

hydrogen: 水素 水素(suiso)

hydrotherapy: 水治療法 水治療法(suichi ryōhō)

hyphen: ハイフン ハイフン(haifun)

hypnosis: 催眠 催眠(saimin)

I

I: 私 私(watashi)

I agree: 賛成です 賛成です(sansei desu)

ice: 氷 氷(kōri)

ice climbing: アイスクライミング アイスクライミング(aisu kuraimingu)

ice cream: アイスクリーム アイスクリーム(aisu kurīmu)

iced coffee: アイスコーヒー アイスコーヒー(aisu kōhī)

ice hockey: アイスホッケー アイスホッケー(aisu hokkē)

Iceland: アイスランド アイスランド(Aisurando)

ice rink: アイスリンク アイスリンク(aisu rinku)

ice skating: アイススケート アイススケート(aisu sukēto)

icing sugar: 粉砂糖 粉砂糖(konazatō)

icon: アイコン アイコン(aikon)

I don't know: 知りません 知りません(shirimasen)

I don't like this: これは好きではありません これは好きではありません(kore wa suki de wa arimasen)

I don't understand: 分かりません 分かりません(wakarimasen)

if: もし もし(moshi)

I have a dog: 犬を飼っています 犬を飼っています(inu o katte imasu)

I know: 知っています 知っています(shitte imasu)

I like you: あなたが好きです あなたが好きです(anata ga suki desu)

I love you: 愛しています 愛しています(aishite imasu)

I miss you: 恋しいです 恋しいです(koishī desu)

immediately: すぐに すぐに(sugu ni)

inbox: 受信ボックス 受信ボックス(jushin bokkusu)

inch: インチ インチ(inchi)

index finger: 人差し指 人差し指(hitosashi yubi)

India: インド インド(Indo)

Indian Ocean: インド洋 インド洋(Indo yō)

indium: インジウム インジウム(injiumu)

Indonesia: インドネシア インドネシア(Indoneshia)

industrial district: 工場地区 工場地区(kōjō chiku)

I need this: これが必要です これが必要です(kore ga hitsuyō desu)

infant: 幼児 幼児(yōji)

infection: 感染症 感染症(kansen shō)

infusion: 点滴 点滴(tenteki)

inhaler: 吸入器 吸入器(kyūnyū ki)

injure: 怪我をする 怪我をする(kega o suru)

injury: 怪我 怪我(kega)

ink: インク インク(inku)

inking roller: インクローラー インクローラー(inku rōrā)

insect repellent: 虫除け 虫除け(mushiyoke)

inside: 中 中(naka)

instant camera: インスタントカメラ インスタントカメラ (insutanto kamera)

instant noodles: インスタントラーメン インスタントラーメン (insutanto rāmen)

insulating tape: 絶縁テープ 絶縁テープ (zetsuen tēpu)

insulin: インスリン インスリン (insurin)

insurance: 保険 保険 (hoken)

intensive care unit: 集中治療室 集中治療室 (shūchū chiryō shitsu)

interest: 利子 利子 (rishi)

intern: 研修員 研修員 (kenshū in)

intersection: 交差点 交差点 (kōsa ten)

intestine: 腸 腸 (chō)

investment: 投資 投資 (tōshi)

iodine: ヨウ素 ヨウ素 (yōso)

ion: イオン イオン (ion)

Iran: イラン イラン (Iran)

Iraq: イラク イラク (Iraku)

Ireland: アイルランド アイルランド (Airurando)

iridium: イリジウム イリジウム (irijiumu)

iris: 燕子花 燕子花 (kakitsubata)

iron: アイロンをかける アイロンをかける (airon o kakeru), 鉄 鉄 (tetsu)

ironing table: アイロン台 アイロン台 (airon dai)

island: 島 島 (shima)

isotope: アイソトープ アイソトープ (aisotōpu)

Israel: イスラエル イスラエル (Isuraeru)

IT: IT IT (IT)

Italy: イタリア イタリア (Itaria)

Ivory Coast: コートジボワール コートジボワール (Kōtojibowāru)

I want more: もっと欲しいです もっと欲しいです (motto hoshī desu)

I want this: これが欲しいです これが欲しいです (kore ga hoshī desu)

J

jack: ジャッキ ジャッキ (jakki)

jacket: ジャケット ジャケット (jaketto)

jackfruit: パラミツ パラミツ (paramitsu)

jade: 翡翠 翡翠 (hisui)

jam: ジャム ジャム (jamu)

Jamaica: ジャマイカ ジャマイカ (Jamaika)

January: 一月 一月 (ichi gatsu)

Japan: 日本 日本 (Nihon/Nippon)

Japanese: 日本語 日本語 (Nippon go)

jar: 瓶 瓶 (bin)

javelin throw: 槍投げ 槍投げ (yarinage)

jawbone: 顎骨 顎骨 (gakkotsu)

jazz: ジャズ ジャズ (jazu)

jeans: ジーンズ ジーンズ (jīnzu)

jellyfish: クラゲ クラゲ (kurage)

jersey: ジャージ ジャージ (jāji)

jet ski: ジェットスキー ジェットスキー (jetto sukī)

jeweller: 宝石商人 宝石商人 (hōseki shōnin)

jive: ジャイブ ジャイブ (jaibu)

job: 仕事 仕事 (shigoto)

jogging bra: スポーツブラジャー スポーツブラジャー(supōtsu burajā)

joke: 冗談 冗談(jōdan)

Jordan: ヨルダン ヨルダン(Yorudan)

journalist: ジャーナリスト ジャーナリスト(jānarisuto)

judge: 裁判官 裁判官(saiban kan)

judo: 柔道 柔道(jūdō)

juicy: ジューシー ジューシー(jūshī)

July: 七月 七月(shichi gatsu)

jump: 跳ぶ 跳ぶ(tobu)

June: 六月 六月(roku gatsu)

junior school: 中学校 中学校(chū gakkō)

Jupiter: 木星 木星(Moku sei)

jury: 陪審 陪審(baishin)

K

kangaroo: カンガルー カンガルー(kangarū)

karate: 空手 空手(karate)

kart: レーシングカート レーシングカート(rēshingu kāto)

Kazakhstan: カザフスタン カザフスタン(Kazafusutan)

kebab: ケバブ ケバブ(kebabu)

kennel: 犬小屋 犬小屋(inugoya)

Kenya: ケニア ケニア(Kenia)

kettle: やかん やかん(yakan)

kettledrum: ケトルドラム ケトルドラム(ketoru doramu)

key: 鍵 鍵(kagi)

keyboard: キーボード キーボード(kībōdo)

key chain: キーチェーン キーチェーン(kī chēn)

keyhole: 鍵穴 鍵穴(kagiana)

kick: 蹴る 蹴る(keru)

kidney: 腎臓 腎臓(jinzō)

kill: 殺す 殺す(korosu)

killer whale: シャチ シャチ(shachi)

kilogram: キログラム キログラム(kiroguramu)

kindergarten: 幼稚園 幼稚園(yōchi en)

kindergarten teacher: 保育士 保育士(hoiku shi)

Kiribati: キリバス キリバス(Kiribasu)

kiss: キスする キスする(kisu suru), キス キス(kisu)

kitchen: キッチン キッチン(kicchin)

kiwi: キウイ キウイ(kiui)

knee: 膝 膝(hiza)

kneecap: 膝頭 膝頭(hizagashira)

knife: ナイフ ナイフ(naifu)

knit cap: ニット帽 ニット帽(nitto bō)

know: 知る 知る(shiru)

koala: コアラ コアラ(koara)

Kosovo: コソボ コソボ(Kosobo)

krone: クローネ クローネ(kurōne)

krypton: クリプトン クリプトン(kuriputon)

Kuwait: クウェート クウェート(Kuwēto)

Kyrgyzstan: キルギスタン キルギスタン(Kirugisutan)

L

laboratory: 実験室 実験室(jikken shitsu)

lace: 靴紐 靴紐(kutsuhimo)

lacrosse: ラクロス ラクロス(rakurosu)

ladder: はしご はしご(hashigo)

ladle: しゃもじ しゃもじ(shamoji)

ladybird: てんとうむし てんとうむし(tentō mushi)

lake: 湖 湖(mizuumi)

lamb: 羊肉 羊肉(yōniku)

lamp: ランプ ランプ(ranpu)

landlord: 大家 大家(ooya)

lanthanum: ランタン ランタン(rantan)

Laos: ラオス ラオス(Raosu)

laptop: ノートパソコン ノートパソコン(nōto pasokon)

larch: カラマツ カラマツ(karamatsu)

lasagne: ラザニア ラザニア(razania)

last month: 先月 先月 (sengetsu)

last week: 先週 先週(senshū)

last year: 去年 去年(kyonen)

Latin: ラテン語 ラテン語(raten go)

Latin dance: ラテンダンス ラテンダンス(raten dansu)

latitude: 緯度 緯度(ido)

Latvia: ラトビア ラトビア(Ratobia)

laugh: 笑う 笑う(warau)

laundry: 洗濯物 洗濯物(sentaku butsu)

laundry basket: 洗濯籠 洗濯籠(sentaku kago)

lava: 溶岩 溶岩(yōgan)

law: 法律 法律(hōritsu)

lawn mower: 芝刈り機 芝刈り機(shibakari ki)

lawrencium: ローレンシウム ローレンシウム(rōrenshiumu)

lawyer: 弁護士 弁護士(bengo shi)

lazy: 怠惰な 怠惰な(taida na)

lead: 鉛 鉛(namari)

leaf: 葉 葉(ha)

leaflet: リーフレット リーフレット(rīfuretto)

lean meat: 赤身 赤身(akami)

leather shoes: 革靴 革靴(kawagutsu)

Lebanon: レバノン レバノン(Rebanon)

lecture: 授業 授業(jugyō)

lecturer: 講演者 講演者(kōen sha)

lecture theatre: 講堂 講堂(kōdō)

leek: 西洋葱 西洋葱(seiyō negi)

left: 左 左(hidari)

leg: 足 足(ashi)

legal department: 法務部 法務部(hōmu bu)

leggings: レギンス レギンス(reginsu)

leg press: レッグプレス レッグプレス(reggu puresu)

lemon: レモン レモン(remon)

lemonade: レモネード レモネード(remonēdo)

lemongrass: レモングラス レモングラス(remon gurasu)

lemur: きつねざる きつねざる(kitsunezaru)

leopard: ヒョウ ヒョウ(hyō)

Lesotho: レソト レソト(Resoto)

less: よりも少ない よりも少ない(yori mo sukunai)

lesson: レッスン レッスン(ressun)

Let's go home: 帰りましょう 帰りましょう (kaerimashō)

letter: 文字 文字(moji), 手紙 手紙(tegami)

lettuce: レタス レタス(retasu)

Liberia: リベリア リベリア(Riberia)

librarian: 司書 司書(shisho)

library: 図書館 図書館(tosho kan)

Libya: リビア リビア(Ribia)

lie: 横になる 横になる(yoko ni naru)

Liechtenstein: リヒテンシュタイン リヒテンシュタイン(Rihitenshutain)

lifeboat: 救命ボート 救命ボート(kyūmei bōto)

life buoy: 救命ブイ 救命ブイ(kyūmei bui)

lifeguard: ライフガード ライフガード(raifu gādo)

life jacket: 救命胴衣 救命胴衣(kyūmei dōi)

lift: 持ち上げる 持ち上げる(mochiageru)

light: 軽い 軽い(karui), 明るい 明るい(akarui)

light bulb: 電球 電球(denkyū)

lighter: ライター ライター(raitā)

lighthouse: 灯台 灯台(tōdai)

lightning: 稲妻 稲妻(inazuma)

light switch: 照明スイッチ 照明スイッチ(shōmei suicchi)

like: 好む 好む(konomu)

lime: ライム ライム(raimu)

limestone: 石灰岩 石灰岩(sekkai gan)

limousine: リムジン リムジン(rimujin)

lingerie: ランジェリー ランジェリー(ranjerī)

lion: ライオン ライオン(raion)

lip: 唇 唇(kuchibiru)

lip balm: リップクリーム リップクリーム(rippu kurīmu)

lip gloss: リップグロス リップグロス(rippu gurosu)

lipstick: 口紅 口紅(kuchibeni)

liqueur: リキュール リキュール(rikyūru)

liquorice: リコリス リコリス(rikorisu)

listen: 聞く 聞く(kiku)

liter: リッター リッター(rittā)

literature: 文学 文学(bungaku)

lithium: リチウム リチウム(richiumu)

Lithuania: リトアニア リトアニア(Ritoania)

little black dress: 黒いワンピース 黒いワンピース(kuroi wan pīsu)

little brother: 弟 弟(otōto)

little finger: 小指 小指(koyubi)

little sister: 妹 妹(imōto)

live: 生きる 生きる(ikiru)

liver: 肝臓 肝臓(kanzō)

livermorium: リバモリウム リバモリウム(ribamoriumu)

living room: リビング リビング(ribingu)

lizard: トカゲ トカゲ(tokage)

llama: ラマ ラマ(rama)

loan: ローン ローン(rōn)
lobby: ロビー ロビー(robī)
lobster: ロブスター ロブスター(robusutā)
lock: 鍵をかける 鍵をかける(kagi o kakeru)
locomotive: 機関車 機関車(kikan sha)
lonely: 寂しい 寂しい(sabishī)
long: 長い 長い(nagai)
longitude: 経度 経度(keido)
long jump: 幅跳び 幅跳び(habatobi)
look for: 探す 探す(sagasu)
loppers: 万能ハサミ 万能ハサミ(bannō hasami)
lorry: トラック トラック(torakku)
lorry driver: トラックの運転手 トラックの運転手(torakku no unten shu)
lose: 負ける 負ける(makeru)
lose weight: 痩せる 痩せる(yaseru)
loss: 損失 損失(sonshitsu)
lotus root: れんこん れんこん(ren kon)
loud: うるさい うるさい(urusai)
loudspeaker: スピーカー スピーカー(supīkā)
love: 愛する 愛する(aisuru), 愛 愛(ai)
lovesickness: 恋の病 恋の病(koi no yamai)
low: 低い 低い(hikui)
lubricant: ラブローション ラブローション(rabu rōshon)
luge: リュージュ リュージュ(ryūju)
luggage: 荷物 荷物(nimotsu)
lunar eclipse: 月食 月食(gesshoku)
lunch: ランチ ランチ(ranchi)
lung: 肺 肺(hai)
lutetium: ルテチウム ルテチウム(rutechiumu)
Luxembourg: ルクセンブルク ルクセンブルク (Rukusenburuku)
lychee: ライチ ライチ(raichi)
lyrics: 歌詞 歌詞(kashi)

M

Macao: マカオ マカオ(Makao)
Macedonia: マケドニア マケドニア(Makedonia)
Madagascar: マダガスカル マダガスカル(Madagasukaru)
magazine: 雑誌 雑誌(zasshi)
magma: マグマ マグマ(maguma)
magnesium: マグネシウム マグネシウム(maguneshiumu)
magnet: 磁石 磁石(jishaku)
magnetic resonance imaging: 磁気共鳴断層撮影装置 磁気共鳴断層撮影装置(jiki kyōmei dansō satsuei sōchi)
magpie: カササギ カササギ(kasasagi)
mailbox: ポスト ポスト(posuto)
Malawi: マラウイ マラウイ(Maraui)
Malaysia: マレーシア マレーシア(Marēshia)
Maldives: モルディブ モルディブ(Morudibu)
Mali: マリ マリ(Mari)
Malta: マルタ マルタ(Maruta)

man: 男 男(otoko)

manager: マネージャー マネージャー(manējā)

Mandarin: 北京語 北京語(Pekin go)

manganese: マンガン マンガン(mangan)

mango: マンゴー マンゴー(mangō)

manhole cover: マンホールの蓋 マンホールの蓋(manhōru no futa)

manicure: マニキュア マニキュア(manikyua)

mannequin: マネキン マネキン(manekin)

many: 多い 多い(ōi)

map: 地図 地図(chizu)

maple: 楓 楓(kaede)

maple syrup: メープルシロップ メープルシロップ(mēpuru shiroppu)

marathon: マラソン マラソン(marason)

March: 三月 三月(san gatsu)

marjoram: マジョラム マジョラム(majoramu)

market: マーケット マーケット(māketto)

marketing: マーケティング マーケティング(māketingu)

marry: 結婚する 結婚する(kekkon suru)

Mars: 火星 火星(Ka sei)

marsh: 沼沢 沼沢(shōtaku)

Marshall Islands: マーシャル諸島 マーシャル諸島(Māsharu Shotō)

marshmallow: マシュマロ マシュマロ(mashumaro)

martini: マティーニ マティーニ(Matīni)

mascara: マスカラ マスカラ(masukara)

mashed potatoes: マッシュポテト マッシュポテト(masshu poteto)

massage: マッサージ マッサージ(massāji)

masseur: マッサージ師 マッサージ師(massāji shi)

mast: マスト マスト(masuto)

master: 修士 修士(shūshi)

match: マッチ棒 マッチ棒(macchi bō)

mathematics: 数学 数学(sūgaku)

mattress: 敷布団 敷布団(shikifuton)

Mauritania: モーリタニア モーリタニア(Mōritania)

Mauritius: モーリシャス モーリシャス(Mōrishasu)

May: 五月 五月(go gatsu)

mayonnaise: マヨネーズ マヨネーズ(mayonēzu)

measles: 麻疹 麻疹(hashika)

measure: 測る 測る(hakaru)

meat: 肉 肉(niku)

meatball: ミートボール ミートボール(mītobōru)

mechanic: 整備士 整備士(seibi shi)

medal: メダル メダル(medaru)

meditation: 瞑想 瞑想(meisō)

Mediterranean Sea: 地中海 地中海(Chichū kai)

meerkat: ミーアキャット ミーアキャット(mīakyatto)

meet: 会う 会う(au)

meeting room: 会議室 会議室(kaigi shitsu)

meitnerium: マイトネリウム マイトネリウム(maitoneriumu)

melody: メロディ メロディ(merodi)

member: メンバー メンバー(menbā)

membership: メンバーシップ メンバーシップ(menbāshippu)

mendelevium: メンデレビウム メンデレビウム(menderebiumu)

menu: メニュー メニュー(menyū)

Mercury: 水星 水星(Sui sei)

mercury: 水銀 水銀(suigin)

metal: 金属 金属(kinzoku)

metalloid: 半金属 半金属(han kinzoku)

meteorite: 隕石 隕石(inseki)

meter: メートル メートル(mētoru)

methane: メタン メタン(metan)

metropolis: 大都市 大都市(dai toshi)

Mexico: メキシコ メキシコ(Mekishiko)

Micronesia: ミクロネシア ミクロネシア(Mikuroneshia)

microscope: 顕微鏡 顕微鏡(kenbi kyō)

microwave: 電子レンジ 電子レンジ(denshi renji)

middle finger: 中指 中指(nakayubi)

midnight: 真夜中 真夜中(ma yonaka)

midwife: 助産婦 助産婦(jo sanpu)

migraine: 頭痛 頭痛(zutsū)

mile: マイル マイル(mairu)

milk: 牛乳 牛乳(gyūnyū)

milk powder: 粉ミルク 粉ミルク(kona miruku)

milkshake: ミルクセーキ ミルクセーキ(miruku sēki)

milk tea: ミルクティー ミルクティー(miruku tī)

Milky Way: 天の川 天の川(amanogawa)

millennium: 千年紀 千年紀(sen nenki)

milliliter: ミリリットル ミリリットル(miririttoru)

millimeter: ミリメートル ミリメートル(mirimētoru)

minced meat: 挽肉 挽肉(hikiniku)

minibar: ミニバー ミニバー(mini bā)

minibus: マイクロバス マイクロバス(maikurobasu)

minister: 大臣 大臣(daijin)

mint: ミント ミント(minto)

minute: 分 分(bun)

mirror: 鏡 鏡(kagami)

miscarriage: 流産 流産(ryūzan)

mitt: ミット ミット(mitto)

mixer: ミキサー ミキサー(mikisā)

mobile phone: 携帯 携帯(keitai)

mocha: モカ モカ(moka)

model: モデル モデル(moderu)

modern pentathlon: 近代五種競技 近代五種競技(kindai go shu kyōgi)

Moldova: モルドバ モルドバ(Morudoba)

molecule: 分子 分子(bunshi)

molybdenum: モリブデン モリブデン(moribuden)

Monaco: モナコ モナコ(Monako)

Monday: 月曜日 月曜日(getsuyōbi)

money: お金 お金(o kane)

Mongolia: モンゴル モンゴル(Mongoru)

monk: 僧侶 僧侶(sōryo)

monkey: 猿 猿(saru)

Monopoly: モノポリー モノポリー(monoporī)

monorail: モノレール モノレール(monorēru)

monsoon: モンスーン モンスーン(monsūn)

Montenegro: モンテネグロ モンテネグロ(Monteneguro)

month: 月 月(tsuki)

Montserrat: モントセラト モントセラト(Montoserato)

monument: 記念碑 記念碑(kinen hi)

moon: 月 月(tsuki)

more: もっと もっと(motto)

morning: 朝 朝(asa), 午前 午前(gozen)

Morocco: モロッコ モロッコ(Morokko)

mosque: モスク モスク(mosuku)

mosquito: 蚊 蚊(ka)

most: ほとんど ほとんど(hotondo)

moth: 蛾 蛾(ga)

mother: 母 母(haha)

mother-in-law: 義母 義母(gibo)

motocross: モトクロス モトクロス(motokurosu)

motor: モーター モーター(mōtā)

motorcycle: バイク バイク(baiku)

motorcycle racing: オートバイレース オートバイレース(ōtobai rēsu)

motor scooter: スクーター スクーター(sukūtā)

motorway: 高速道路 高速道路(kōsoku dōro)

mountain: 山 山(yama)

mountain biking: マウンテンバイク マウンテンバイク(maunten baiku)

mountaineering: 登山 登山(tozan)

mountain range: 山脈 山脈(sanmyaku)

mouse: ねずみ ねずみ(nezumi), マウス マウス(mausu)

mouth: 口 口(kuchi)

mouthguard: マウスピース マウスピース(mausupīsu)

Mozambique: モザンビーク モザンビーク(Mozanbīku)

mozzarella: モッツァレラ モッツァレラ(mottsarera)

MP3 player: MP3プレーヤー MP3プレーヤー(MP3 purēyā)

muesli: ミューズリー ミューズリー(myūzurī)

muffin: マフィン マフィン(mafin)

mufti: ムフティー ムフティー(mufu tī)

multiplication: 掛け算 掛け算(kakezan)

mum: ママ ママ(mama)

mumps: おたふく風邪 おたふく風邪(otafukukaze)

muscle: 筋肉 筋肉(kinniku)

museum: 博物館 博物館(hakubutsu kan)

mushroom: マッシュルーム マッシュルーム(masshurūmu)

musician: ミュージシャン ミュージシャン(myūjishan)

mustard: マスタード マスタード(masutādo)

mute: 口がきけない 口がきけない(kuchi ga kikenai)

my dog: 私の犬 私の犬(watashi no inu)

N

nachos: ナチョス ナチョス(nachosu)

nail: 釘 釘(kugi)

nail clipper: 爪切り 爪切り(tsumekiri)

nail file: 爪やすり 爪やすり (tsumeyasuri)

nail polish: マニキュア マニキュア (manikyua)

nail scissors: 爪切ハサミ 爪切ハサミ (tsumekire hasami)

nail varnish remover: マニキュア落とし マニキュア落とし (manikyua otoshi)

Namibia: ナミビア ナミビア (Namibia)

nape: 項 項 (kō)

narrow: 狭い 狭い (semai)

nasal bone: 鼻骨 鼻骨 (bikotsu)

nasal spray: 鼻腔用スプレー 鼻腔用スプレー (bikū yō supurē)

national park: 国立公園 国立公園 (kokuritsu kōen)

Nauru: ナウル ナウル (Nauru)

nausea: 吐き気 吐き気 (hakike)

neck: 首 首 (kubi)

neck brace: ネックカラー ネックカラー (nekku karā)

necklace: ネックレス ネックレス (nekkuresu)

nectar: 蜜 蜜 (mitsu)

needle: 針 針 (hari)

negligee: ネグリジェ ネグリジェ (negurije)

neighbour: 隣人 隣人 (rinjin)

neodymium: ネオジム ネオジム (neojimu)

neon: ネオン ネオン (neon)

Nepal: ネパール ネパール (Nepāru)

nephew: 甥 甥 (oi)

Neptune: 海王星 海王星 (Kaiō sei)

neptunium: ネプツニウム ネプツニウム (neputsuniumu)

nerve: 神経 神経 (shinkei)

net: ネット ネット (netto)

Netherlands: オランダ オランダ (Oranda)

network: ネットワーク ネットワーク (nettowāku)

neurology: 神経科 神経科 (shinkei ka)

neutron: 中性子 中性子 (chūseishi)

new: 新しい 新しい (atarashī)

New Caledonia: ニューカレドニア ニューカレドニア (Nyūkaredonia)

news: ニュース ニュース (nyūsu)

newsletter: ニュースレター ニュースレター (nyūsuretā)

newspaper: 新聞 新聞 (shinbun)

New Year: 新年 新年 (shinnen)

New Zealand: ニュージーランド ニュージーランド (Nyūjīrando)

next month: 来月 来月 (raigetsu)

next week: 来週 来週 (raishū)

next year: 来年 来年 (rainen)

Nicaragua: ニカラグア ニカラグア (Nikaragua)

nickel: ニッケル ニッケル (nikkeru)

niece: 姪 姪 (mei)

Niger: ニジェール ニジェール (Nijēru)

Nigeria: ナイジェリア ナイジェリア (Naijeria)

night: 夜 夜 (yoru)

night club: ナイトクラブ ナイトクラブ (naitokurabu)

nightie: パジャマ パジャマ (pajama)

night table: ナイトテーブル ナイトテーブル (naitotēburu)

niobium: ニオブ ニオブ (niobu)

nipple: 乳首 乳首(chikubi)

nitrogen: 窒素 窒素(chisso)

Niue: ニウエ ニウエ(Niue)

nobelium: ノーベリウム ノーベリウム(nōberiumu)

non-metal: 非金属 非金属(hi kinzoku)

none: 何もない 何もない(nanimonai)

noodle: 麺 麺(men)

noon: 正午 正午(shōgo)

Nordic combined: ノルディックコンバインド ノルディックコンバインド (norudikku konbaindo)

north: 北 北(kita)

northern hemisphere: 北半球 北半球(kita hankyū)

North Korea: 北朝鮮 北朝鮮(Kitachōsen)

North Pole: 北極 北極(Hokkyoku)

Norway: ノルウェー ノルウェー(Noruwē)

nose: 鼻 鼻(hana)

nosebleed: 鼻血 鼻血(hanadi)

nostril: 鼻孔 鼻孔(bikō)

not: ではない ではない(de wa nai)

note: 音符 音符(onpu), メモ メモ(memo), 紙幣 紙幣(shihei)

notebook: ノート ノート(nōto)

nougat: ヌガー ヌガー(nugā)

novel: 小説 小説(shōsetsu)

November: 十一月 十一月(jū ichi gatsu)

now: 今 今(ima)

no worries: 大丈夫 大丈夫(daijōbu)

nuclear power plant: 原子力発電所 原子力発電所(genshi ryoku hatsuden sho)

numerator: 分子 分子(bunshi)

nun: 修道女 修道女(shūdō onna)

nurse: 看護婦 看護婦(kango fu)

nursery: 子供部屋 子供部屋(kodomo heya), 保育園 保育園(hoiku en)

nut: ナッツ ナッツ(nattsu)

nutmeg: ナツメグ ナツメグ(natsumegu)

nylon: ナイロン ナイロン(nairon)

O

oak: 柏 柏(kashiwa)

oat: オート麦 オート麦(ōto mugi)

oatmeal: オートミール オートミール(ōtomīru)

oboe: オーボエ オーボエ(ōboe)

ocean: 海洋 海洋(kaiyō)

octagon: 八角形 八角形(hakkaku kei)

October: 十月 十月(jū gatsu)

octopus: たこ たこ(tako)

oesophagus: 食道 食道(shokudō)

of course: もちろん もちろん(mochiron)

office: オフィス オフィス(ofisu)

often: たいてい たいてい(taitei)

oil: 油 油(abura)

oil paint: 油性塗料 油性塗料(yusei toryō)

oil pastel: オイルパステル オイルパステル(oiru pasuteru)

ok: はい はい(hai)
okra: オクラ オクラ(okura)
old: 古い 古い(furui), 年寄り 年寄り(toshiyori)
olive: オリーブ オリーブ(orību)
olive oil: オリーブオイル オリーブオイル(orību oiru)
Oman: オマーン オマーン(Omān)
oncology: 腫瘍学 腫瘍学(shuyō gaku)
one-way street: 一方通行 一方通行(ippō tsūkō)
one o'clock in the morning: 午前一時 午前一時(gozen ichi ji)
onion: タマネギ タマネギ(tamanegi)
onion ring: オニオンリング オニオンリング(onion ringu)
opal: オパール オパール(opāru)
open: 開く 開く(hiraku), 開ける 開ける(akeru)
opera: オペラ オペラ(opera)
operating theatre: 手術室 手術室(shujutsu shitsu)
optician: 眼鏡商人 眼鏡商人(megane shōnin)
or: 又は 又は(mata wa)
orange: 橙 橙(daidai), オレンジ オレンジ(orenji)
orange juice: オレンジジュース オレンジジュース(orenji jūsu)
orchestra: オーケストラ オーケストラ(ōkesutora)
oregano: オレガノ オレガノ(oregano)
organ: オルガン オルガン(orugan)
origami: 折り紙 折り紙(origami)
orphan: 孤児 孤児(koji)
orthopaedics: 整形外科 整形外科(seikei geka)
osmium: オスミウム オスミウム(osumiumu)
ostrich: ダチョウ ダチョウ(dachō)
other: 他人 他人(tanin)
otter: かわうそ かわうそ(kawauso)
ounce: オンス オンス(onsu)
our home: 私達の家 私達の家(watashitachi no ie)
outpatient: 外来患者 外来患者(gairai kanja)
outside: 外 外(soto)
ovary: 卵巣 卵巣(ransō)
oven: オーブン オーブン(ōbun)
overpass: 陸橋 陸橋(rikkyō)
oviduct: 卵管 卵管(rankan)
ovum: 卵子 卵子(ranshi)
owl: フクロウ フクロウ(fukurō)
oxygen: 酸素 酸素(sanso)

P

Pacific Ocean: 太平洋 太平洋(Taihei yō)
package: パッケージ パッケージ(pakkēji)
paediatrics: 小児科 小児科(shōni ka)
painkiller: 鎮痛剤 鎮痛剤(chintsū zai)
paint: 塗る 塗る(nuru), ペンキ ペンキ(penki)
painting: 絵画 絵画(kaiga)
Pakistan: パキスタン パキスタン(Pakisutan)
Palau: パラオ パラオ(Parao)

pale: 青白い 青白い(aojiroi)

Palestine: パレスチナ パレスチナ(Paresuchina)

palette: パレット パレット(paretto)

palladium: パラジウム パラジウム(parajiumu)

pallet: パレット パレット(paretto)

palm: 手のひら 手のひら(tenohira)

palm tree: 椰子 椰子(yashi)

pan: フライパン フライパン(furaipan)

Panama: パナマ パナマ(Panama)

pancake: ホットケーキ ホットケーキ(hottokēki)

pancreas: 膵臓 膵臓(suizō)

panda: パンダ パンダ(panda)

panties: パンティー パンティー(pantī)

pantyhose: パンスト パンスト(pansuto)

panty liner: パンティライナー パンティライナー(panti rainā)

papaya: パパイヤ パパイヤ(papaiya)

paperclip: ペーパークリップ ペーパークリップ(pēpā kurippu)

paprika: パプリカ パプリカ(papurika)

Papua New Guinea: パプアニューギニア パプアニューギニア(Papuanyūginia)

parachute: パラシュート パラシュート(parashūto)

parachuting: パラシューティング パラシューティング(para shūtingu)

paragraph: 段落 段落(danraku)

Paraguay: パラグアイ パラグアイ(Paraguai)

parasol: 日傘 日傘(higasa)

parcel: 小包 小包(kozutsumi)

parents: 両親 両親(ryōshin)

parents-in-law: 舅姑 舅姑(kyūko)

park: 公園 公園(kōen)

parking meter: パーキングメーター パーキングメーター(pākingu mētā)

parmesan: パルメザン パルメザン(parumezan)

parrot: オウム オウム(ōmu)

passport: パスポート パスポート(pasupōto)

password: パスワード パスワード(pasuwādo)

pathology: 病理学 病理学(byōri gaku)

patient: 患者 患者(kanja)

pavement: 歩道 歩道(hodō)

pay: 支払う 支払う(shiharau)

pea: エンドウマメ エンドウマメ(endoumame)

peach: 桃 桃(momo)

peacock: くじゃく くじゃく(kujaku)

peanut: ピーナツ ピーナツ(pīnatsu)

peanut butter: ピーナッツバター ピーナッツバター(pīnattsu batā)

peanut oil: ピーナッツ油 ピーナッツ油(pīnattsu abura)

pear: 梨 梨(nashi)

pearl necklace: パールネックレス パールネックレス(pāru nekkuresu)

pedestrian area: 歩行者天国 歩行者天国(hokō sha tengoku)

pedestrian crossing: 横断歩道 横断歩道(ōdan hodō)

pedicure: ペディキュア ペディキュア(pedikyua)

peel: 皮 皮(kawa)

peg: 洗濯ばさみ 洗濯ばさみ(sentaku basami)

pelican: ペリカン ペリカン(perikan)

pelvis: 骨盤 骨盤(kotsuban)

pen: ペン ペン(pen)

pencil: 鉛筆 鉛筆(enpitsu)

pencil case: 筆箱 筆箱(fudebako)

pencil sharpener: 鉛筆削り 鉛筆削り(enpitsu kezuri)

penguin: ペンギン ペンギン(pengin)

peninsula: 半島 半島(hantō)

penis: 陰茎 陰茎(inkei)

pepper: パプリカ パプリカ(papurika), 胡椒 胡椒(koshō)

perfume: 香水 香水(kōsui)

periodic table: 周期表 周期表(shūki hyō)

Peru: ペルー ペルー(Perū)

petal: 花びら 花びら(hanabira)

Petri dish: ペトリ皿 ペトリ皿(Petori sara)

petrol: ガソリン ガソリン(gasorin)

petrol station: ガソリンスタンド ガソリンスタンド(gasorin sutando)

pet shop: ペットショップ ペットショップ(petto shoppu)

pharmacist: 薬剤師 薬剤師(yakuzai shi)

pharmacy: 薬局 薬局(yakkyoku)

PhD: 博士 博士(hakase)

Philippines: フィリピン フィリピン(Firipin)

philosophy: 哲学 哲学(tetsugaku)

phoalbum: フォトアルバム フォトアルバム(foto arubamu)

phosphorus: リン リン(rin)

photographer: 写真家 写真家(shashin ka)

physical education: 体育 体育(taiiku)

physician: 内科医 内科医(naika i)

physicist: 物理学者 物理学者(butsuri gakusha)

physics: 物理学 物理学(butsuri gaku)

physiotherapist: 理学療法士 理学療法士(rigaku ryōhō shi)

physiotherapy: 理学療法 理学療法(rigaku ryōhō)

piano: ピアノ ピアノ(piano)

picnic: ピクニック ピクニック(pikunikku)

picture: 写真 写真(shashin)

picture frame: 額縁 額縁(gakubuchi)

pie: パイ パイ(pai)

pier: 桟橋 桟橋(sanbashi)

pig: 豚 豚(buta)

pigeon: 鳩 鳩(hato)

piglet: 子豚 子豚(kobuta)

Pilates: ピラティス ピラティス(piratisu)

pill: 錠剤 錠剤(jōzai)

pillow: 枕 枕(makura)

pilot: パイロット パイロット(pairotto)

pincers: 釘抜き 釘抜き(kuginuki)

pine: 松 松(matsu)

pineapple: パイナップル パイナップル(painappuru)

pink: 桃色 桃色(momoiro)

pipette: ピペット ピペット(pipetto)

pistachio: ピスタチオ ピスタチオ(pisutachio)

pit: 種 種(tane)

pitchfork: ピッチフォーク ピッチフォーク (picchifōku)

pizza: ピザ ピザ (piza)

plane: 飛行機 飛行機 (hikō ki)

planet: 惑星 惑星 (wakusei)

plaster: カットバン カットバン (katto ban)

plastic: プラスチック プラスチック (purasuchikku)

plastic bag: ビニール袋 ビニール袋 (binīru bukuro)

plate: 皿 皿 (sara)

platform: プラットホーム プラットホーム (purattohōmu)

platinum: プラチナ プラチナ (purachina)

play: 遊ぶ 遊ぶ (asobu), 演劇 演劇 (engeki)

playground: 遊び場 遊び場 (asobiba)

please: お願いします お願いします (o negaishimasu)

plug: プラグ プラグ (puragu)

plum: 梅 梅 (ume)

plumber: 水道屋 水道屋 (suidō ya)

plump: 豊満 豊満 (hōman)

Pluto: 冥王星 冥王星 (Meiō sei)

plutonium: プルトニウム プルトニウム (purutoniumu)

pocket: ポケット ポケット (poketto)

poisoning: 中毒 中毒 (chūdoku)

poker: ポーカー ポーカー (pōkā)

Poland: ポーランド ポーランド (Pōrando)

polar bear: シロクマ シロクマ (shirokuma)

pole: 極 極 (kyoku)

pole vault: 棒高跳び 棒高跳び (bō takatobi)

police: 警察 警察 (keisatsu)

police car: パトカー パトカー (patokā)

policeman: 警察官 警察官 (keisatsu kan)

police station: 警察署 警察署 (keisatsu sho)

politician: 政治家 政治家 (seiji ka)

politics: 政治学 政治学 (seiji gaku)

polo: ポロ ポロ (poro)

polonium: ポロニウム ポロニウム (poroniumu)

polo shirt: ポロシャツ ポロシャツ (poro shatsu)

polyester: ポリエステル ポリエステル (poriesuteru)

pond: 池 池 (ike)

ponytail: ポニーテール ポニーテール (ponītēru)

poor: 貧しい 貧しい (mazushī)

pop: ポップ ポップ (poppu)

popcorn: ポップコーン ポップコーン (poppukōn)

pork: 豚肉 豚肉 (butaniku)

porridge: ポリッジ ポリッジ (porijji)

portfolio: ポートフォリオ ポートフォリオ (pōtoforio)

portrait: 肖像画 肖像画 (shōzō ga)

Portugal: ポルトガル ポルトガル (Porutogaru)

postcard: ポストカード ポストカード (posutokādo)

postman: 郵便配達人 郵便配達人 (yūbin haitatsu nin)

post office: 郵便局 郵便局 (yūbin kyoku)

pot: 鍋 鍋 (nabe)

potasalad: ポテトサラダ ポテトサラダ (poteto sarada)

potassium: カリウム カリウム(kariumu)

potato: じゃがいも じゃがいも(jagaimo)

potawedges: ポテトウェッジ ポテトウェッジ(poteto wejji)

pottery: 陶器 陶器(tōki)

pound: ポンド ポンド(pondo)

powder: 粉薬 粉薬(kogusuri)

powder puff: パフ パフ(pafu)

power: 電気 電気(denki)

power line: 配電線 配電線(haiden sen)

power outlet: 電源 電源(dengen)

practice: 練習する 練習する(renshū suru)

praseodymium: プラセオジム プラセオジム(puraseojimu)

pray: 祈る 祈る(inoru)

praying mantis: かまきり かまきり(kamakiri)

preface: 序章 序章(joshō)

pregnancy test: 妊娠検査 妊娠検査(ninshin kensa)

present: プレゼント プレゼント(purezento)

presentation: プレゼンテーション プレゼンテーション(purezentēshon)

president: 大統領 大統領(daitōryō)

press: 押す 押す(osu)

priest: 神父 神父(shinpu)

primary school: 小学校 小学校(shō gakkō)

prime minister: 総理大臣 総理大臣(sōri daijin)

print: 印刷する 印刷する(insatsu suru)

printer: プリンター プリンター(purintā)

prison: 刑務所 刑務所(keimu sho)

professor: 教授 教授(kyōju)

profit: 利益 利益(rieki)

programmer: プログラマー プログラマー(puroguramā)

projector: プロジェクター プロジェクター(purojekutā)

promenade: プロムナード プロムナード(puromunādo)

promethium: プロメチウム プロメチウム(puromechiumu)

prosecutor: 検察官 検察官(kensatsu kan)

prostate: 前立腺 前立腺(zenritsu sen)

prostitute: 売春婦 売春婦(baishun fu)

protactinium: プロトアクチニウム プロトアクチニウム(purotoakuchiniumu)

proton: プロトン プロトン(puroton)

proud: 誇り高い 誇り高い(hokori takai)

province: 州 州(shū)

psychiatry: 精神科 精神科(seishin ka)

psychoanalysis: 精神分析 精神分析(seishin bunseki)

psychotherapy: 心理療法 心理療法(shinri ryōhō)

publisher: 出版社 出版社(shuppan sha)

puck: パック パック(pakku)

pudding: プリン プリン(purin)

PuerRico: プエルトリコ プエルトリコ(Puerutoriko)

pull: 引く 引く(hiku)

pulse: 脈拍 脈拍(myakuhaku)

pumpkin: かぼちゃ かぼちゃ(kabocha)

punk: パンク パンク(panku)

pupil: 瞳孔 瞳孔(dōkō)

purple: 紫 紫(murasaki)

purse: 財布 財布(saifu)

push: 押す 押す(osu)

push-up: 腕立て伏せ 腕立て伏せ(udetate fuse)

pushchair: ベビーカー ベビーカー(bebī kā)

put: 置く 置く(oku)

putty: へら へら(hera)

puzzle: パズル パズル(pazuru)

pyjamas: パジャマ パジャマ(pajama)

pyramid: ピラミッド ピラミッド(piramiddo)

Q

Qatar: カタール カタール(Katāru)

quarter of an hour: 十五分 十五分(jū go fun)

quartz: 石英 石英(sekiei)

question mark: 疑問符 疑問符(gimon fu)

quick: 速い 速い(hayai)

quickstep: クイックステップ クイックステップ(kuikku suteppu)

quiet: 静かな 静かな(shizuka na)

quote: 引用する 引用する(in yō suru)

R

rabbi: ラビ ラビ(rabi)

rabbit: うさぎ うさぎ(usagi)

raccoon: アライグマ アライグマ(araiguma)

racing bicycle: レース用自転車 レース用自転車(rēsu yō jiten sha)

radar: レーダー レーダー(rēdā)

radiator: ラジエーター ラジエーター(rajiētā)

radio: ラジオ ラジオ(rajio)

radiology: 放射線科 放射線科(hōsha sen ka)

radish: 大根 大根(daikon)

radium: ラジウム ラジウム(rajiumu)

radius: 半径 半径(hankei)

radon: ラドン ラドン(radon)

rafting: ラフティング ラフティング(rafutingu)

railtrack: レール レール(rēru)

rain: 雨 雨(ame)

rainbow: 虹 虹(niji)

raincoat: レインコート レインコート(rein kōto)

rainforest: 雨林 雨林(urin)

rainy: 雨の 雨の(ame no)

raisin: レーズン レーズン(rēzun)

rake: 熊手 熊手(kumade)

rally racing: ラリー ラリー(rarī)

Ramadan: ラマダン ラマダン(ramadan)

ramen: ラーメン ラーメン(rāmen)

random access memory (RAM): RAM RAM(RAM)

rap: ラップ ラップ(rappu)

rapeseed oil: 菜種油 菜種油(natane abura)

rash: 湿疹 湿疹(shisshin)

raspberry: ラズベリー ラズベリー(razuberī)

rat: ラット ラット(ratto)

rattle: ガラガラ ガラガラ(garagara)

raven: カラス カラス(karasu)

raw: 生 生(nama)

razor: 剃刀 剃刀(kamisori)

razor blade: かみそりの刃 かみそりの刃(kamisori no ha)

read: 読む 読む(yomu)

reading room: 読書室 読書室(dokusho shitsu)

real-estate agent: 不動産業者 不動産業者(fu dōsan gyōsha)

really: 本当に 本当に(hontō ni)

rear light: テールライト テールライト(tēruraito)

rear mirror: バックミラー バックミラー(bakku mirā)

rear trunk: トランク トランク(toranku)

receptionist: 受付係 受付係(uketsuke kakari)

record player: レコードプレーヤー レコードプレーヤー(rekōdo purēyā)

rectangle: 長方形 長方形(chō hōkei)

recycle bin: ゴミ箱 ゴミ箱(gomibako)

red: 赤 赤(aka)

red panda: レッサーパンダ レッサーパンダ(ressā panda)

Red Sea: 紅海 紅海(Kōkai)

red wine: 赤ワイン 赤ワイン(aka wain)

reed: 葦 葦(ashi)

referee: 審判員 審判員(shinpan in)

reggae: レゲエ レゲエ(regē)

region: 地域 地域(chiiki)

relax: 楽にして 楽にして(raku ni shite)

remote control: リモコン リモコン(rimokon)

reporter: レポーター レポーター(repōtā)

Republic of the Congo: コンゴ共和国 コンゴ共和国(Kongo Kyōwakoku)

rescue: 救う 救う(sukū)

research: 研究 研究(kenkyū)

reservation: 予約 予約(yoyaku)

respiratory machine: 人工呼吸器 人工呼吸器(jinkō kokyū ki)

rest: 休憩する 休憩する(kyūkei suru)

restaurant: レストラン レストラン(resutoran)

result: 結果 結果(kekka)

retirement: 退職 退職(taishoku)

rhenium: レニウム レニウム(reniumu)

rhino: サイ サイ(sai)

rhodium: ロジウム ロジウム(rojiumu)

rhomboid: 平行四辺形 平行四辺形(heikō shihen kei)

rhombus: 菱形 菱形(ryōkei)

rhythmic gymnastics: 新体操 新体操(shin taisō)

rib: 肋骨 肋骨(rokkotsu)

rice: 米 米(kome)

rice cooker: 炊飯器 炊飯器(suihan ki)

rich: 豊富な 豊富な(hōfu na)

right: 右 右(migi)

right angle: 直角 直角(chokkaku)

ring: 指輪 指輪(yubiwa)

ring finger: 薬指 薬指(kusuriyubi)

river: 川 川(kawa)

road: 道路 道路(dōro)

road roller: ロードローラー ロードローラー(rōdo rōrā)

roast chicken: ローストチキン ローストチキン(rōsuto chikin)

roast pork: ローストポーク ローストポーク(rōsuto pōku)

robot: ロボット ロボット(robotto)

rock: ロック ロック(rokku), 岩石 岩石(ganseki)

rock 'n' roll: ロックンロール ロックンロール(rokkunrōru)

rocket: ロケット ロケット(roketto)

rocking chair: ロッキングチェア ロッキングチェア(rokkingu chea)

roentgenium: レントゲニウム レントゲニウム(rentogeniumu)

roll: 転がる 転がる(korogaru)

roller coaster: ローラーコースター ローラーコースター(rōrā kōsutā)

roller skating: ローラースケーティング ローラースケーティング(rōrā sukētingu)

Romania: ルーマニア ルーマニア(Rūmania)

roof: 屋根 屋根(yane)

roof tile: 屋根瓦 屋根瓦(yanegawara)

room key: ルームキー ルームキー(rūmu kī)

room number: ルームナンバー ルームナンバー(rūmu nanbā)

room service: ルームサービス ルームサービス(rūmu sābisu)

root: 根 根(ne)

rose: 薔薇 薔薇(bara)

rosemary: ローズマリー ローズマリー(rōzumarī)

round: 丸い 丸い(marui)

roundabout: ロータリー ロータリー(rōtarī)

router: ルーター ルーター(rūtā)

row: 列 列(retsu)

rowing: ボート競技 ボート競技(bōto kyōgi)

rowing boat: ボート ボート(bōto)

rubber: 消しゴム 消しゴム(keshi gomu)

rubber band: 輪ゴム 輪ゴム(wa gomu)

rubber boat: ゴムボート ゴムボート(gomu bōto)

rubber stamp: スタンプ スタンプ(sutanpu)

rubidium: ルビジウム ルビジウム(rubijiumu)

ruby: ルビー ルビー(rubī)

rugby: ラグビー ラグビー(ragubī)

ruin: 廃墟 廃墟(haikyo)

ruler: ものさし ものさし(monosashi)

rum: ラム酒 ラム酒(ramu shu)

rumba: ルンバ ルンバ(runba)

run: 走る 走る(hashiru)

running: ランニング ランニング(ranningu)

runway: 滑走路 滑走路(kassō ro)

rush hour: ラッシュアワー ラッシュアワー(rasshu awā)

Russia: ロシア ロシア(Roshia)

ruthenium: ルテニウム ルテニウム(ruteniumu)

rutherfordium: ラザホージウム ラザホージウム(razahōjiumu)

Rwanda: ルワンダ ルワンダ(Ruwanda)

S

sad: 悲しい 悲しい(kanashī)

saddle: サドル サドル(sadoru)

safe: 安心な 安心な(anshin na), 金庫 金庫(kinko)

safety glasses: 保護眼鏡 保護眼鏡(hogo megane)

Sahara: サハラ サハラ(Sahara)

sail: 帆 帆(ho)

sailing: セーリング セーリング(sēringu)

sailing boat: 帆船 帆船(hansen)

Saint Kitts and Nevis: セントキッツ・ネイビス連邦 セントキッツ・ネイビス連邦(Sentokittsu Neibisu Renpō)

Saint Lucia: セントルシア セントルシア(Sentorushia)

Saint Vincent and the Grenadines: セントビンセント・グレナディーン セントビンセント・グレナディーン(Sentobinsento Gurenadīn)

sake: 日本酒 日本酒(Nippon shu)

salad: サラダ サラダ(sarada)

salami: サラミ サラミ(sarami)

salary: 給料 給料(kyūryō)

sales: 営業 営業(eigyō)

salmon: 鮭 鮭(sake)

salsa: サルサ サルサ(sarusa)

salt: 塩 塩(shio)

salty: 塩辛い 塩辛い(shiokarai)

samarium: サマリウム サマリウム(samariumu)

samba: サンバ サンバ(sanba)

Samoa: サモア サモア(Samoa)

sand: 砂 砂(suna)

sandals: サンダル サンダル(sandaru)

sandbox: 砂場 砂場(sunaba)

sandwich: サンドイッチ サンドイッチ(sandoicchi)

sanitary towel: ナプキン ナプキン(napukin)

San Marino: サンマリノ サンマリノ(Sanmarino)

sapphire: サファイア サファイア(safaia)

sardine: 鰯 鰯(iwashi)

satellite: 衛星 衛星(eisei)

satellite dish: テレビ受信用アンテナ テレビ受信用アンテナ(terebi jushin yō antena)

Saturday: 土曜日 土曜日(doyōbi)

Saturn: 土星 土星(Do sei)

Saudi Arabia: サウジアラビア サウジアラビア(Saujiarabia)

sauna: サウナ サウナ(sauna)

sausage: ソーセージ ソーセージ(sōsēji)

savings: 積み立て 積み立て(tsumitate)

saw: 挽く 挽く(hiku), 鋸 鋸(nokogiri)

saxophone: サクソフォン サクソフォン(sakusofon)

scaffolding: 足場 足場(ashiba)

scale: 体重計 体重計(taijū kei)

scalpel: メス メス(mesu)

scan: スキャンする スキャンする(sukyan suru)

scandium: スカンジウム スカンジウム(sukanjiumu)

scanner: スキャナー スキャナー(sukyanā)

scarf: スカーフ スカーフ(sukāfu)

scholarship: 奨学金 奨学金(shōgaku kin)

school: 学校 学校(gakkō)

schoolbag: 通学鞄 通学鞄(tsūgaku kaban)

school bus: スクールバス スクールバス(sukūru basu)

school uniform: 制服 制服(seifuku)

schoolyard: 校庭 校庭(kōtei)

science: 科学 科学(kagaku)

science fiction: サイエンスフィクション サイエンスフィクション(saiensu fikushon)

scientist: 科学者 科学者(kagaku sha)

scissors: ハサミ ハサミ(hasami)

scorpion: サソリ サソリ(sasori)

scrambled eggs: スクランブルエッグ スクランブルエッグ(sukuranburu eggu)

screen: スクリーン スクリーン(sukurīn), ディスプレイ ディスプレイ(disupurei)

screwdriver: スクリュードライバー スクリュードライバー(sukuryū doraibā)

screw wrench: スパナ スパナ(supana)

script: 台本 台本(daihon)

scrollbar: スクロールバー スクロールバー(sukurōru bā)

scrotum: 陰嚢 陰嚢(innō)

scrunchy: ヘアーゴム ヘアーゴム(heā gomu)

sculpting: 彫刻 彫刻(chōkoku)

sea: 海 海(umi)

seaborgium: シーボーギウム シーボーギウム(shībōgiumu)

seafood: シーフード シーフード(shīfūdo)

seagull: カモメ カモメ(kamome)

sea horse: タツノオトシゴ タツノオトシゴ(tatsunootoshigo)

seal: アザラシ アザラシ(azarashi)

sea lion: アシカ アシカ(ashika)

seat: シート シート(shīto)

seatbelt: シートベルト シートベルト(shīto beruto)

seaweed: 海藻 海藻(kaisō)

second: 秒 秒(byō), 第二 第二(dai ni)

second-hand shop: リサイクルショップ リサイクルショップ(risaikuru shoppu)

second basement floor: 地下二階 地下二階(chika ni kai)

secretary: 秘書 秘書(hisho)

security camera: 監視カメラ 監視カメラ(kanshi kamera)

security guard: 警備員 警備員(keibi in)

seed: 種 種(tane)

see you later: 行って来ます 行って来ます(itte kimasu)

selenium: セレン セレン(seren)

sell: 売る 売る(uru)

semicolon: セミコロン セミコロン(semikoron)

Senegal: セネガル セネガル(Senegaru)

September: 九月 九月(kyū gatsu)

Serbia: セルビア セルビア(Serubia)

server: サーバー サーバー(sābā)

sewage plant: 下水処理場 下水処理場(gesui shori jō)

sewing machine: ミシン ミシン(mishin)

sex: セックス セックス(sekkusu)

sexy: セクシー セクシー(sekushī)

Seychelles: セイシェル セイシェル(Seisheru)

shallow: 浅い 浅い(asai)

shampoo: シャンプー シャンプー(shanpū)

share: 分け合う 分け合う(wakeau), 株 株(kabu)

share price: 株価 株価(kabuka)

shark: サメ サメ(same)

shaver: 髭剃り器 髭剃り器(higesori ki)

shaving foam: シェービングフォーム シェービングフォーム(shēbingu fōmu)

she: 彼女 彼女(kanojo)

shed: 小屋 小屋(koya)

sheep: 羊 羊(hitsuji)

shelf: 棚 棚(tana)

shell: 貝 貝(kai)

shinpad: すね当て すね当て(suneate)

ship: 船 船(fune)

shirt: シャツ シャツ(shatsu)

shiver: 震える 震える(furueru)

shock absorber: ショックアブソーバ ショックアブソーバ(shokku abusōba)

shoe cabinet: 靴箱 靴箱(kutsubako)

shoot: 撃つ 撃つ(utsu)

shooting: 射撃 射撃(shageki)

shop assistant: 店員 店員(ten in)

shopping basket: ショッピングバスケット ショッピングバスケット (shoppingu basuketto)

shopping cart: ショッピングカート ショッピングカート (shoppingu kāto)

shopping mall: ショッピングセンター ショッピングセンター(shoppingu sentā)

shore: 海岸 海岸(kaigan)

short: 短い 短い(mijikai), 背が低い 背が低い(se ga hikui)

shorts: 短パン 短パン(tanpan)

short track: ショートトラック ショートトラック (shōto torakku)

shot put: 砲丸投げ 砲丸投げ(hōgan nage)

shoulder: 肩 肩(kata)

shoulder blade: 肩胛骨 肩胛骨(kenkōkotsu)

shout: 叫ぶ 叫ぶ(sakebu)

shovel: シャベル シャベル(shaberu)

shower: シャワー シャワー(shawā)

shower cap: シャワーキャップ シャワーキャップ(shawā kyappu)

shower curtain: シャワーカーテン シャワーカーテン(shawā kāten)

shower gel: シャワージェル シャワージェル(shawā jeru)

show jumping: 障害飛越競技 障害飛越競技(shōgai tobikoshi kyōgi)

shrink: 収縮する 収縮する(shūshuku suru)

shuttlecock: シャトルコック シャトルコック(shatoru kokku)

shy: 恥ずかしそうな 恥ずかしそうな(hazukashi sō na)

siblings: 兄弟姉妹 兄弟姉妹(kyōdai shimai)

sick: 病気の 病気の(byōki no)

side dish: 副菜 副菜(fukusai)

side door: サイドドア サイドドア(saido doa)

side effect: 副作用 副作用(fuku sayō)

Sierra Leone: シエラレオネ シエラレオネ(Shierareone)

signal: 信号 信号(shingō)

signature: 署名 署名(shomei)

silent: 静か 静か(shizuka)

silicon: シリコン シリコン(shirikon)

silk: シルク シルク(shiruku)

silly: ばかばかしい ばかばかしい(bakabakashī)

silver: 銀 銀(gin)

silver medal: 銀メダル 銀メダル(gin medaru)

sing: 歌う 歌う(utau)

Singapore: シンガポール シンガポール(Shingapōru)

singer: 歌手 歌手(kashu)

single room: シングルルーム シングルルーム(shinguru rūmu)

sink: シンク シンク(shinku)

siren: サイレン サイレン(sairen)

sister-in-law: 義姉妹 義姉妹(gi shimai)

sit: 座る 座る(suwaru)

sit-ups: シットアップ シットアップ(shitto appu)

skateboarding: スケートボーディング スケートボーディング(sukēto bōdingu)

skates: スケート スケート(sukēto)

skeleton: スケルトン スケルトン(sukeruton), 骸骨 骸骨(gaikotsu)

skewer: 串もの 串もの(kushi mono)

ski: スキー スキー(sukī)

skiing: スキー スキー(sukī)

ski jumping: スキージャンプ スキージャンプ(sukī janpu)

skinny: 細身 細身(hosomi)

ski pole: スキーストック スキーストック(sukī sutokku)

ski resort: スキー場 スキー場(sukī ba)

skirt: スカート スカート(sukāto)

ski suit: スキーウェア スキーウェア(sukī wea)

skull: 頭蓋骨 頭蓋骨(zugaikotsu)

skyscraper: 摩天楼 摩天楼(maten rō)

sledge: そり そり(sori)

sleep: 寝る 寝る(neru)

sleeping bag: 寝袋 寝袋(nebukuro)

sleeping mask: アイマスク アイマスク(ai masuku)

sleeping pill: 睡眠薬 睡眠薬(suimin yaku)

sleeve: スリーブ スリーブ(surību)

slide: 滑り台 滑り台(suberidai)

slim: スリム スリム(surimu)

slippers: スリッパ スリッパ(surippa)

slope: 坂 坂(saka)

Slovakia: スロバキア スロバキア(Surobakia)

Slovenia: スロベニア スロベニア(Surobenia)

slow: 遅い 遅い(osoi)

small: 小さい 小さい(chīsai)

small intestine: 小腸 小腸(shōchō)

smartphone: スマートフォン スマートフォン(sumāto fon)

smell: 匂いを嗅ぐ 匂いを嗅ぐ(nioi o kagu)

smile: 笑顔になる 笑顔になる(egao ni naru)

smoke: 吸う 吸う(sū)

smoke detector: 煙感知器 煙感知器(kemuri kanchi ki)

smoothie: スムージー スムージー(sumūjī)

smoothing plane: かんな かんな(kanna)

snack: スナック スナック(sunakku)

snail: カタツムリ カタツムリ(katatsumuri)

snake: ヘビ ヘビ(hebi)

snare drum: スネアドラム スネアドラム (sunea doramu)

snooker: スヌーカー スヌーカー (sunūkā)

snooker table: ビリヤード台 ビリヤード台 (biriyādo dai)

snow: 雪 雪 (yuki)

snowboarding: スノーボーディング スノーボーディング (sunō bōdingu)

snowmobile: スノーモービル スノーモービル (sunō mōbiru)

soap: 石鹸 石鹸 (sekken)

sober: しらふ しらふ (shirafu)

social media: ソーシャルメディア ソーシャルメディア (sōsharu media)

sock: 靴下 靴下 (kutsushita)

soda: ソーダ ソーダ (sōda)

sodium: ナトリウム ナトリウム (natoriumu)

sofa: ソファ ソファ (sofa)

soft: 柔らかい 柔らかい (yawarakai)

soil: 土 土 (tsuchi)

solar eclipse: 日食 日食 (nisshoku)

solar panel: ソーラーパネル ソーラーパネル (sōrā paneru)

soldier: 兵士 兵士 (heishi)

sole: ソール ソール (sōru)

solid: 固体 固体 (kotai)

Solomon Islands: ソロモン諸島 ソロモン諸島 (Soromon Shotō)

Somalia: ソマリア ソマリア (Somaria)

son: 息子 息子 (musuko)

son-in-law: 婿 婿 (muko)

soother: おしゃぶり おしゃぶり (oshaburi)

sore throat: 喉の痛み 喉の痛み (nodo no itami)

sorry: ごめんなさい ごめんなさい (gomen nasai)

soup: スープ スープ (sūpu)

sour: 酸っぱい 酸っぱい (suppai)

sour cream: サワークリーム サワークリーム (sawā kurīmu)

south: 南 南 (minami)

South Africa: 南アフリカ 南アフリカ (Minamiafurika)

southern hemisphere: 南半球 南半球 (minami hankyū)

South Korea: 韓国 韓国 (Kankoku)

South Pole: 南極 南極 (Nankyoku)

South Sudan: 南スーダン 南スーダン (Minami Sūdan)

souvenir: お土産 お土産 (o miyage)

soy: 大豆 大豆 (daizu)

soy milk: 豆乳 豆乳 (tōnyū)

space: スペース スペース (supēsu)

space shuttle: スペースシャトル スペースシャトル (supēsu shatoru)

space station: 宇宙ステーション 宇宙ステーション (uchū sutēshon)

space suit: 宇宙服 宇宙服 (uchū fuku)

spaghetti: スパゲティ スパゲティ (supageti)

Spain: スペイン スペイン (Supein)

Spanish: スペイン語 スペイン語 (Supein go)

sparkling wine: スパークリングワイン スパークリングワイン (supākuringu wain)

speed limit: 制限速度 制限速度 (seigen sokudo)

speedometer: メーター メーター (mētā)

speed skating: スピードスケート スピードスケート (supīdo sukēto)

sperm: 精子 精子 (seishi)

sphere: 球体 球体(kyūtai)

spider: 蜘蛛 蜘蛛(kumo)

spinach: ほうれん草 ほうれん草(hōren sō)

spinal cord: 脊髄 脊髄(sekizui)

spine: 背骨 背骨(sebone)

spirit level: 水平器 水平器(suihei ki)

spit: 唾を吐く 唾を吐く(tsuba o haku)

spleen: 脾臓 脾臓(hizō)

sponge: スポンジ スポンジ(suponji)

spoon: スプーン スプーン(supūn)

sports ground: 運動場 運動場(undō jō)

sports shop: スポーツ用品店 スポーツ用品店(supōtsu yōhin ten)

spray: スプレー スプレー(supurē)

spring: 春 春(haru)

spring onion: 葱 葱(negi)

spring roll: 春巻き 春巻き(harumaki)

sprint: スプリント スプリント(supurinto)

square: 角ばった 角ばった(kakubatta), 正四角形 正四角形(sei shikaku kei), スクエア スクエア(sukuea)

square meter: 平方メートル 平方メートル(heihō mētoru)

squat: スクワット スクワット(sukuwatto)

squid: イカ イカ(ika)

squirrel: リス リス(risu)

Sri Lanka: スリランカ スリランカ(Suriranka)

staff: スタッフ スタッフ(sutaffu)

stage: ステージ ステージ(sutēji)

stairs: 階段 階段(kaidan)

stalk: 茎 茎(kuki)

stamp: 切手 切手(kitte)

stand: 立つ 立つ(tatsu)

stapler: ホッチキス ホッチキス(hocchikisu)

star: 星 星(hoshi)

stare: 見つめる 見つめる(mitsumeru)

starfish: ヒトデ ヒトデ(hitode)

starter: 前菜 前菜(zensai)

state: 州 州(shū)

steak: ステーキ ステーキ(sutēki)

steal: 盗む 盗む(nusumu)

steam train: 蒸気機関車 蒸気機関車(jōki kikan sha)

steel: スチール スチール(suchīru)

steel beam: 鋼桁 鋼桁(hagane keta)

steep: 急な 急な(kyū na)

steering wheel: ハンドル ハンドル(handoru)

stepdaughter: 継娘 継娘(mamamusume)

stepfather: 継父 継父(keifu)

stepmother: 継母 継母(mamahaha)

stepson: 継息子 継息子(mamamusuko)

stethoscope: 聴診器 聴診器(chōshin ki)

stewardess: 客室乗務員 客室乗務員(kyakushitsu jōmu in)

stockbroker: 株式仲買人 株式仲買人(kabushiki nakagai nin)

stock exchange: 証券取引所 証券取引所(shōken torihiki sho)

stocking: ストッキング ストッキング(sutokkingu)

stomach: 胃 胃(i)

stomach ache: 腹痛 腹痛(fukutsū)

stool: スツール スツール(sutsūru)

stopwatch: ストップウオッチ ストップウオッチ(sutoppuuocchi)

stork: コウノトリ コウノトリ(kōnotori)

storm: 嵐 嵐(arashi)

straight: まっすぐな まっすぐな(massugu na), ストレート ストレート(sutorēto)

straight line: 直線 直線(chokusen)

strange: 風変わりな 風変わりな(fūgawari na)

strawberry: 苺 苺(ichigo)

stream: 川 川(kawa)

street food: ストリートフード ストリートフード(sutorīto fūdo)

street light: 街灯 街灯(gaitō)

stress: ストレス ストレス(sutoresu)

stretching: ストレッチ ストレッチ(sutorecchi)

strict: 厳しい 厳しい(kibishī)

stroke: 脳卒中 脳卒中(nō socchū)

strong: 強い 強い(tsuyoi)

strontium: ストロンチウム ストロンチウム(sutoronchiumu)

study: 勉強する 勉強する(benkyō suru)

stupid: 愚かな 愚かな(oroka na)

submarine: 潜水艦 潜水艦(sensui kan)

subtraction: 引き算 引き算(hikizan)

suburb: 郊外 郊外(kōgai)

subway: 地下鉄 地下鉄(chika tetsu)

Sudan: スーダン スーダン(Sūdan)

suddenly: 突然 突然(totsuzen)

Sudoku: 数独 数独(sūdoku)

sugar: 砂糖 砂糖(satō)

sugar beet: 甜菜 甜菜(tensai)

sugar cane: サトウキビ サトウキビ(satō kibi)

sugar melon: ハニーデューメロン ハニーデューメロン(hanī dyū meron)

suit: スーツ スーツ(sūtsu)

sulphur: 硫黄 硫黄(iō)

summer: 夏 夏(natsu)

sun: 太陽 太陽(taiyō)

sunburn: 日焼け 日焼け(hiyake)

Sunday: 日曜日 日曜日(nichiyōbi)

sunflower: ひまわり ひまわり(himawari)

sunflower oil: ひまわり油 ひまわり油(himawariabura)

sunglasses: サングラス サングラス(sangurasu)

sun hat: サンハット サンハット(san hatto)

sunny: 晴れ 晴れ(hare)

sunscreen: 日焼け止めクリーム 日焼け止めクリーム(hiyake tome kurīmu)

sunshine: 日光 日光(nikkō)

supermarket: スーパマーケット スーパマーケット(sūpa māketto)

surfboard: サーフボード サーフボード(sāfubōdo)

surfing: サーフィン サーフィン(sāfin)

surgeon: 外科医 外科医(geka i)

surgery: 手術 手術(shujutsu), 外科 外科(geka)

Suriname: スリナム スリナム(Surinamu)

surprised: 驚いた 驚いた(odoroita)

sushi: 寿司 寿司(sushi)

suspect: 容疑者 容疑者(yōgi sha)

suture: 縫合 縫合(hōgō)

swallow: 飲む 飲む(nomu)

swan: 白鳥 白鳥(hakuchō)

Swaziland: スワジランド スワジランド (Suwajirando)

sweatband: スエットバンド スエットバンド (suetto bando)

sweater: セーター セーター(sētā)

sweatpants: スエットパンツ スエットパンツ (suetto pantsu)

Sweden: スウェーデン スウェーデン (Suwēden)

sweet: 甘い 甘い(amai)

sweet potato: サツマイモ サツマイモ (satsuma imo)

swim: 泳ぐ 泳ぐ(oyogu)

swim cap: 水泳帽 水泳帽(suiei bō)

swim goggles: ゴーグル ゴーグル(gōguru)

swimming: 水泳 水泳(suiei)

swimming pool: スイミングプール スイミングプール(suimingu pūru)

swimsuit: 水着 水着(mizugi)

swim trunks: 水泳パンツ 水泳パンツ (suiei pantsu)

swing: ブランコ ブランコ (buranko)

Switzerland: スイス スイス(Suisu)

symphony: シンフォニー シンフォニー(shinfonī)

synagogue: シナゴーグ シナゴーグ(shinagōgu)

synchronized swimming: シンクロナイズドスイミング シンクロナイズドスイミング (shinkuronaizudo suimingu)

Syria: シリア シリア(Shiria)

syringe: シリンジ シリンジ(shirinji)

São Tomé and Príncipe: サントメプリンシペ サントメプリンシペ(Santomepurinshipe)

T

T-shirt: Tシャツ Tシャツ(tī shatsu)

table: テーブル テーブル(tēburu)

tablecloth: テーブルクロス テーブルクロス(tēburukurosu)

table of contents: 目次 目次(mokuji)

table tennis: 卓球 卓球(takkyū)

table tennis table: 卓球台 卓球台(takkyū dai)

taekwondo: テコンドー テコンドー(tekondō)

tailor: テーラー テーラー(tērā)

Taiwan: 台湾 台湾(Taiwan)

Tajikistan: タジキスタン タジキスタン (Tajikisutan)

take: 取る 取る(toru)

take a shower: シャワーを浴びる シャワーを浴びる (shawā o abiru)

take care: 気を付けて 気を付けて (ki o tsukete)

talk: 話す 話す(hanasu)

tall: 背が高い 背が高い(se ga takai)

tambourine: タンバリン タンバリン(tanbarin)

tampon: タンポン タンポン(tanpon)

tandem: タンデム タンデム(tandemu)

tangent: 正接 正接(seisetsu)

tango: タンゴ タンゴ(tango)

tank: 戦車 戦車(sensha)

tantalum: タンタル タンタル(tantaru)

Tanzania: タンザニア タンザニア(Tanzania)

tap: 蛇口 蛇口(jaguchi)

tape measure: 巻き尺 巻き尺(makijaku)

tapir: バク バク(baku)

tap water: 水道水 水道水(suidō sui)

tar: タール タール(tāru)

tarantula: タランチュラ タランチュラ(taranchura)

tattoo: 刺青 刺青(irezumi)

tax: 税金 税金(zeikin)

taxi: タクシー タクシー(takushī)

taxi driver: タクシーの運転手　タクシーの運転手　(takushī no unten shu)

tea: お茶 お茶(o cha)

teacher: 教師 教師(kyōshi)

teapot: ティーポット ティーポット(tīpotto)

technetium: テクネチウム テクネチウム(tekunechiumu)

telephone: 電話 電話(denwa)

telephone number: 電話番号 電話番号(denwa bangō)

telescope: 望遠鏡 望遠鏡(bōen kyō)

tellurium: テルル テルル(teruru)

temperature: 気温 気温(kion)

temple: こめかみ こめかみ(komekami), お寺 お寺(o tera)

tendon: 腱 腱(ken)

tennis: テニス テニス(tenisu)

tennis ball: テニスボール テニスボール(tenisu bōru)

tennis court: テニスコート テニスコート(tenisu kōto)

tennis racket: テニスラケット テニスラケット(tenisu raketto)

tent: テント テント(tento)

tequila: テキーラ テキーラ(tekīra)

terbium: テルビウム テルビウム(terubiumu)

term: 学期 学期(gakki)

termite: シロアリ シロアリ(shiroari)

terrace: テラス テラス(terasu)

territory: 領土 領土(ryōdo)

testament: 遺言書 遺言書(yuigon sho)

testicle: 睾丸 睾丸(kōgan)

Tetris: テトリス テトリス(tetorisu)

text: テキスト テキスト(tekisuto)

textbook: 教科書 教科書(kyōka sho)

text message: テキストメッセージ テキストメッセージ(tekisuto messēji)

Thailand: タイ タイ(Tai)

thallium: タリウム タリウム(tariumu)

Thanksgiving: サンクスギビング サンクスギビング(sankusugibingu)

thank you: ありがとうございます ありがとうございます(arigatō gozaimasu)

that: あれ あれ(are)

theatre: 劇場 劇場(gekijō)

The Bahamas: バハマ バハマ(Bahama)

the day after tomorrow: 明後日 明後日(asatte)

the day before yesterday: 一昨日 一昨日(issakujitsu)

The Gambia: ガンビア ガンビア(Ganbia)

their company: 彼らの会社 彼らの会社(kare ra no kaisha)

theme park: テーマパーク テーマパーク(tēma pāku)

then: そして そして(soshite)

theory of relativity: 相対性理論 相対性理論(sōtai sei riron)

there: あそこ あそこ(asoko)

thermal underwear: 保温インナー 保温インナー(hoon innā)

thermos jug: 魔法瓶 魔法瓶(mahō bin)

thesis: 論文 論文(ronbun)

The United States of America: アメリカ合衆国 アメリカ合衆国(Amerika Gasshūkoku)

they: 彼ら 彼ら(kare ra)

thief: 泥棒 泥棒(dorobō)

think: 考える 考える(kangaeru)

third: 第三 第三(dai san)

thirsty: 渇く 渇く(kawaku)

this: これ これ(kore)

this month: 今月 今月(kongetsu)

this week: 今週 今週(konshū)

this year: 今年 今年(kotoshi)

thong: Tバック Tバック(T bakku)

thorium: トリウム トリウム(toriumu)

threaten: 脅す 脅す(odosu)

three quarters of an hour: 四十五分 四十五分(yonjū go fun)

thriller: スリラー スリラー(surirā)

throttle: アクセルペダル アクセルペダル(akuseru pedaru)

throw: 投げる 投げる(nageru)

thulium: ツリウム ツリウム(tsuriumu)

thumb: 親指 親指(oyayubi)

thunder: 雷 雷(kaminari)

thunderstorm: 雷雨 雷雨(raiu)

Thursday: 木曜日 木曜日(mokuyōbi)

thyme: タイム タイム(taimu)

ticket: チケット チケット(chiketto)

ticket office: 切符売り場 切符売り場(kippu uriba)

ticket vending machine: 券売機 券売機(kenbai ki)

tidal wave: 津波 津波(tsunami)

tie: ネクタイ ネクタイ(nekutai)

tiger: 虎 虎(tora)

tile: タイル タイル(tairu)

timetable: 時刻表 時刻表(jikoku hyō)

tin: 錫 錫(suzu), 缶 缶(kan)

tip: チップ チップ(chippu)

tired: 疲れた 疲れた(tsukareta)

tissue: ティッシュペーパー ティッシュペーパー(tisshu pēpā)

titanium: チタン チタン(chitan)

toaster: トースター トースター(tōsutā)

tobacco: タバコ タバコ(tabako)

today: 今日 今日(kyō)

toe: つま先 つま先(tsumasaki)

tofu: 豆腐 豆腐(tōfu)

together: 一緒に 一緒に(issho ni)

Togo: トーゴ トーゴ(Tōgo)

toilet: トイレ トイレ(toire)

toilet brush: トイレブラシ トイレブラシ(toire burashi)

toilet paper: トイレットペーパー トイレットペーパー(toirettopēpā)

toll: 通行料金 通行料金(tsūkō ryōkin)

tomasauce: トマトソース トマトソース(tomato sōsu)

tomato: トマト トマト(tomato)

tomorrow: 明日 明日(ashita)

ton: トン トン(ton)

Tonga: トンガ トンガ(Tonga)

tongue: 舌 舌(shita)

tooth: 歯 歯(ha)

toothache: 歯痛 歯痛(shitsū)

toothbrush: 歯ブラシ 歯ブラシ(ha burashi)

toothpaste: 歯磨き粉 歯磨き粉(hamigakiko)

torch: 懐中電灯 懐中電灯(kaichū dentō)

tornado: 竜巻 竜巻(tatsumaki)

tortoise: 陸亀 陸亀(rikugame)

touch: 触る 触る(sawaru)

tour guide: ツアーガイド ツアーガイド(tsuā gaido)

tourist attraction: 観光の名所 観光の名所(kankō no meisho)

tourist guide: ガイドブック ガイドブック(gaidobukku)

tourist information: 観光案内 観光案内(kankō annai)

towel: タオル タオル(taoru)

town hall: 市役所 市役所(shi yakusho)

toy shop: おもちゃ屋 おもちゃ屋(omochaya)

track cycling: トラックレース トラックレース(torakku rēsu)

tracksuit: 運動着 運動着(undō gi)

tractor: トラクター トラクター(torakutā)

traffic jam: 交通渋滞 交通渋滞(kōtsū jūtai)

traffic light: 信号 信号(shingō)

trailer: トレーラー トレーラー(torērā)

train: 列車 列車(ressha)

train driver: 電車の運転手 電車の運転手(densha no unten shu)

trainers: スニーカー スニーカー(sunīkā)

train station: 駅 駅(eki)

tram: 路面電車 路面電車(romen densha)

trampoline: トランポリン トランポリン(toranporin)

trapezoid: 台形 台形(daikei)

travel: 旅行する 旅行する(ryokō suru)

travel agent: 旅行代理店 旅行代理店(ryokō dairi ten)

treadmill: トレッドミル トレッドミル(toreddomiru)

tree: 木 木(ki)

tree house: ツリーハウス ツリーハウス(tsurī hausu)

triangle: トライアングル トライアングル(toraianguru), 三角形 三角形(sankaku kei)

triathlon: トライアスロン トライアスロン(toraiasuron)

Trinidad and Tobago: トリニダードトバゴ トリニダードトバゴ(Torinidādotobago)

triple jump: 三段跳び 三段跳び(san dan tobi)

triplets: 三つ子 三つ子(mitsu go)

tripod: 三脚 三脚(sankyaku)

trombone: トロンボーン トロンボーン(toronbōn)

tropics: 熱帯 熱帯(nettai)

trousers: ズボン ズボン(zubon)

truffle: トリュフ トリュフ(toryufu)

trumpet: トランペット トランペット(toranpetto)

trunk: 幹 幹(miki)

tuba: チューバ チューバ(chūba)

Tuesday: 火曜日 火曜日(kayōbi)

tulip: チューリップ チューリップ(chūrippu)

tuna: マグロ マグロ(maguro)

tungsten: タングステン タングステン(tangusuten)

Tunisia: チュニジア チュニジア(Chunijia)

Turkey: トルコ トルコ(Toruko)

turkey: 七面鳥 七面鳥(shichimenchō), 七面鳥肉 七面鳥肉(shichimenchō niku)

Turkmenistan: トルクメニスタン トルクメニスタン(Torukumenisutan)

turnip cabbage: コールラビ コールラビ(kōrurabi)

turn left: 左に曲がる 左に曲がる(hidari ni magaru)

turn off: 消す 消す(kesu)

turn on: つける つける(tsukeru)

turn right: 右に曲がる 右に曲がる(migi ni magaru)

turtle: 亀 亀(kame)

Tuvalu: ツバル ツバル(Tsubaru)

TV: テレビ テレビ(terebi)

TV series: 連続番組 連続番組(renzoku bangumi)

TV set: テレビセット テレビセット(terebi setto)

tweezers: ピンセット ピンセット(pinsetto)

twins: 双子 双子(futago)

twisting: ねじれた ねじれた(nejireta)

two o'clock in the afternoon: 午後二時 午後二時(gogo ni ji)

typhoon: 台風 台風(taifū)

tyre: タイヤ タイヤ(taiya)

U

Uganda: ウガンダ ウガンダ(Uganda)

ugly: 醜い 醜い(minikui)

Ukraine: ウクライナ ウクライナ(Ukuraina)

ukulele: ウクレレ ウクレレ(ukurere)

ultrasound machine: 超音波検査 超音波検査(chō onpa kensa)

umbrella: 傘 傘(kasa)

uncle: 叔父 叔父(oji)

underpants: パンツ パンツ(pantsu)

underpass: 地下道 地下道(chika dō)

underscore: アンダースコア アンダースコア(andā sukoa)

undershirt: アンダーシャツ アンダーシャツ(andāshatsu)

unfair: 不公平な 不公平な(fu kōhei na)

uniform: 制服 制服(seifuku)

United Arab Emirates: アラブ首長国連邦 アラブ首長国連邦(Arabu Shuchōkoku Renpō)

United Kingdom: イギリス イギリス(Igirisu)

university: 大学 大学(daigaku)

uranium: ウラン ウラン(uran)

Uranus: 天王星 天王星(Tennō sei)

url: URL URL(URL)

urn: 骨壺 骨壺(kotsutsubo)

urology: 泌尿器科 泌尿器科(hinyō ki ka)

Uruguay: ウルグアイ ウルグアイ (Uruguai)

USB stick: USBメモリー USBメモリー(USB memorī)

uterus: 子宮 子宮(shikyū)

utility knife: 万能ナイフ 万能ナイフ (bannō naifu)

Uzbekistan: ウズベキスタン ウズベキスタン (Uzubekisutan)

V

vacuum: 掃除機をかける 掃除機をかける(sōji ki o kakeru)

vacuum cleaner: 掃除機 掃除機(sōji ki)

vagina: 膣 膣(chitsu)

valley: 谷 谷(tani)

vanadium: バナジウム バナジウム(banajiumu)

vanilla: バニラ バニラ(banira)

vanilla sugar: バニラシュガー バニラシュガー(banira shugā)

Vanuatu: バヌアツ バヌアツ(Banuatsu)

varnish: ニス ニス(nisu)

vase: 花瓶 花瓶(kabin)

Vatican City: バチカン市国 バチカン市国(Bachikan Shikoku)

veal: 子牛肉 子牛肉(ko gyūniku)

vector: ベクトル ベクトル(bekutoru)

vein: 静脈 静脈(jōmyaku)

Venezuela: ベネズエラ ベネズエラ(Benezuera)

Venus: 金星 金星(Kin sei)

vertebra: 椎骨 椎骨(tsuikotsu)

very: とっても とっても(tottemo)

vet: 獣医 獣医(jūi)

Viennese waltz: ウィンナワルツ ウィンナワルツ(winna warutsu)

Vietnam: ベトナム ベトナム(Betonamu)

village: 村 村(mura)

vinegar: 酢 酢(su)

viola: ビオラ ビオラ(biora)

violin: バイオリン バイオリン(baiorin)

virus: ウィルス ウィルス(wirusu)

visa: ビザ ビザ(biza)

visiting hours: 面会時間 面会時間(menkai jikan)

visitor: 訪問者 訪問者(hōmon sha)

vitamin: ビタミン ビタミン(bitamin)

vocational training: 職業訓練 職業訓練(shokugyō kunren)

vodka: ウォッカ ウォッカ(wokka)

voice message: 音声メール 音声メール(onsei mēru)

volcano: 火山 火山(kazan)

volleyball: バレーボール バレーボール(barēbōru)

volt: ヴォルト ヴォルト(boruto)

volume: 体積 体積(taiseki)

vomit: 吐く 吐く(haku)

vote: 投票する 投票する(tōhyō suru)

W

waffle: ワッフル ワッフル(waffuru)

waist: ウエスト ウエスト(uesuto)

wait: 待つ 待つ(matsu)

waiter: ウェイター ウェイター(weitā)

waiting room: 待合室 待合室(machiai shitsu)

walk: 歩く 歩く(aruku)

walkie-talkie: トランシーバー トランシーバー(toranshībā)

wall: 壁 壁(kabe)

wallet: 財布 財布(saifu)

walnut: クルミ クルミ(kurumi)

walrus: セイウチ セイウチ(seiuchi)

waltz: ワルツ ワルツ(warutsu)

wardrobe: クローゼット クローゼット(kurōzetto)

warehouse: 倉庫 倉庫(sōko)

warm: 暖かい 暖かい(atatakai)

warm-up: ウオームアップ ウオームアップ(uōmu appu)

warn: 警告する 警告する(keikoku suru)

warning light: 警告灯 警告灯(keikoku tō)

warranty: 保証 保証(hoshō)

wash: 洗う 洗う(arau)

washing machine: 洗濯機 洗濯機(sentaku ki)

washing powder: 洗濯用洗剤 洗濯用洗剤(sentaku yō senzai)

wasp: スズメバチ スズメバチ(suzumebachi)

watch: 見る 見る(miru), 腕時計 腕時計(ude tokei)

water: 水 水(mizu)

water bottle: 水筒 水筒(suitō)

water can: じょうろ じょうろ(jōro)

waterfall: 滝 滝(taki)

water melon: スイカ スイカ(suika)

water park: 親水公園 親水公園(shinsui kōen)

water polo: 水球 水球(suikyū)

waterskiing: 水上スキー 水上スキー(suijō sukī)

water slide: ウォータースライダー ウォータースライダー(wōtā suraidā)

watt: ワット ワット(watto)

we: 私達 私達(watashi tachi)

weak: 弱い 弱い(yowai)

webcam: ウェブカム ウェブカム(webu kamu)

website: ウェブサイト ウェブサイト(webusaito)

wedding: 結婚式 結婚式(kekkon shiki)

wedding cake: ウエディングケーキ ウエディングケーキ(uedingu kēki)

wedding dress: ウエディングドレス ウエディングドレス(uedingu doresu)

wedding ring: 結婚指輪 結婚指輪(kekkon yubiwa)

Wednesday: 水曜日 水曜日(suiyōbi)

weed: 雑草 雑草(zassō)

week: 週 週(shū)

weightlifting: 重量挙げ 重量挙げ(jūryō age)

welcome: ようこそ ようこそ(yō koso)

well-behaved: 行儀のよい 行儀のよい(gyōgi no yoi)

wellington boots: ウェリントンブーツ ウェリントンブーツ(Werinton būtsu)

west: 西 西(nishi)

western film: 西洋映画 西洋映画(seiyō eiga)

wet: 濡れた 濡れた(nureta)

wetsuit: ウエットスーツ ウエットスーツ (uetto sūtsu)

whale: 鯨 鯨(kujira)

what: 何 何(nani)

What's your name?: 名前はなんですか？ 名前はなんですか？ (namae wa nan desu ka)

wheat: 小麦 小麦(komugi)

wheelbarrow: 手押し車 手押し車 (teoshi sha)

wheelchair: 車いす 車いす (kuruma isu)

when: いつ いつ(itsu)

where: どこ どこ(doko)

Where is the toilet?: トイレはどこですか？ トイレはどこですか？ (toire wa doko desu ka)

which: どれ どれ(dore)

whip: 鞭 鞭(muchi)

whipped cream: ホイップクリーム ホイップクリーム (hoippu kurīmu)

whiskey: ウイスキー ウイスキー (uisukī)

whisper: 囁く 囁く (sasayaku)

white: 白 白(shiro)

white wine: 白ワイン 白ワイン (shiro wain)

who: 誰 誰(dare)

why: なぜ なぜ(naze)

widow: 未亡人 未亡人(mibōjin)

widower: やもめ やもめ(yamome)

width: 横幅 横幅(yokohaba)

wife: 妻 妻(tsuma)

wig: かつら かつら(katsura)

willow: 柳 柳(yanagi)

win: 勝つ 勝つ(katsu)

wind: 風 風(kaze)

wind farm: 風力発電所 風力発電所(fūryoku hatsuden sho)

window: 窓 窓(mado), 窓側 窓側(madogawa)

windpipe: 気管 気管(kikan)

windscreen: フロントガラス フロントガラス(furonto garasu)

windscreen wiper: ワイパー ワイパー(waipā)

windsurfing: ウインドサーフィン ウインドサーフィン (uindosāfin)

windy: 風が強い 風が強い (kaze ga tsuyoi)

wine: ワイン ワイン(wain)

wing: ウイング ウイング(uingu)

wing mirror: サイドミラー サイドミラー(saido mirā)

winter: 冬 冬(fuyu)

wire: ワイヤー ワイヤー(waiyā)

witness: 証人 証人(shōnin)

wolf: 狼 狼(ōkami)

woman: 女 女(onna)

womb: 子宮 子宮(shikyū)

wooden beam: 木造梁 木造梁(mokuzō hari)

wooden spoon: しゃもじ しゃもじ(shamoji)

woodwork: 木細工 木細工(ki zaiku)

wool: ウール ウール(ūru)

work: 働く 働く(hataraku)

workroom: 仕事部屋 仕事部屋(shigoto heya)

world record: 世界記録 世界記録(sekai kiroku)

worried: 心配している 心配している(shinpai shite iru)

wound: 傷口 傷口(kizuguchi)

wrestling: レスリング レスリング(resuringu)

wrinkle: 皺 皺(shiwa)

wrist: 手首 手首(tekubi)

write: 書く 書く(kaku)

wrong: 間違った 間違った(machigatta)

X

X-ray photograph: レントゲン写真 レントゲン写真(rentogen shashin)

xenon: キセノン キセノン(kisenon)

xylophone: 木琴 木琴(mokkin)

Y

yacht: ヨット ヨット(yotto)

yard: ヤード ヤード(yādo)

year: 年 年(toshi)

yeast: イースト イースト(īsuto)

yellow: 黄色 黄色(kiiro)

Yemen: イエメン イエメン(Iemen)

yen: 円 円(en)

yesterday: 昨日 昨日(kinō)

yoga: ヨガ ヨガ(yoga)

yoghurt: ヨーグルト ヨーグルト(yōguruto)

yolk: 卵黄 卵黄(ranō)

you: あなた あなた(anata), あなた達 あなた達(anata tachi)

young: 若い 若い(wakai)

your cat: あなたの猫 あなたの猫(anata no neko)

your team: あなたのチーム あなたのチーム(anata no chīmu)

ytterbium: イッテルビウム イッテルビウム(itterubiumu)

yttrium: イットリウム イットリウム(ittoriumu)

yuan: 元 元(moto)

Z

Zambia: ザンビア ザンビア(Zanbia)

zebra: シマウマ シマウマ(shimauma)

Zimbabwe: ジンバブエ ジンバブエ(Jinbabue)

zinc: 亜鉛 亜鉛(aen)

zip code: 郵便番号 郵便番号(yūbin bangō)

zipper: ジッパー ジッパー(jippā)

zirconium: ジルコニウム ジルコニウム(jirukoniumu)

zoo: 動物園 動物園(dōbutsu en)

Japanese - English

A

abokado (アボカド): avocado

abura (油): oil

aburami (脂身): fat meat

aen (亜鉛): zinc

Afuganisutan (アフガニスタン): Afghanistan

afutā shēbu (アフターシェーブ): aftershave

age sōsēji (揚げソーセージ): fried sausage

ago (顎): chin

ai (愛): love

aibeya (相部屋): dorm room

aiburō penshiru (アイブローペンシル): eyebrow pencil

aikon (アイコン): icon

ai masuku (アイマスク): sleeping mask

ainsutainiumu (アインスタイニウム): einsteinium

airainā (アイライナー): eyeliner

airon dai (アイロン台): ironing table

airon o kakeru (アイロンをかける): to iron

Airurando (アイルランド): Ireland

ai shadō (アイシャドウ): eye shadow

aishite imasu (愛しています): I love you

aisotōpu (アイソトープ): isotope

aisu hokkē (アイスホッケー): ice hockey

aisu kuraimingu (アイスクライミング): ice climbing

aisu kurīmu (アイスクリーム): ice cream

aisu kōhī (アイスコーヒー): iced coffee

Aisurando (アイスランド): Iceland

aisu rinku (アイスリンク): ice rink

aisuru (愛する): to love

aisu sukēto (アイススケート): ice skating

aka (赤): red

akachan (赤ちゃん): baby

akage no (赤毛の): ginger

akami (赤身): lean meat

akarui (明るい): light

akashia (アカシア): acacia

aka wain (赤ワイン): red wine

akeru (開ける): to open

aki (秋): autumn

Akiresu ken (アキレス腱): Achilles tendon

akuchiniumu (アクチニウム): actinium

akuseru pedaru (アクセルペダル): throttle

akōdion (アコーディオン): accordion

amai (甘い): sweet

amanogawa (天の川): Milky Way

Amazon (アマゾン): Amazon

ame (雨): rain

ame no (雨の): rainy

Amerika Gasshūkoku (アメリカ合衆国): The United States of America

amerikan futtobōru (アメリカンフットボール): American football

Amerikaryō Samoa (アメリカ領サモア): American Samoa

amerishiumu (アメリシウム): americium

anaake panchi (穴あけパンチ): hole puncher

anata (あなた): you

anata ga suki desu (あなたが好きです): I like you

anata no chīmu (あなたのチーム): your team

anata no neko (あなたの猫): your cat

anata tachi (あなた達): you

anchimon (アンチモン): antimony

Andesu (アンデス): Andes

Andora (アンドラ): Andorra

andāshatsu (アンダーシャツ): undershirt

andā sukoa (アンダースコア): underscore

ane (姉): big sister

Angora (アンゴラ): Angola

ani (兄): big brother

ankā (アンカー): anchor

anorakku (アノラック): anorak

an pea (アンペア): ampere

anshin na (安心な): safe

Antigua Bābūda (アンティグア・バーブーダ): Antigua and Barbuda

anzu (杏子): apricot

ao (青): blue

aojiroi (青白い): pale

aomushi (あおむし): caterpillar

aposutorofi (アポストロフィ): apostrophe

appuru pai (アップルパイ): apple pie

apuri (アプリ): app

apāto (アパート): apartment

Arabia go (アラビア語): Arabic

Arabu Shuchōkoku Renpō (アラブ首長国連邦): United Arab Emirates

araiguma (アライグマ): raccoon

arashi (嵐): storm

arau (洗う): to wash

are (あれ): that

arerugī (アレルギー): allergy

ari (アリ): ant

arigatō gozaimasu (ありがとうございます): thank you

arikui (アリクイ): ant-eater

aromaserapī (アロマセラピー): aromatherapy

Aruba (アルバ): Aruba

Arubania (アルバニア): Albania

arufabetto (アルファベット): alphabet

arugon (アルゴン): argon

Arujeria (アルジェリア): Algeria

aruku (歩く): to walk

Arumenia (アルメニア): Armenia

arumi (アルミ): aluminium

Aruzenchin (アルゼンチン): Argentina

asa (朝): morning
asai (浅い): shallow
asatte (明後日): the day after tomorrow
ashi (脚): foot
ashi (葦): reed
ashi (足): leg
ashiba (足場): scaffolding
ashika (アシカ): sea lion
ashisutanto (アシスタント): assistant
ashita (明日): tomorrow
asobiba (遊び場): playground
asobu (遊ぶ): to play
asoko (あそこ): there
asufaruto (アスファルト): asphalt
asupirin (アスピリン): aspirin
asutachin (アスタチン): astatine
ataeru (与える): to give
atarashī (新しい): new
atatakai (暖かい): warm
ATM (ATM): cash machine
atopī (アトピー): eczema
atotsugi (跡継ぎ): heir
atsui (暑い): hot
au (会う): to meet
azarashi (アザラシ): seal
Azerubaijan (アゼルバイジャン): Azerbaijan

B

Bachikan Shikoku (バチカン市国): Vatican City
badominton (バドミントン): badminton
baffarō (バッファロー): buffalo
baggu (バッグ): bag
Bahama (バハマ): The Bahamas
baiasuron (バイアスロン): biathlon
baiku (バイク): motorcycle
baiorin (バイオリン): violin
baishin (陪審): jury
baishun fu (売春婦): prostitute
baison (バイソン): bison
bajiru (バジル): basil
bakabakashī (ばかばかしい): silly
baketsu (バケツ): bucket
bakkin (罰金): fine
bakkugyamon (バックギャモン): backgammon
bakku mirā (バックミラー): rear mirror
bakkupakku (バックパック): backpack
baku (バク): tapir
banajiumu (バナジウム): vanadium
banana (バナナ): banana
Banguradeshu (バングラデシュ): Bangladesh

banira (バニラ): vanilla

banira shugā (バニラシュガー): vanilla sugar

banjī janpu (バンジージャンプ): bungee jumping

bannō hasami (万能ハサミ): loppers

bannō naifu (万能ナイフ): utility knife

banpā (バンパー): bumper

Banuatsu (バヌアツ): Vanuatu

bara (薔薇): rose

baretta (バレッタ): barrette

bariumu (バリウム): barium

Barubadosu (バルバドス): Barbados

barē (バレエ): ballet

barēbōru (バレーボール): volleyball

barē shūzu (バレエシューズ): ballet shoes

basu (バス): bus

basuketto (バスケット): basket

basukettobōru (バスケットボール): basketball

basu no unten shu (バスの運転手): bus driver

basurōbu (バスローブ): bathrobe

basurūmu (バスルーム): bathroom

basu taoru (バスタオル): bath towel

basu tei (バス停): bus stop

batta (バッタ): grasshopper

batterī (バッテリー): battery

batto (バット): bat

batā (バター): butter

batā miruku (バターミルク): buttermilk

bebī kā (ベビーカー): pushchair

bebī monitā (ベビーモニター): baby monitor

beddo (ベッド): bed

beddo saido ranpu (ベッドサイドランプ): bedside lamp

beikudo bīnzu (ベイクドビーンズ): baked beans

bekutoru (ベクトル): vector

benchi (ベンチ): bench

benchi puresu (ベンチプレス): bench press

Benezuera (ベネズエラ): Venezuela

bengo shi (弁護士): lawyer

Benin (ベニン): Benin

benkyō suru (勉強する): to study

beranda (ベランダ): balcony

Berarūshi (ベラルーシ): Belarus

beririumu (ベリリウム): beryllium

Berugī (ベルギー): Belgium

beruto (ベルト): belt

Berīzu (ベリーズ): Belize

Betonamu (ベトナム): Vietnam

bideo kamera (ビデオカメラ): camcorder

bijinesu dinā (ビジネスディナー): business dinner

bijinesu kurasu (ビジネスクラス): business class

bijinesu sukūru (ビジネススクール): business school

bijutsu (美術): art

bijutsu kan (美術館): art gallery

bikini (ビキニ): bikini

bikotsu (鼻骨): nasal bone

bikō (鼻孔): nostril

bikū yō supurē (鼻腔用スプレー): nasal spray

bin (瓶): jar

binīru bukuro (ビニール袋): plastic bag

biora (ビオラ): viola

biriyādo (ビリヤード): billiards

biriyādo dai (ビリヤード台): snooker table

bisuketto (ビスケット): biscuit

bisumasu (ビスマス): bismuth

bitamin (ビタミン): vitamin

biza (ビザ): visa

bobusurē (ボブスレー): bobsleigh

bochi (墓地): cemetery

bodībirudingu (ボディービルディング): bodybuilding

bodīgādo (ボディーガード): bodyguard

bodī rōshon (ボディーローション): body lotion

bokushingu (ボクシング): boxing

bokushingu ringu (ボクシングリング): boxing ring

bokushingu yō gurōbu (ボクシング用グローブ): boxing glove

bonnetto (ボンネット): bonnet

Boribia (ボリビア): Bolivia

boruto (ヴォルト): volt

Bosunia (ボスニア): Bosnia

botan (ボタン): button

botoru (ボトル): bottle

Botsuwana (ボツワナ): Botswana

budō (ぶどう): grape

bumon (部門): department

bun (分): minute

buna (橅): beech

bunbo (分母): denominator

bungaku (文学): literature

bunshi (分子): numerator, molecule

bunsū (分数): fraction

buraindo (ブラインド): blind

Burajiru (ブラジル): Brazil

burajā (ブラジャー): bra

burakkuberī (ブラックベリー): blackberry

burakku hōru (ブラックホール): black hole

burandē (ブランデー): brandy

buranko (ブランコ): swing

burashi (ブラシ): brush

buraunī (ブラウニー): brownie

burauza (ブラウザ): browser

bureiku dansu (ブレイクダンス): breakdance

buresuretto (ブレスレット): bracelet

burezā (ブレザー): blazer

burijj i (ブリッジ): bridge

burokkorī (ブロッコリー): broccoli

burondo (ブロンド): blond

Burugaria (ブルガリア): Bulgaria

Burukinafaso (ブルキナファソ): Burkina Faso

Burunei (ブルネイ): Brunei

burunetto (ブルネット): brunette

Burunji (ブルンジ): Burundi

burēki (ブレーキ): brake

burēki raito (ブレーキライト): brake light

burīfukēsu (ブリーフケース): briefcase

burōchi (ブローチ): brooch

burūberī (ブルーベリー): blueberry

burūsu (ブルース): blues

buta (豚): pig

butaniku (豚肉): pork

butsuri gaku (物理学): physics

butsuri gakusha (物理学者): physicist

byuffe (ビュッフェ): buffet

byō (秒): second

byōga (描画): drawing

byōin (病院): hospital

byōki no (病気の): sick

byōri gaku (病理学): pathology

bā (バー): bar

bābekyū (バーベキュー): barbecue

bāberu (バーベル): barbell

bāgen (バーゲン): bargain

bākuriumu (バークリウム): berkelium

bā kōdo (バーコード): bar code

bā kōdo sukyanā (バーコードスキャナー): bar code scanner

Bārēn (バーレーン): Bahrain

bāsudē kēki (バースデーケーキ): birthday cake

bātendā (バーテンダー): barkeeper

bēju (ベージュ): beige

bēkingu paudā (ベーキングパウダー): baking powder

bēkon (ベーコン): bacon

bēsubōru kyappu (ベースボールキャップ): baseball cap

bēsu gitā (ベースギター): bass guitar

bīchi (ビーチ): beach

bīchi barē (ビーチバレー): beach volleyball

bīchi sandaru (ビーチサンダル): flip-flops

bīru (ビール): beer

bōdo gēmu (ボードゲーム): board game

bōen kyō (望遠鏡): telescope

bōkō (膀胱): bladder

bōringu (ボーリング): bowling

bōringu bōru (ボーリングボール): bowling ball

bōriumu (ボーリウム): bohrium

bōru (ボウル): bowl

bōru pen (ボールペン): ball pen

bōshi (帽子): hat

bō takatobi (棒高跳び): pole vault
bōto (ボート): rowing boat
bōto kyōgi (ボート競技): rowing
Būtan (ブータン): Bhutan

C

CD purēyā (CDプレーヤー): CD player
chachacha (チャチャチャ): cha-cha
Chado (チャド): Chad
chaibu (チャイブ): chive
chairo (茶色): brown
chairudo shīto (チャイルドシート): child seat
channeru (チャンネル): channel
chatto (チャット): chat
chekku in kauntā (チェックインカウンター): check-in desk
chekkā (チェッカー): draughts
Cheko Kyōwakoku (チェコ共和国): Czech Republic
chero (チェロ): cello
chesu (チェス): chess
chiarīdā (チアリーダー): cheerleader
chichi (父): father
Chichū kai (地中海): Mediterranean Sea
chiiki (地域): region
chika dō (地下道): underpass
chikai (近い): close
chika ikkai (地下一階): first basement floor
chikaku (地核): earth's core
chikaku (地殻): earth's crust
chika ni kai (地下二階): second basement floor
chikara (力): force
chika shitsu (地下室): basement
chika tetsu (地下鉄): subway
chiketto (チケット): ticket
chikin nagetto (チキンナゲット): chicken nugget
chikin uingu (チキンウイング): chicken wings
chikubi (乳首): nipple
chikyū (地球): earth
chimamire (血まみれ): bloody
chintsū zai (鎮痛剤): painkiller
chippu (チップ): tip
chippusu (チップス): chips
chirashi (チラシ): flyer
Chiri (チリ): Chile
chiri (地理): geography
chisso (窒素): nitrogen
chitan (チタン): titanium
chitsu (膣): vagina
chizu (地図): map
chokkaku (直角): right angle
chokorēto (チョコレート): chocolate

chokorēto supureddo (チョコレートスプレッド): chocolate cream

chokusen (直線): straight line

Chunijia (チュニジア): Tunisia

chāhan (チャーハン): fried rice

chēn (チェーン): chain

chēn sō (チェーンソー): chainsaw

chīsai (小さい): small

chītā (チーター): cheetah

chīzu (チーズ): cheese

chīzubāgā (チーズバーガー): cheeseburger

chīzu kēki (チーズケーキ): cheesecake

chō (腸): intestine

chō (蝶): butterfly

chō hōkei (長方形): rectangle

chōkoku (彫刻): sculpting

chōku (チョーク): chalk

chō nekutai (蝶ネクタイ): bow tie

chō onpa kensa (超音波検査): ultrasound machine

chōshin ki (聴診器): stethoscope

chōshoku (朝食): breakfast

chūba (チューバ): tuba

chūdoku (中毒): poisoning

chū gakkō (中学校): junior school

Chūgoku (中国): China

chūrippu (チューリップ): tulip

chūseishi (中性子): neutron

chūsha jō (駐車場): car park

Chūō Afurika Kyōwakoku (中央アフリカ共和国): Central African Republic

CPU (CPU): central processing unit (CPU)

CT sukyanā (CTスキャナー): CT scanner

D

daboku (打撲): bruise

daburu bēsu (ダブルベース): double bass

daburu rūmu (ダブルルーム): double room

dachō (ダチョウ): ostrich

daen (楕円): ellipse

daibingu (ダイビング): diving

daibingu masuku (ダイビングマスク): diving mask

daidai (橙): orange

daigaku (大学): university

daihon (台本): script

dai ichi (第一): first

daijin (大臣): minister

daijōbu (大丈夫): no worries

daijōbu desu ka (大丈夫ですか？): Are you ok?

daikei (台形): trapezoid

daikon (大根): radish

daiku (大工): carpenter

dai ni (第二): second

dai san (第三): third
dai seidō (大聖堂): cathedral
dai toshi (大都市): metropolis
daitōryō (大統領): president
daiyamondo (ダイヤモンド): diamond
dai yon (第四): fourth
daizu (大豆): soy
da kara (だから): because
damu (ダム): dam
danberu (ダンベル): dumbbell
danbō sōchi (暖房装置): heating
danraku (段落): paragraph
dansu (ダンス): dancing
dansu shūzu (ダンスシューズ): dancing shoes
dansā (ダンサー): dancer
dare (誰): who
dasshubōdo (ダッシュボード): dashboard
deijī (デイジー): daisy
dejikame (デジカメ): digital camera
dekki (デッキ): deck
dekki chea (デッキチェア): deck chair
de mo (でも): but
dengen (電源): power outlet
denki (電気): power
denki airon (電気アイロン): electric iron
denki gishi (電気技師): electrician
denki shokku (電気ショック): electric shock
denkyū (電球): light bulb
Denmāku (デンマーク): Denmark
densha no unten shu (電車の運転手): train driver
denshi (電子): electron
denshi mēru (電子メール): e-mail
denshi renji (電子レンジ): microwave
denwa (電話): telephone
denwa bangō (電話番号): telephone number
denwa suru (電話する): to call
deshimētoru (デシメートル): decimeter
de wa nai (ではない): not
dezainā (デザイナー): designer
dezāto (デザート): dessert
dinā (ディナー): dinner
dipuroma (ディプロマ): diploma
direkutā (ディレクター): director
diru (ディル): dill
disupurei (ディスプレイ): screen
DJ (DJ): DJ
doa (ドア): door
doa nobu (ドアノブ): door handle
doboku sagyō in (土木作業員): construction worker
dobu niumu (ドブニウム): dubnium
Doitsu (ドイツ): Germany

Doitsu go (ドイツ語): German

doko (どこ): where

dokusho shitsu (読書室): reading room

Dominika (ドミニカ): Dominica

Dominika Kyōwakoku (ドミニカ共和国): Dominican Republic

domino (ドミノ): dominoes

dono yō ni (どのように): how

dorai furūtsu (ドライフルーツ): dried fruit

doramu (ドラム): drums

dore (どれ): which

doreddo hea (ドレッドヘア): dreadlocks

doresu (ドレス): dress

doriru (ドリル): drilling machine

doriru suru (ドリルする): to drill

dorobō (泥棒): thief

doru (ドル): dollar

Do sei (土星): Saturn

doyōbi (土曜日): Saturday

DVD purēyā (DVDプレーヤー): DVD player

dāmusutachiumu (ダームスタチウム): darmstadtium

dātsu (ダーツ): darts

dētabēsu (データベース): database

dētsu (デーツ): date

dīzeru (ディーゼル): diesel

dō (銅): copper

dōbutsu en (動物園): zoo

dōkutsu (洞窟): cave

dōkō (瞳孔): pupil

dō medaru (銅メダル): bronze medal

dōmyaku (動脈): artery

dōnatsu (ドーナツ): doughnut

dōro (道路): road

dōru hausu (ドールハウス): dollhouse

dōryō (同僚): colleague

E

ea baggu (エアバッグ): airbag

eakon (エアコン): air conditioner

ea matto (エアマット): air mattress

earobikusu (エアロビクス): aerobics

Echiopia (エチオピア): Ethiopia

eda (枝): branch

egao ni naru (笑顔になる): to smile

eiga (映画): cinema

eigo (英語): English

eigyō (営業): sales

eisei (衛星): satellite

eiyō dorinku (栄養ドリンク): energy drink

Ejiputo (エジプト): Egypt

eki (駅): train station

ekitai (液体): fluid

ekonomī kurasu (エコノミークラス): economy class

Ekuadoru (エクアドル): Ecuador

ekubo (えくぼ): dimple

en (円): circle, yen

enban nage (円盤投げ): discus throw

endoumame (エンドウマメ): pea

engan (沿岸): coast

engeki (演劇): play

enjin (エンジン): engine

enjinia (エンジニア): engineer

enjin rūmu (エンジンルーム): engine room

enpitsu (鉛筆): pencil

enpitsu kezuri (鉛筆削り): pencil sharpener

enso (塩素): chlorine

ensui kei (円錐形): cone

entotsu (煙突): chimney

entō (円筒): cylinder

erabu (選ぶ): to choose

erebētā (エレベーター): elevator

ereki gitā (エレキギター): electric guitar

eri (襟): collar

Eritoria (エリトリア): Eritrea

erubiumu (エルビウム): erbium

Erusarubadoru (エルサルバドル): El Salvador

esupuresso (エスプレッソ): espresso

Esutonia (エストニア): Estonia

F

F1 (F1): Formula 1

fagotto (ファゴット): bassoon

fairu (ファイル): file

fakkusu (ファックス): fax

fandēshon (ファンデーション): foundation

feisharu kurīmu (フェイシャルクリーム): face cream

feisu pakku (フェイスパック): face mask

feisu paudā (フェイスパウダー): face powder

fenneru (フェンネル): fennel

fenshingu (フェンシング): fencing

fensu (フェンス): fence

ferumiumu (フェルミウム): fermium

ferī (フェリー): ferry

Ferō Shotō (フェロー諸島): Faroe Islands

feta chīzu (フェタチーズ): feta

figyua sukēto (フィギュアスケート): figure skating

Fijī (フィジー): Fiji

fin (フィン): fin

Finrando (フィンランド): Finland

Firipin (フィリピン): Philippines

firutā (フィルター): filter

fisshu ando chippusu (フィッシュアンドチップス): fish and chips

fittonesu baiku (フィットネスバイク): exercise bike

forudā (フォルダー): folder

foto arubamu (フォトアルバム): photo album

fudebako (筆箱): pencil case

fu dōsan gyōsha (不動産業者): real-estate agent

fujin ka (婦人科): gynaecology

fukai (深い): deep

fuke (フケ): dandruff

fukurō (フクロウ): owl

fukusai (副菜): side dish

fuku sayō (副作用): side effect

fukutsū (腹痛): stomach ache

fu kōhei na (不公平な): unfair

funabashi (船橋): bridge

fune (船): ship

funsui (噴水): fountain

furaido poteto (フライドポテト): French fries

furaipan (フライパン): pan

furamingo (フラミンゴ): flamingo

furanshiumu (フランシウム): francium

Furansu (フランス): France

Furansu go (フランス語): French

Furansuryō Porineshia (フランス領ポリネシア): French Polynesia

furasshu (フラッシュ): flash

furenchi horun (フレンチホルン): French horn

furendorī na (フレンドリーな): friendly

furerobiumu (フレロビウム): flerovium

furippu chāto (フリップチャート): flip chart

furonto garasu (フロントガラス): windscreen

furonto raito (フロントライト): front light

furonto shīto (フロントシート): front seat

furueru (震える): to shiver

furui (古い): old

furī sutairu sukī (フリースタイルスキー): freestyle skiing

furūto (フルート): flute

furūtsu gamu (フルーツガム): fruit gum

furūtsu sarada (フルーツサラダ): fruit salad

fusso (フッ素): fluorine

futago (双子): twins

futoru (太る): to gain weight

futotta (太った): chubby

futtobōru (フットボール): football

futō eki (不凍液): antifreeze fluid

fuyu (冬): winter

fāsuto kurasu (ファーストクラス): first class

fīto (フィート): foot

fōku (フォーク): fork

Fōkurando Shotō (フォークランド諸島): Falkland Islands

fōkurifuto (フォークリフト): forklift truck

fūgawari na (風変わりな): strange

fūryoku hatsuden sho (風力発電所): wind farm

fūshi ga (風刺画): caricature

fūsui (風水): feng shui

fūtō (封筒): envelope

G

ga (蛾): moth

Gabon (ガボン): Gabon

gachō (ガチョウ): goose

gadoriniumu (ガドリニウム): gadolinium

Gaiana (ガイアナ): Guyana

gaidobukku (ガイドブック): tourist guide

gaikotsu (骸骨): skeleton

gairai kanja (外来患者): outpatient

gaitō (街灯): street light

gake (崖): cliff

gakki (学期): term

gakkotsu (顎骨): jawbone

gakkō (学校): school

gakubuchi (額縁): picture frame

gakui (学位): degree

gakushi (学士): bachelor

gamu (ガム): chewing gum

gan (癌): cancer

Ganbia (ガンビア): The Gambia

ganseki (岩石): rock

garagara (ガラガラ): rattle

gariumu (ガリウム): gallium

gasorin (ガソリン): petrol

gasorin sutando (ガソリンスタンド): petrol station

gasu (ガス): gas

geka (外科): surgery

geka i (外科医): surgeon

gekijō (劇場): theatre

genki desu ka (元気ですか？): How are you?

genshi (原子): atom

genshi bangō (原子番号): atomic number

genshi ryoku hatsuden sho (原子力発電所): nuclear power plant

geri (下痢): diarrhea

gerumaniumu (ゲルマニウム): germanium

gesshoku (月食): lunar eclipse

gesui shori jō (下水処理場): sewage plant

gesuto (ゲスト): guest

getsuyōbi (月曜日): Monday

gia shifuto (ギアシフト): gear shift

gibo (義母): mother-in-law

gifu (義父): father-in-law

gi kyōdai (義兄弟): brother-in-law

gimon fu (疑問符): question mark

gin (銀): silver

ginga (銀河): galaxy

Ginia (ギニア): Guinea

Giniabisau (ギニアビサウ): Guinea-Bissau

ginkō furikomi (銀行振込): bank transfer

ginkō kōza (銀行口座): bank account

gin medaru (銀メダル): silver medal

gipusu (ギプス): cast

Girisha (ギリシャ): Greece

gishi (義歯): dental prostheses

gi shimai (義姉妹): sister-in-law

gitā (ギター): guitar

go gatsu (五月): May

gogo (午後): afternoon

gogo ni ji (午後二時): two o'clock in the afternoon

gomen nasai (ごめんなさい): sorry

gomibako (ゴミ箱): garbage bin, recycle bin

gomu bōto (ゴムボート): rubber boat

gorufu (ゴルフ): golf

gorufu bōru (ゴルフボール): golf ball

gorufu jō (ゴルフ場): golf course

gorufu kurabu (ゴルフクラブ): golf club

goto (ごと): every

gozen (午前): morning

gozen ichi ji (午前一時): one o'clock in the morning

GPS (GPS): GPS

Guatemara (グアテマラ): Guatemala

gurafaito (グラファイト): graphite

guraidā (グライダー): glider

gurajiorasu (グラジオラス): gladiolus

guramu (グラム): gram

guranyū tō (グラニュー糖): granulated sugar

gurasu (グラス): glass

Gurenada (グレナダ): Grenada

guruten (グルテン): gluten

gurēpufurūtsu (グレープフルーツ): grapefruit

Gurīn Rando (グリーンランド): Greenland

gurūpu serapī (グループセラピー): group therapy

gyanburu suru (ギャンブルする): to gamble

gyosen (漁船): fishing boat

gyōgi no yoi (行儀のよい): well-behaved

gyōza (餃子): dumpling

gyūniku (牛肉): beef

gyūnyū (牛乳): milk

Gāna (ガーナ): Ghana

gōguru (ゴーグル): swim goggles

gōru (ゴール): goal

gūrasshu (グーラッシュ): goulash

H

ha (歯): tooth

ha (葉): leaf
habahiroi (幅広い): broad
habatobi (幅跳び): long jump
ha burashi (歯ブラシ): toothbrush
hachi (蜂): bee
hachi (鉢): flower pot
hachi gatsu (八月): August
hachimitsu (蜂蜜): honey
hachiue (鉢植え): houseplant
hae (ハエ): fly
hafuniumu (ハフニウム): hafnium
hagane keta (鋼桁): steel beam
hagata (歯型): bite
hageatama (はげ頭): bald head
haha (母): mother
hai (はい): ok
hai (灰): ash
hai (肺): lung
Haichi (ハイチ): Haiti
haiden sen (配電線): power line
haifun (ハイフン): hyphen
hai hīru (ハイヒール): high heels
haiiro (灰色): grey
haiki kan (排気管): exhaust pipe
haikingu (ハイキング): hiking
haikingu būtsu (ハイキングブーツ): hiking boots
haikyo (廃墟): ruin
ha isha (歯医者): dentist
haitō (配当): dividend
haiyū (俳優): actor
haka (墓): grave
hakaru (測る): to measure
hakase (博士): PhD
hakike (吐き気): nausea
hakkaku kei (八角形): octagon
hakobu (運ぶ): to carry
haku (吐く): to vomit
hakubutsu kan (博物館): museum
hakuchō (白鳥): swan
hamaki (葉巻): cigar
hamigakiko (歯磨き粉): toothpaste
hamu (ハム): ham
hamusutā (ハムスター): hamster
hana (花): flower, blossom
hana (鼻): nose
hanabira (花びら): petal
hanadi (鼻血): nosebleed
hanamuko (花婿): groom
hanasu (話す): to talk
hanaya (花屋): florist
hanayome (花嫁): bride

hanbāgā (ハンバーガー): burger, hamburger

handobaggu (ハンドバッグ): handbag

hando burēki (ハンドブレーキ): hand brake

handobōru (ハンドボール): handball

handoru (ハンドル): steering wheel

hanemūn (ハネムーン): honeymoon

Hangarī (ハンガリー): Hungary

hankei (半径): radius

han kinzoku (半金属): metalloid

hanmā (ハンマー): hammer

hanmā nage (ハンマー投げ): hammer throw

hansamu (ハンサム): handsome

hansen (帆船): sailing boat

hantō (半島): peninsula

hanzai sha (犯罪者): criminal

hanī dyū meron (ハニーデューメロン): sugar melon

hara (腹): belly

harapeko (腹ペコ): hungry

hare (晴れ): sunny

hari (針): needle

hari chiryō (鍼治療): acupuncture

harikēn (ハリケーン): hurricane

harinezumi (ハリネズミ): hedgehog

harowīn (ハロウィーン): Halloween

haru (春): spring

harumaki (春巻き): spring roll

hasami (ハサミ): scissors

hashi (箸): chopstick

hashigo (はしご): ladder

hashika (麻疹): measles

hashiru (走る): to run

hasshiumu (ハッシウム): hassium

hataraku (働く): to work

hato (鳩): pigeon

hatsuden ki (発電機): generator

hau (這う): to crawl

hayabusa (ハヤブサ): falcon

hayai (速い): quick

hazukashi sō na (恥ずかしそうな): shy

hea airon (ヘアアイロン): curling iron

hea burashi (ヘアブラシ): brush

hea doraiyā (ヘアドライヤー): hairdryer

hea doressā (ヘアドレッサー): hairdresser

hea jeru (ヘアジェル): hair gel

hebi (ヘビ): snake

hebī metaru (ヘビーメタル): heavy metal

heihō mētoru (平方メートル): square meter

heikō shihen kei (平行四辺形): rhomboid

heishi (兵士): soldier

hera (へら): putty

herajika (ヘラジカ): elk

herikoputā (ヘリコプター): helicopter
heriumu (ヘリウム): helium
herumetto (ヘルメット): helmet
heso (臍): belly button
heā gomu (ヘアーゴム): scrunchy
hi (日): day
hi (火): fire
hidari (左): left
hidari ni magaru (左に曲がる): turn left
hifu ka (皮膚科): dermatology
higasa (日傘): parasol
higashi (東): east
Higashichimōru (東チモール): East Timor
hige (髭): beard
higesori ki (髭剃り器): shaver
hiji (肘): elbow
hijō guchi (非常口): emergency exit
hikidashi (引き出し): drawer
hikiniku (挽肉): minced meat
hi kinzoku (非金属): non-metal
hikizan (引き算): subtraction
hikoku nin (被告人): defendant
hiku (引く): to pull
hiku (挽く): to saw
hikui (低い): low
hikō ki (飛行機): plane
Himaraya (ヒマラヤ): Himalayas
himawari (ひまわり): sunflower
himawariabura (ひまわり油): sunflower oil
hina (雛): chick
hinin yō piru (避妊用ピル): birth control pill
hinyō ki ka (泌尿器科): urology
hiraku (開く): to open
hiroi (広い): huge
hisho (秘書): secretary
hiso (ヒ素): arsenic
hisui (翡翠): jade
hitai (額): forehead
hitode (ヒトデ): starfish
hitosashi yubi (人差し指): index finger
hitsuji (羊): sheep
hiyake (日焼け): sunburn
hiyake tome kurīmu (日焼け止めクリーム): sunscreen
hiza (膝): knee
hizagashira (膝頭): kneecap
hizō (脾臓): spleen
ho (帆): sail
hocchikisu (ホッチキス): stapler
hodō (歩道): pavement
hogo megane (保護眼鏡): safety glasses
hoiku en (保育園): nursery

hoiku shi (保育士): kindergarten teacher

hoippu kurīmu (ホイップクリーム): whipped cream

hoken (保険): insurance

Hokkyoku (北極): North Pole

hokkē sutikku (ホッケースティック): hockey stick

hokori takai (誇り高い): proud

hokō sha tengoku (歩行者天国): pedestrian area

homeopashī (ホメオパシー): homoeopathy

hon (本): book

hondana (本棚): bookshelf

hone (骨): bone

Honjurasu (ホンジュラス): Honduras

Honkon (香港): Hong Kong

hontō ni (本当に): really

honyū bin (哺乳瓶): baby bottle

hoon innā (保温インナー): thermal underwear

horu (掘る): to dig

horumiumu (ホルミウム): holmium

horā eiga (ホラー映画): horror movie

hoshi (星): star

hoshō (保証): warranty

hosomi (細身): skinny

hosuteru (ホステル): hostel

hosuto (ホスト): host

hoteru (ホテル): hotel

hotondo (ほとんど): most

hotto chokorēto (ホットチョコレート): hot chocolate

hotto dokku (ホットドック): hot dog

hottokēki (ホットケーキ): pancake

hyō (ヒョウ): leopard

hyōga (氷河): glacier

hādodisuku (ハードディスク): hard drive

hādoru kyōgi (ハードル競技): hurdles

hāmonika (ハーモニカ): harmonica

hāpu (ハープ): harp

hēzerunattsu (ヘーゼルナッツ): hazelnut

hīru (ヒール): heel

hō (頬): cheek

hōfu na (豊富な): rich

hōgan nage (砲丸投げ): shot put

hōgō (縫合): suture

hōkaiseki (方解石): calcite

hōki (箒): broom

hōman (豊満): plump

hōmon sha (訪問者): visitor

hōmu bu (法務部): legal department

hōren sō (ほうれん草): spinach

hōritsu (法律): law

hōseki shōnin (宝石商人): jeweller

hōsha sen ka (放射線科): radiology

hōso (ホウ素): boron

hōsu (ホース): hose
hōtai (包帯): bandage
hōtei shiki (方程式): equation

I

i (胃): stomach
ibo ji (イボ痔): hemorrhoid
ibuningu doresu (イブニングドレス): evening dress
ichi gatsu (一月): January
ichigo (苺): strawberry
ichijiku (イチジク): fig
ido (緯度): latitude
Iemen (イエメン): Yemen
Igirisu (イギリス): United Kingdom
iji warui (意地悪い): evil
ika (イカ): squid
ikari (怒り): angry
ike (池): pond
ikegaki (生垣): hedge
iki o suru (息をする): to breathe
ikiru (生きる): to live
ikkai (一階): ground floor
ikura (いくら？): how much?
iku tsu desu ka (いくつですか？): how many?
ima (今): now
imōto (妹): little sister
inazuma (稲妻): lightning
inchi (インチ): inch
Indo (インド): India
Indoneshia (インドネシア): Indonesia
Indo yō (インド洋): Indian Ocean
infuruenza (インフルエンザ): flu
injiumu (インジウム): indium
inkei (陰茎): penis
inku (インク): ink
inku rōrā (インクローラー): inking roller
innō (陰嚢): scrotum
inoru (祈る): to pray
insatsu suru (印刷する): to print
inseki (隕石): meteorite
insurin (インスリン): insulin
insutanto kamera (インスタントカメラ): instant camera
insutanto rāmen (インスタントラーメン): instant noodles
inu (犬): dog
inugoya (犬小屋): kennel
inu o katte imasu (犬を飼っています): I have a dog
in yō suru (引用する): to quote
ion (イオン): ion
ippō tsūkō (一方通行): one-way street
Iraku (イラク): Iraq

Iran (イラン): Iran

irezumi (刺青): tattoo

irijiumu (イリジウム): iridium

iro enpitsu (色鉛筆): coloured pencil

iruka (イルカ): dolphin

isan (遺産): heritage

isha (医者): doctor

isogashī (忙しい): busy

issakujitsu (一昨日): the day before yesterday

issankatanso (一酸化炭素): carbon monoxide

issho ni (一緒に): together

issho ni o ide (一緒においで): Come with me

isu (椅子): chair

Isuraeru (イスラエル): Israel

IT (IT): IT

itameru (炒める): to fry

Itaria (イタリア): Italy

itsu (いつ): when

itsu mo (いつも): always

itte kimasu (行って来ます): see you later

itterubiumu (イッテルビウム): ytterbium

ittoriumu (イットリウム): yttrium

iwashi (鰯): sardine

iwau (祝う): to celebrate

iyafon (イヤフォン): earphone

iyaringu (イヤリング): earring

iō (硫黄): sulphur

J

jagaimo (じゃがいも): potato

jaguchi (蛇口): tap

jaibu (ジャイブ): jive

jaketto (ジャケット): jacket

jakki (ジャッキ): jack

Jamaika (ジャマイカ): Jamaica

jamu (ジャム): jam

jazu (ジャズ): jazz

jetto sukī (ジェットスキー): jet ski

ji (時): hour

Jibuchi (ジブチ): Djibouti

Jiburarutaru (ジブラルタル): Gibraltar

jiken (事件): case

jiki kyōmei dansō satsuei sōchi (磁気共鳴断層撮影装置): magnetic resonance imaging

jikken shitsu (実験室): laboratory

jiko (事故): accident

jikoku hyō (時刻表): timetable

jin (ジン): gin

Jinbabue (ジンバブエ): Zimbabwe

jinji (人事): human resources

jinkō kokyū ki (人工呼吸器): respiratory machine

jinzō (腎臓): kidney

jippā (ジッパー): zipper

jirukoniumu (ジルコニウム): zirconium

jishaku (磁石): magnet

jishin (地震): earthquake

jisho (辞書): dictionary

jisupuroshiumu (ジスプロシウム): dysprosium

jiten sha (自転車): bicycle

jitsu wa (実は): actually

jo sanpu (助産婦): midwife

joshō (序章): preface

jugyō (授業): lecture

jushin bokkusu (受信ボックス): inbox

jāji (ジャージ): jersey

jānarisuto (ジャーナリスト): journalist

jīnzu (ジーンズ): jeans

jōdan (冗談): joke

Jōjia (ジョージア): Georgia

jōki kikan sha (蒸気機関車): steam train

jōmyaku (静脈): vein

jōro (じょうろ): water can

jōzai (錠剤): pill

jū (銃): gun

jūdō (柔道): judo

jū gatsu (十月): October

jū go fun (十五分): quarter of an hour

jūgyō in (従業員): employee

jūi (獣医): vet

jū ichi gatsu (十一月): November

jūkeitei (従兄弟): cousin

jū nen (十年): decade

jū ni gatsu (十二月): December

jūnishichō (十二指腸): duodenum

jūryoku (重力): gravity

jūryō age (重量挙げ): weightlifting

jūshimai (従姉妹): cousin

jūsho (住所): address

jūshī (ジューシー): juicy

K

ka (蚊): mosquito

kaba (カバ): hippo

kaba (樺): birch

kabe (壁): wall

kabin (花瓶): vase

kabocha (かぼちゃ): pumpkin

kabu (株): share

kabuka (株価): share price

kabushiki nakagai nin (株式仲買人): stockbroker

kadan (花壇): flower bed

kadomiumu (カドミウム): cadmium

kaede (楓): maple

kaerimashō (帰りましょう): Let's go home

kaeru (カエル): frog

kafeteria (カフェテリア): canteen

kafun shō (花粉症): hay fever

kagaku (化学): chemistry

kagaku (科学): science

kagaku hannō (化学反応): chemical reaction

kagaku kōzō (化学構造): chemical structure

kagaku sha (化学者): chemist

kagaku sha (科学者): scientist

kagami (鏡): mirror

kagi (鍵): key

kagiana (鍵穴): keyhole

kagi o kakeru (鍵をかける): to lock

kagu ya (家具屋): furniture store

kagō butsu (化合物): chemical compound

kahei (貨幣): coin

kai (貝): shell

kaichō (会長): chairman

kaichū dentō (懐中電灯): torch

kaidan (階段): stairs

kaiga (絵画): painting

kaigan (海岸): shore

kaigi shitsu (会議室): meeting room

kaiinsekkai jutsu (会陰切開術): episiotomy

kaikei shi (会計士): accountant

kairopurakutā (カイロプラクター): chiropractor

kaisoku densha (快速電車): high-speed train

kaisō (海藻): seaweed

kaiyō (海洋): ocean

Kaiō sei (海王星): Neptune

kaji (火事): fire

kajino (カジノ): casino

kakato (かかと): heel

kakeru (賭ける): to bet

kakezan (掛け算): multiplication

kakitsubata (燕子花): iris

kakko ī (かっこいい): cool

kaku (書く): to write

kakubatta (角ばった): square

kakudo (角度): angle

kakusu (隠す): to hide

kakuteru (カクテル): cocktail

kakō gan (花崗岩): granite

kamakiri (かまきり): praying mantis

kame (亀): turtle

kamera (カメラ): camera

kameraman (カメラマン): camera operator

kamereon (カメレオン): chameleon

Kamerūn (カメルーン): Cameroon

kaminari (雷): thunder

kaminoke (髪の毛): hair

kamisori (剃刀): razor

kamisori no ha (かみそりの刃): razor blade

kamo (鴨): duck

kamome (カモメ): seagull

kamotsu kōkū ki (貨物航空機): cargo aircraft

kamotsu ressha (貨物列車): freight train

kamu (噛む): to bite

kan (缶): tin

Kanada (カナダ): Canada

kanashī (悲しい): sad

Kanbojia (カンボジア): Cambodia

kanboku (灌木): bush

kandai na (寛大な): generous

kangaeru (考える): to think

kangarū (カンガルー): kangaroo

kango fu (看護婦): nurse

kani (カニ): crab

kanja (患者): patient

kankei nai (関係ない): doesn't matter

kanketsu sen (間欠泉): geyser

kanki sen (換気扇): fan

Kankoku (韓国): South Korea

kankyaku (観客): audience

kankō annai (観光案内): tourist information

kankō no meisho (観光の名所): tourist attraction

kanmuri (冠): crown

kanna (かんな): smoothing plane

kanojo (彼女): girlfriend, she

kanojo no doresu (彼女のドレス): her dress

kanoke (棺桶): coffin

kanpai (乾杯): cheers

kanpō yaku (漢方薬): Chinese medicine

kansei tō (管制塔): control tower

kansen shō (感染症): infection

kanshi kamera (監視カメラ): security camera

kantan fu (感嘆符): exclamation mark

kantan na (簡単な): easy

kanzei (関税): customs

kanzō (肝臓): liver

kanū (カヌー): canoe

kanū kyōgi (カヌー競技): canoeing

kaoku (家屋): house

kappu (カップ): cup

kapuchīno (カプチーノ): cappuccino

kapuseru (カプセル): capsule

karamatsu (カラマツ): larch

karappo (空っぽ): empty

karasu (カラス): crow, raven

karate (空手): karate

kare (彼): he

karendā (カレンダー): calendar

kare no kuruma (彼の車): his car

kare ra (彼ら): they

kare ra no kaisha (彼らの会社): their company

kareshi (彼氏): boyfriend

karifurawā (カリフラワー): cauliflower

karihoruniumu (カリホルニウム): californium

kariumu (カリウム): potassium

karui (軽い): light

karushiumu (カルシウム): calcium

karē (カレー): curry

karūseru (カルーセル): carousel

kasa (傘): umbrella

kasai keihō (火災警報): fire alarm

kasasagi (カササギ): magpie

Ka sei (火星): Mars

kashi (歌詞): lyrics

kashi (華氏): Fahrenheit

kashikoi (賢い): clever

kashiwa (柏): oak

kashu (歌手): singer

kashū nattsu (カシューナッツ): cashew

kassō ro (滑走路): runway

kasutādo (カスタード): custard

kata (肩): shoulder

katai (固い): hard

katatsumuri (カタツムリ): snail

katorarī (カトラリー): cutlery

katsu (勝つ): to win

katsura (かつら): wig

katto ban (カットバン): plaster

Katāru (カタール): Qatar

katēteru (カテーテル): catheter

kau (買う): to buy

kawa (川): river, stream

kawa (皮): peel

kawagutsu (革靴): leather shoes

kawaita (乾いた): dry

kawakasu (乾かす): to dry

kawaku (渇く): thirsty

kawauso (かわうそ): otter

kawaī (可愛い): cute

kayōbi (火曜日): Tuesday

Kazafusutan (カザフスタン): Kazakhstan

kazan (火山): volcano

kaze (風): wind

kaze (風邪): cold

kaze ga tsuyoi (風が強い): windy

kazoeru (数える): to count

kazoku ryōhō (家族療法): family therapy

kazoku shashin (家族写真): family picture

kebabu (ケバブ): kebab

kecchō (結腸): colon

kega (怪我): injury

kega o suru (怪我をする): to injure

keibi in (警備員): security guard

keiburu (ケーブル): cable

keibō (警棒): baton

keido (経度): longitude

keifu (継父): stepfather

keiji ban (掲示板): bulletin board

keikoku (渓谷): canyon

keikoku suru (警告する): to warn

keikoku tō (警告灯): warning light

Keiman shotō (ケイマン諸島): Cayman Islands

keimu sho (刑務所): prison

keiniku (鶏肉): chicken

keiren (けいれん): cramp

keiri (経理): accounting

keisan suru (計算する): to calculate

keisatsu (警察): police

keisatsu kan (警察官): policeman

keisatsu sho (警察署): police station

keitai (携帯): mobile phone

keizai gaku (経済学): economics

kekka (結果): result

kekkon shiki (結婚式): wedding

kekkon suru (結婚する): to marry

kekkon yubiwa (結婚指輪): wedding ring

kemuri kanchi ki (煙感知器): smoke detector

ken (腱): tendon

kenbai ki (券売機): ticket vending machine

kenbi kyō (顕微鏡): microscope

kenchiku ka (建築家): architect

Kenia (ケニア): Kenya

kenka suru (喧嘩する): to argue

kenkyū (研究): research

kenkōkotsu (肩胛骨): shoulder blade

kenkōteki na (健康的な): healthy

kensatsu kan (検察官): prosecutor

kenshū in (研修員): intern

keru (蹴る): to kick

keshi gomu (消しゴム): rubber

keshō sui (化粧水): facial toner

kesu (消す): to turn off

ketoru doramu (ケトルドラム): kettledrum

ketsueki kensa (血液検査): blood test

ki (木): tree

kiatsu (気圧): air pressure

kibishī (厳しい): strict

kicchin (キッチン): kitchen

kigyō ka (起業家): entrepreneur

kiiro (黄色): yellow

kiji (記事): article

kika gaku (幾何学): geometry

kikan (気管): windpipe

kikan sha (機関車): locomotive

kiku (聞く): to listen

kin (金): gold

kindai go shu kyōgi (近代五種競技): modern pentathlon

kinen hi (記念碑): monument

kingaku (金額): amount

ki ni shinaide (気にしないで): don't worry

kinko (金庫): safe

kinkyū (緊急): emergency

kin medaru (金メダル): gold medal

kinniku (筋肉): muscle

kinpōge (金鳳花): buttercup

Kin sei (金星): Venus

kin wa gin yori mo takai desu (金は銀よりも高いです): Gold is more expensive than silver

kin yōbi (金曜日): Friday

kinzoku (金属): metal

kinō (昨日): yesterday

kion (気温): temperature

ki o tsukete (気を付けて): take care

kippu uriba (切符売り場): ticket office

Kipurosu (キプロス): Cyprus

kirei (きれい): clean

kiri (霧): fog

Kiribasu (キリバス): Kiribati

kirigirisu (キリギリス): cricket

kirin (キリン): giraffe

kiri no kakatta (霧のかかった): foggy

kiroguramu (キログラム): kilogram

kiru (切る): to cut

Kirugisutan (キルギスタン): Kyrgyzstan

kisenon (キセノン): xenon

kisu (キス): kiss

kisu suru (キスする): to kiss

kita (北): north

Kitachōsen (北朝鮮): North Korea

kita hankyū (北半球): northern hemisphere

kitanai (汚い): dirty

kitsune (きつね): fox

kitsunezaru (きつねざる): lemur

kitte (切手): stamp

kiui (キウイ): kiwi

ki zaiku (木細工): woodwork

kizetsu suru (気絶する): to faint

kizuguchi (傷口): wound

koara (コアラ): koala

kobaruto (コバルト): cobalt

kobushi (拳): fist

kobuta (子豚): piglet

kodomo (子供): child

kodomo heya (子供部屋): nursery

kogitte (小切手): cheque

kogusuri (粉薬): powder

ko gyūniku (子牛肉): veal

koi no yamai (恋の病): lovesickness

koishī desu (恋しいです): I miss you

koji (孤児): orphan

Kokkai (黒海): Black Sea

kokku (コック): cook

kokkupitto (コックピット): cockpit

koko (ここ): here

kokonattsu (ココナッツ): coconut

kokuban (黒板): blackboard

kokuritsu kōen (国立公園): national park

kokyaku (顧客): customer

kome (米): rice

komedi (コメディ): comedy

komekami (こめかみ): temple

komentētā (コメンテーター): commentator

Komoro (コモロ): Comoros

komugi (小麦): wheat

komugiko (小麦粉): flour

kona miruku (粉ミルク): milk powder

konazatō (粉砂糖): icing sugar

konbain (コンバイン): combine harvester

kondōmu (コンドーム): condom

kongetsu (今月): this month

Kongo Kyōwakoku (コンゴ共和国): Republic of the Congo

Kongo Minshu Kyōwakoku (コンゴ民主共和国): Democratic Republic of the Congo

konkurīto (コンクリート): concrete

konkurīto mikisā (コンクリートミキサー): concrete mixer

konnichiwa (こんにちは): hello

konomu (好む): to like

konpasu (コンパス): compass

konro (焜炉): cooker

konsarutanto (コンサルタント): consultant

konshīrā (コンシーラー): concealer

konshū (今週): this week

konsāto (コンサート): concert

kontakuto renzu (コンタクトレンズ): contact lens

kontena (コンテナ): container

kontena sen (コンテナ船): container ship

kon yaku (婚約): engagement

kon yaku sha (婚約者): fiancé, fiancée

kon yaku yubiwa (婚約指輪): engagement ring

koperunishiumu (コペルニシウム): copernicium

koppu (コップ): cup

kopī suru (コピーする): to copy

kore (これ): this

kore ga hitsuyō desu (これが必要です): I need this

kore ga hoshī desu (これが欲しいです): I want this

kore wa ikura desu ka (これはいくらですか？): How much is this?

kore wa suki de wa arimasen (これは好きではありません): I don't like this

koriandā (コリアンダー): coriander

korogaru (転がる): to roll

koron (コロン): colon

Koronbia (コロンビア): Colombia

korosu (殺す): to kill

koshō (胡椒): pepper

Kosobo (コソボ): Kosovo

kossetsu (骨折): fracture

Kosutarika (コスタリカ): Costa Rica

kotaeru (答える): to answer

kotai (固体): solid

kotoshi (今年): this year

kotsuban (骨盤): pelvis

kotsutsubo (骨壺): urn

kotsuzui (骨髄): bone marrow

koya (小屋): shed

koyubi (小指): little finger

koyō shu (雇用主): employer

kozutsumi (小包): parcel

ku (区): district

kubi (首): neck

kuchi (口): mouth

kuchibeni (口紅): lipstick

kuchibiru (唇): lip

kuchi ga kikenai (口がきけない): mute

kugi (釘): nail

kuginuki (釘抜き): pincers

kuikku suteppu (クイックステップ): quickstep

kujaku (くじゃく): peacock

kujira (鯨): whale

kuki (茎): stalk

Kukku Shotō (クック諸島): Cook Islands

kukkī (クッキー): cookie

kuma (熊): bear

kumade (熊手): rake

kumo (蜘蛛): spider

kumo (雲): cloud

kumotta (曇った): cloudy

kuni (国): country

kuracchi (クラッチ): clutch

kurage (クラゲ): jellyfish

kurai (暗い): dark

kuraimingu (クライミング): climbing

kurakushon (クラクション): horn

kuranberī (クランベリー): cranberry

kurarinetto (クラリネット): clarinet

kurashikku kā (クラシックカー): classic car

kurashikku ongaku (クラシック音楽): classical music

kurejitto kādo (クレジットカード): credit card

kurifu daibingu (クリフダイビング): cliff diving

kuriketto (クリケット): cricket

kurinikku (クリニック): clinic

kurippu bōdo (クリップボード): clipboard

kuriputon (クリプトン): krypton

kurisumasu (クリスマス): Christmas

kuritorisu (クリトリス): clitoris

kuro (黒): black

Kuroachia (クロアチア): Croatia

kuroi wan pīsu (黒いワンピース): little black dress

kuromu (クロム): chromium

kurosu kantorī sukī (クロスカントリースキー): cross-country skiing

kurosu torēnā (クロストレーナー): cross trainer

kurosuwādo (クロスワード): crosswords

kurowassan (クロワッサン): croissant

kuru (来る): to come

kurubushi (踝): ankle

kuruma (車): car

kuruma isu (車いす): wheelchair

kurumi (クルミ): walnut

kurutta (狂った): crazy

kurēn (クレーン): crane

kurēn sha (クレーン車): crane truck

kurēpu (クレープ): crêpe

kurētā (クレーター): crater

kurīmu (クリーム): cream

kurōbā (クローバー): clover

kurōne (クローネ): krone

kurōzetto (クローゼット): wardrobe

kurūzu sen (クルーズ船): cruise ship

kusa (草): grass

kushi (櫛): comb

kushi mono (串もの): skewer

kussaku ki (掘削機): excavator

kusuriyubi (薬指): ring finger

kuten (句点): full stop

kutsubako (靴箱): shoe cabinet

kutsuhimo (靴紐): lace

kutsushita (靴下): sock

kuwa (鍬): hoe

Kuwēto (クウェート): Kuwait

kyabetsu (キャベツ): cabbage

kyabin (キャビン): cabin

kyacchi suru (キャッチする): to catch

kyakushitsu jōmu in (客室乗務員): stewardess

kyandī (キャンディー): candy

kyanpu (キャンプ): camping

kyanpu faiyā (キャンプファイヤー): campfire

kyanpu jō (キャンプ場): camping site

kyaputen (キャプテン): captain

kyaraban (キャラバン): caravan

kyarameru (キャラメル): caramel

kyasuto (キャスト): cast

kyoku (極): pole

kyokusen (曲線): curve

kyonen (去年): last year

kyuriumu (キュリウム): curium

kyō (今日): today

kyōbu (胸部): chest

kyōdai shimai (兄弟姉妹): siblings

kyōju (教授): professor

kyōkai (教会): church

kyōka sho (教科書): textbook

kyōkotsu (胸骨): breastbone

kyōryū (恐竜): dinosaur

kyōsei gu (矯正具): dental brace

kyōshi (教師): teacher

kyō wa (今日は): good day

kyū (キュー): cue

Kyūba (キューバ): Cuba

kyū gatsu (九月): September

kyūkei suru (休憩する): to rest

kyūko (舅姑): parents-in-law

kyūkyū sha (救急車): ambulance

kyūmei bui (救命ブイ): life buoy

kyūmei bōto (救命ボート): lifeboat

kyūmei dōi (救命胴衣): life jacket

kyūmei sentā (救命センター): emergency room

kyū na (急な): steep

kyūnyū ki (吸入器): inhaler

kyūri (キュウリ): cucumber

kyūryō (給料): salary

kyūtai (球体): sphere

Kābo Berude (カーボベルデ): Cape Verde

kādigan (カーディガン): cardigan

kādo gēmu (カードゲーム): card game

kāpetto (カーペット): carpet

kāringu (カーリング): curling

kā rēsu (カーレース): car racing

kāten (カーテン): curtain

kēki (ケーキ): cake

kībōdo (キーボード): keyboard

kī chēn (キーチェーン): key chain

kō (項): nape

kōbu zaseki (後部座席): back seat

kōcha (紅茶): black tea

kōchi (コーチ): coach

kōdō (講堂): lecture theatre

212

kōdō ryōhō (行動療法): behaviour therapy
kōen (公園): park
kōen sha (講演者): lecturer
kōgai (郊外): suburb
kōgan (睾丸): testicle
kōgeki suru (攻撃する): to attack
kōhei na (公平な): fair
kōhī (コーヒー): coffee
kōhī mashin (コーヒーマシン): coffee machine
kōhī tēburu (コーヒーテーブル): coffee table
kōi shitsu (更衣室): changing room
kōji genba (工事現場): construction site
kōjō (工場): factory
kōjō chiku (工場地区): industrial district
Kōkai (紅海): Red Sea
kō ketsuatsu shō (高血圧症): high blood pressure
kōkoku (広告): advertisement
kōkō (高校): high school
kōkū kaisha (航空会社): airline
kōkū kōtsū kansei kan (航空交通管制官): air traffic controller
kōmon (肛門): anus
kōmori (コウモリ): bat
kōn oiru (コーンオイル): corn oil
kōnotori (コウノトリ): stork
kōra (コーラ): coke
kōri (氷): ice
kōrurabi (コールラビ): turnip cabbage
kōsa ten (交差点): intersection
kōsei busshitsu (抗生物質): antibiotics
kōsoku dōro (高速道路): motorway
kōsui (香水): perfume
kōtei (校庭): schoolyard
kōto (コート): coat
Kōtojibowāru (コートジボワール): Ivory Coast
kōtsū jūtai (交通渋滞): traffic jam
kōza bangō (口座番号): account number
kōzui (洪水): flood
kūbo (空母): aircraft carrier
kūkō (空港): airport

M

macchi bō (マッチ棒): match
machiai shitsu (待合室): waiting room
machigatta (間違った): wrong
Madagasukaru (マダガスカル): Madagascar
mado (窓): window
madogawa (窓側): window
mae (前): front
mafin (マフィン): muffin
mago (孫): grandson, grandchild

magomusume (孫娘): granddaughter

maguma (マグマ): magma

maguneshiumu (マグネシウム): magnesium

maguro (マグロ): tuna

mahō bin (魔法瓶): thermos jug

maikurobasu (マイクロバス): minibus

mairu (マイル): mile

maitoneriumu (マイトネリウム): meitnerium

majoramu (マジョラム): marjoram

Makao (マカオ): Macao

Makedonia (マケドニア): Macedonia

makeru (負ける): to lose

makigami (巻き髪): curly

makijaku (巻き尺): tape measure

makura (枕): pillow

mama (ママ): mum

mamahaha (継母): stepmother

mamamusuko (継息子): stepson

mamamusume (継娘): stepdaughter

mame (豆): bean

mamoru (守る): to defend

manaita (まな板): chopping board

manekin (マネキン): mannequin

manga (漫画): cartoon

manga hon (漫画本): comic book

mangan (マンガン): manganese

mangō (マンゴー): mango

manhōru no futa (マンホールの蓋): manhole cover

manikyua (マニキュア): manicure, nail polish

manikyua otoshi (マニキュア落とし): nail varnish remover

manpuku (満腹): full

mantan (満タン): full

manējā (マネージャー): manager

marason (マラソン): marathon

Maraui (マラウイ): Malawi

Mari (マリ): Mali

marui (丸い): round

Maruta (マルタ): Malta

Marēshia (マレーシア): Malaysia

mashumaro (マシュマロ): marshmallow

masshu poteto (マッシュポテト): mashed potatoes

masshurūmu (マッシュルーム): mushroom

massugu iku (真っすぐ行く): go straight

massugu na (まっすぐな): straight

massāji (マッサージ): massage

massāji o suru (マッサージをする): to give a massage

massāji shi (マッサージ師): masseur

masukara (マスカラ): mascara

masuto (マスト): mast

masutādo (マスタード): mustard

mata ne (またね): bye bye

mata wa (又は): or
maten rō (摩天楼): skyscraper
matsu (待つ): to wait
matsu (松): pine
matsuba tsue (松葉杖): crutch
matsuge (睫毛): eyelashes
Matīni (マティーニ): martini
maunten baiku (マウンテンバイク): mountain biking
mausu (マウス): mouse
mausupīsu (マウスピース): mouthguard
ma yonaka (真夜中): midnight
mayonēzu (マヨネーズ): mayonnaise
mayu (眉): eyebrow
mazushī (貧しい): poor
me (目): eye
medaru (メダル): medal
me ga mienai (目が見えない): blind
megane (眼鏡): glasses
megane shōnin (眼鏡商人): optician
mei (姪): niece
meishi (名刺): business card
meisō (瞑想): meditation
Meiō sei (冥王星): Pluto
Mekishiko (メキシコ): Mexico
me kyabetsu (芽キャベツ): Brussels sprouts
memo (メモ): note
men (綿): cotton
men (麺): noodle
menbā (メンバー): member
menbāshippu (メンバーシップ): membership
menderebiumu (メンデレビウム): mendelevium
menkai jikan (面会時間): visiting hours
menseki (面積): area
menyū (メニュー): menu
merodi (メロディ): melody
mesu (メス): scalpel
metan (メタン): methane
mezamashi tokei (目覚まし時計): alarm clock
mibōjin (未亡人): widow
midashi (見出し): heading
midori (緑): green
migi (右): right
migi ni magaru (右に曲がる): turn right
mijikai (短い): short
miki (幹): trunk
mikisā (ミキサー): mixer
Mikuroneshia (ミクロネシア): Micronesia
mimi (耳): ear
mimi ga kikoenai (耳が聞こえない): deaf
mimisen (耳栓): earplug
minami (南): south

Minamiafurika (南アフリカ): South Africa

minami hankyū (南半球): southern hemisphere

Minami Sūdan (南スーダン): South Sudan

minarai (見習い): apprentice

minato (港): harbour

mini bā (ミニバー): minibar

minikui (醜い): ugly

minna (みんな): everybody

minto (ミント): mint

minzoku ongaku (民族音楽): folk music

mirimētoru (ミリメートル): millimeter

miririttoru (ミリリットル): milliliter

miru (見る): to watch

miruku sēki (ミルクセーキ): milkshake

miruku tī (ミルクティー): milk tea

mishin (ミシン): sewing machine

mitsu (蜜): nectar

mitsubachi (ミツバチ): bumblebee

mitsu go (三つ子): triplets

mitsukeru (見つける): to find

mitsumeru (見つめる): to stare

mitto (ミット): mitt

mizu (水): water

mizu bōsō (水疱瘡): chickenpox

mizugi (水着): swimsuit

mizuumi (湖): lake

mochiageru (持ち上げる): to lift

mochiron (もちろん): of course

moderu (モデル): model

moji (文字): letter, character

moka (モカ): mocha

mokkin (木琴): xylophone

mokuji (目次): table of contents

Moku sei (木星): Jupiter

mokuyōbi (木曜日): Thursday

mokuzō hari (木造梁): wooden beam

momo (桃): peach

momoiro (桃色): pink

Monako (モナコ): Monaco

Mongoru (モンゴル): Mongolia

monoporī (モノポリー): Monopoly

monorēru (モノレール): monorail

monosashi (ものさし): ruler

monsūn (モンスーン): monsoon

Meneguro (モンテネグロ): Montenegro

Montoserato (モントセラト): Montserrat

mori (森): forest

moribuden (モリブデン): molybdenum

Morokko (モロッコ): Morocco

Morudibu (モルディブ): Maldives

Morudoba (モルドバ): Moldova

morumotto (モルモット): guinea pig

moshi (もし): if

mosuku (モスク): mosque

moto (元): yuan

motokurosu (モトクロス): motocross

motto (もっと): more

motto hoshī desu (もっと欲しいです): I want more

mottsarera (モッツァレラ): mozzarella

Mozanbīku (モザンビーク): Mozambique

MP3 purēyā (MP3プレーヤー): MP3 player

muchi (鞭): whip

mufu tī (ムフティー): mufti

muko (婿): son-in-law

mune (胸): bosom

mura (村): village

murasaki (紫): purple

mushi (虫): bug

mushiba (虫歯): caries

mushiyoke (虫除け): insect repellent

musuko (息子): son

musume (娘): daughter

muzukashī (難しい): difficult

myakuhaku (脈拍): pulse

Myanmā (ミャンマー): Burma

myūjishan (ミュージシャン): musician

myūzurī (ミューズリー): muesli

māketingu (マーケティング): marketing

māketto (マーケット): market

Māsharu Shotō (マーシャル諸島): Marshall Islands

mēpuru shiroppu (メープルシロップ): maple syrup

mēru adoresu (メールアドレス): e-mail address

mētoru (メートル): meter

mētā (メーター): speedometer

mīakyatto (ミーアキャット): meerkat

mītobōru (ミートボール): meatball

mōchō (盲腸): appendix

mōfu (毛布): blanket

Mōrishasu (モーリシャス): Mauritius

Mōritania (モーリタニア): Mauritania

mōtā (モーター): motor

N

nabe (鍋): pot

nabe ryōri (鍋料理): hot pot

nachosu (ナチョス): nachos

nagai (長い): long

nageru (投げる): to throw

nai bunpitsu gaku (内分泌学): endocrinology

naifu (ナイフ): knife

Naijeria (ナイジェリア): Nigeria

naika i (内科医): physician

nairon (ナイロン): nylon

naitokurabu (ナイトクラブ): night club

naitotēburu (ナイトテーブル): night table

naiyō (内容): content

naka (中): inside

nakayubi (中指): middle finger

naku (泣く): to cry

nama (生): raw

namae wa nan desu ka (名前はなんですか？): What's your name?

namari (鉛): lead

Namibia (ナミビア): Namibia

nani (何): what

nanimonai (何もない): none

nankotsu (軟骨): cartilage

Nankyoku (南極): South Pole

napukin (ナプキン): sanitary towel

nashi (梨): pear

nasu (茄子): aubergine

natane abura (菜種油): rapeseed oil

natoriumu (ナトリウム): sodium

natsu (夏): summer

natsumegu (ナツメグ): nutmeg

nattsu (ナッツ): nut

Nauru (ナウル): Nauru

naze (なぜ): why

ne (根): root

nebukuro (寝袋): sleeping bag

negi (葱): spring onion

negurije (ネグリジェ): negligee

nejireta (ねじれた): twisting

nekku karā (ネックカラー): neck brace

nekkuresu (ネックレス): necklace

neko (猫): cat

nekutai (ネクタイ): tie

nendo (粘土): clay

neojimu (ネオジム): neodymium

neon (ネオン): neon

neputsuniumu (ネプツニウム): neptunium

Nepāru (ネパール): Nepal

neru (寝る): to sleep

netsu (熱): fever

netsu kikyū (熱気球): hot-air balloon

nettai (熱帯): tropics

netto (ネット): net

nettowāku (ネットワーク): network

nezumi (ねずみ): mouse

nichiyōbi (日曜日): Sunday

ni dan beddo (二段ベッド): bunk bed

ni gatsu (二月): February

Nihon/Nippon (日本): Japan

niji (虹): rainbow
Nijēru (ニジェール): Niger
ni kai (二階): first floor
Nikaragua (ニカラグア): Nicaragua
nikkeru (ニッケル): nickel
nikki (日記): diary
nikkō (日光): sunshine
niku (肉): meat
nikuya (肉屋): butcher
nimotsu (荷物): luggage
ningyō (人形): doll
ninjin (人参): carrot
ninniku (ニンニク): garlic
ninshin kensa (妊娠検査): pregnancy test
niobu (ニオブ): niobium
nioi o kagu (匂いを嗅ぐ): to smell
Nippon go (日本語): Japanese
Nippon shu (日本酒): sake
ni sanka tanso (二酸化炭素): carbon dioxide
nishi (西): west
nisshoku (日食): solar eclipse
nisu (ニス): varnish
nitto bō (ニット帽): knit cap
Niue (ニウエ): Niue
niwa (庭): garden
niwashi (庭師): gardener
niwatori (鶏): chicken
noboru (登る): to climb
nodo no itami (喉の痛み): sore throat
nokogiri (鋸): saw
nomu (飲む): to drink, to swallow
nori (のり): glue
norudikku konbaindo (ノルディックコンバインド): Nordic combined
Noruwē (ノルウェー): Norway
nugā (ヌガー): nougat
nuigurumi (ぬいぐるみ): cuddly toy
nuno (布): fabric
nureta (濡れた): wet
nuru (塗る): to paint
nusumu (盗む): to steal
Nyūjīrando (ニュージーランド): New Zealand
Nyūkaredonia (ニューカレドニア): New Caledonia
nyūsu (ニュース): news
nyūsukyasutā (ニュースキャスター): anchor
nyūsuretā (ニュースレター): newsletter
nō (脳): brain
nōberiumu (ノーベリウム): nobelium
nōjō (農場): farm
nōka (農家): farmer
nō shintō (脳震盪): concussion
nō socchū (脳卒中): stroke

nōto (ノート): notebook
nōto pasokon (ノートパソコン): laptop

O

oba (叔母): aunt
o cha (お茶): tea
ochiru (落ちる): to fall
odoroita (驚いた): surprised
odosu (脅す): to threaten
ofisu (オフィス): office
oi (甥): nephew
oiru pasuteru (オイルパステル): oil pastel
oji (叔父): uncle
oka (丘): hill
o kane (お金): money
oku (置く): to put
okura (オクラ): okra
o miyage (お土産): souvenir
omochaya (おもちゃ屋): toy shop
omoi (重い): heavy
omoshiroi (面白い): funny
omotegenkan (表玄関): front door
omutsu (おむつ): diaper
Omān (オマーン): Oman
on bu kigō (音部記号): clef
ondori (おんどり): cockerel
o negaishimasu (お願いします): please
onion ringu (オニオンリング): onion ring
onna (女): woman
onnanoko (女の子): girl
ono (斧): axe
onpu (音符): note
onsei mēru (音声メール): voice message
onshitsu (温室): greenhouse
onsu (オンス): ounce
ooya (大家): landlord
opera (オペラ): opera
opāru (オパール): opal
Oranda (オランダ): Netherlands
oregano (オレガノ): oregano
orenji (オレンジ): orange
orenji jūsu (オレンジジュース): orange juice
origami (折り紙): origami
oroka na (愚かな): stupid
oroshigane (おろし金): grater
orugan (オルガン): organ
orību (オリーブ): olive
orību oiru (オリーブオイル): olive oil
oshaburi (おしゃぶり): soother
osoi (遅い): slow

osu (押す): to push, to press
osumiumu (オスミウム): osmium
otafukukaze (おたふく風邪): mumps
o tera (お寺): temple
otoko (男): man
otokonoko (男の子): boy
otto (夫): husband
otōto (弟): little brother
oushi (雄牛): bull
oyayubi (親指): thumb
oyogu (泳ぐ): to swim

P

pafu (パフ): powder puff
pai (パイ): pie
painappuru (パイナップル): pineapple
pairotto (パイロット): pilot
pajama (パジャマ): pyjamas, nightie
Pakisutan (パキスタン): Pakistan
pakku (パック): puck
pakkēji (パッケージ): package
pan (パン): bread
Panama (パナマ): Panama
panda (パンダ): panda
panku (パンク): punk
pansuto (パンスト): pantyhose
panti rainā (パンティライナー): panty liner
pantsu (パンツ): underpants
pantī (パンティー): panties
papa (パパ): dad
papaiya (パパイヤ): papaya
Papuanyūginia (パプアニューギニア): Papua New Guinea
papurika (パプリカ): pepper, paprika
Paraguai (パラグアイ): Paraguay
parajiumu (パラジウム): palladium
paramitsu (パラミツ): jackfruit
Parao (パラオ): Palau
para shūtingu (パラシューティング): parachuting
parashūto (パラシュート): parachute
Paresuchina (パレスチナ): Palestine
paretto (パレット): palette, pallet
parumezan (パルメザン): parmesan
pasupōto (パスポート): passport
pasuwādo (パスワード): password
patokā (パトカー): police car
pazuru (パズル): puzzle
pedikyua (ペディキュア): pedicure
Pekin dakku (北京ダック): Beijing duck
Pekin go (北京語): Mandarin
pen (ペン): pen

pengin (ペンギン): penguin

penki (ペンキ): paint

perikan (ペリカン): pelican

Perū (ペルー): Peru

Petori sara (ペトリ皿): Petri dish

petto shoppu (ペットショップ): pet shop

piano (ピアノ): piano

picchifōku (ピッチフォーク): pitchfork

pikunikku (ピクニック): picnic

pinsetto (ピンセット): tweezers

pipetto (ピペット): pipette

piramiddo (ピラミッド): pyramid

piratisu (ピラティス): Pilates

pisutachio (ピスタチオ): pistachio

piza (ピザ): pizza

poketto (ポケット): pocket

pondo (ポンド): pound

ponītēru (ポニーテール): ponytail

poppu (ポップ): pop

poppukōn (ポップコーン): popcorn

poriesuteru (ポリエステル): polyester

porijji (ポリッジ): porridge

poro (ポロ): polo

poroniumu (ポロニウム): polonium

poro shatsu (ポロシャツ): polo shirt

Porutogaru (ポルトガル): Portugal

posuto (ポスト): mailbox

posutokādo (ポストカード): postcard

poteto sarada (ポテトサラダ): potato salad

poteto wejji (ポテトウェッジ): potato wedges

Puerutoriko (プエルトリコ): Puerto Rico

purachina (プラチナ): platinum

puragu (プラグ): plug

puraseojimu (プラセオジム): praseodymium

purasuchikku (プラスチック): plastic

purattohōmu (プラットホーム): platform

purezento (プレゼント): present

purezentēshon (プレゼンテーション): presentation

purin (プリン): pudding

purintā (プリンター): printer

puroguramā (プログラマー): programmer

purojekutā (プロジェクター): projector

puromechiumu (プロメチウム): promethium

puromunādo (プロムナード): promenade

purotoakuchiniumu (プロトアクチニウム): protactinium

puroton (プロトン): proton

purutoniumu (プルトニウム): plutonium

pākingu mētā (パーキングメーター): parking meter

pāru nekkuresu (パールネックレス): pearl necklace

pēpā kurippu (ペーパークリップ): paperclip

pīnatsu (ピーナツ): peanut

222

pīnattsu abura (ピーナッツ油): peanut oil
pīnattsu batā (ピーナッツバター): peanut butter
pōkā (ポーカー): poker
Pōrando (ポーランド): Poland
pōtoforio (ポートフォリオ): portfolio

R

rabi (ラビ): rabbi
rabu rōshon (ラブローション): lubricant
radon (ラドン): radon
rafutingu (ラフティング): rafting
ragubī (ラグビー): rugby
raichi (ライチ): lychee
raifu gādo (ライフガード): lifeguard
raigetsu (来月): next month
raimu (ライム): lime
rainen (来年): next year
raion (ライオン): lion
raishū (来週): next week
raitā (ライター): lighter
raiu (雷雨): thunderstorm
rajio (ラジオ): radio
rajiumu (ラジウム): radium
rajiētā (ラジエーター): radiator
rakuda (らくだ): camel
raku ni shite (楽にして): relax
rakurosu (ラクロス): lacrosse
RAM (RAM): random access memory (RAM)
rama (ラマ): llama
ramadan (ラマダン): Ramadan
ramu shu (ラム酒): rum
ranchi (ランチ): lunch
ranjerī (ランジェリー): lingerie
rankan (卵管): oviduct
ranningu (ランニング): running
ranpaku (卵白): egg white
ranpu (ランプ): lamp
ranshi (卵子): ovum
ransō (卵巣): ovary
rantan (ランタン): lanthanum
ranō (卵黄): yolk
Raosu (ラオス): Laos
rappu (ラップ): rap
rarī (ラリー): rally racing
rasshu awā (ラッシュアワー): rush hour
raten dansu (ラテンダンス): Latin dance
raten go (ラテン語): Latin
Ratobia (ラトビア): Latvia
ratto (ラット): rat
razahōjiumu (ラザホージウム): rutherfordium

razania (ラザニア): lasagne

razuberī (ラズベリー): raspberry

Rebanon (レバノン): Lebanon

reggu puresu (レッグプレス): leg press

reginsu (レギンス): leggings

regē (レゲエ): reggae

rein kōto (レインコート): raincoat

reitō ko (冷凍庫): freezer

reizō ko (冷蔵庫): fridge

reji (レジ): cash register

reji kakari (レジ係): cashier

rekishi (歴史): history

rekōdo purēyā (レコードプレーヤー): record player

remon (レモン): lemon

remon gurasu (レモングラス): lemongrass

remonēdo (レモネード): lemonade

renga (レンガ): brick

reniumu (レニウム): rhenium

renji fūdo (レンジフード): cooker hood

ren kon (れんこん): lotus root

renshū suru (練習する): to practice

rentogeniumu (レントゲニウム): roentgenium

rentogen shashin (レントゲン写真): X-ray photograph

renzoku bangumi (連続番組): TV series

repōtā (レポーター): reporter

Resoto (レソト): Lesotho

ressha (列車): train

ressun (レッスン): lesson

ressā panda (レッサーパンダ): red panda

resuringu (レスリング): wrestling

resutoran (レストラン): restaurant

retasu (レタス): lettuce

retsu (列): row

ribamoriumu (リバモリウム): livermorium

Riberia (リベリア): Liberia

Ribia (リビア): Libya

ribingu (リビング): living room

richiumu (リチウム): lithium

rieki (利益): profit

rigaku ryōhō (理学療法): physiotherapy

rigaku ryōhō shi (理学療法士): physiotherapist

Rihitenshutain (リヒテンシュタイン): Liechtenstein

rikkyō (陸橋): overpass

rikon (離婚): divorce

rikorisu (リコリス): liquorice

rikugame (陸亀): tortoise

rikujō hokkē (陸上ホッケー): field hockey

rikyūru (リキュール): liqueur

rimokon (リモコン): remote control

rimujin (リムジン): limousine

rin (リン): phosphorus

ringo (リンゴ): apple
ringo jūsu (リンゴジュース): apple juice
rinjin (隣人): neighbour
rippu gurosu (リップグロス): lip gloss
rippu kurīmu (リップクリーム): lip balm
rippō mētoru (立方メートル): cubic meter
rippō tai (立方体): cube
risaikuru shoppu (リサイクルショップ): second-hand shop
rishi (利子): interest
risu (リス): squirrel
Ritoania (リトアニア): Lithuania
rittā (リッター): liter
roba (ロバ): donkey
robotto (ロボット): robot
robusutā (ロブスター): lobster
robī (ロビー): lobby
roji (路地): alley
rojiumu (ロジウム): rhodium
roketto (ロケット): rocket
rokkaku kei (六角形): hexagon
rokkingu chea (ロッキングチェア): rocking chair
rokkotsu (肋骨): rib
rokku (ロック): rock
rokkunrōru (ロックンロール): rock 'n' roll
roku gatsu (六月): June
roku kai (六階): fifth floor
romen densha (路面電車): tram
ronbun (論文): essay, thesis
Roshia (ロシア): Russia
rubijiumu (ルビジウム): rubidium
rubī (ルビー): ruby
Rukusenburuku (ルクセンブルク): Luxembourg
runba (ルンバ): rumba
rutechiumu (ルテチウム): lutetium
ruteniumu (ルテニウム): ruthenium
Ruwanda (ルワンダ): Rwanda
ryokucha (緑茶): green tea
ryokō dairi ten (旅行代理店): travel agent
ryokō suru (旅行する): to travel
ryōdo (領土): territory
ryōkei (菱形): rhombus
ryōri suru (料理する): to cook
ryōshi (漁師): fisherman
ryōshin (両親): parents
ryūju (リュージュ): luge
ryūzan (流産): miscarriage
rāmen (ラーメン): ramen
rēdā (レーダー): radar
rēru (レール): railtrack
rēshingu kāto (レーシングカート): kart
rēsu yō jiten sha (レース用自転車): racing bicycle

rēzun (レーズン): raisin

rīfuretto (リーフレット): leaflet

rōdo rōrā (ロードローラー): road roller

rōka (廊下): corridor

rōn (ローン): loan

rōpuuē (ロープウエー): cable car

rōrenshiumu (ローレンシウム): lawrencium

rōrā kōsutā (ローラーコースター): roller coaster

rōrā sukētingu (ローラースケーティング): roller skating

rōsoku (蝋燭): candle

rōsuto chikin (ローストチキン): roast chicken

rōsuto pōku (ローストポーク): roast pork

rōtarī (ロータリー): roundabout

rōto (漏斗): funnel

rōzumarī (ローズマリー): rosemary

Rūmania (ルーマニア): Romania

rūmu kī (ルームキー): room key

rūmu nanbā (ルームナンバー): room number

rūmu sābisu (ルームサービス): room service

rūtā (ルーター): router

S

sabaku (砂漠): desert

sabishī (寂しい): lonely

saboten (サボテン): cactus

sadoru (サドル): saddle

safaia (サファイア): sapphire

sagasu (探す): to look for

Sahara (サハラ): Sahara

sai (サイ): rhino

saiban kan (裁判官): judge

saiban sho (裁判所): court

saido (再度): again

saido doa (サイドドア): side door

saido mirā (サイドミラー): wing mirror

saidā (サイダー): cider

saiensu fikushon (サイエンスフィクション): science fiction

saifu (財布): wallet, purse

saikin (細菌): bacterium

saikuringu (サイクリング): cycling

saimin (催眠): hypnosis

sairen (サイレン): siren

saka (坂): slope

sakana (魚): fish

sakana no hone (魚の骨): fishbone

sake (鮭): salmon

sakebu (叫ぶ): to shout

sakka (作家): author

sakkā (サッカー): football

sakkā bōru (サッカーボール): football

sakkā sutajiamu (サッカースタジアム): football stadium

sakotsu (鎖骨): collarbone

sakuranbo (サクランボ): cherry

sakusofon (サクソフォン): saxophone

samariumu (サマリウム): samarium

same (サメ): shark

Samoa (サモア): Samoa

samui (寒い): cold

sanba (サンバ): samba

sanbashi (桟橋): pier

san dan tobi (三段跳び): triple jump

sandaru (サンダル): sandals

sandoicchi (サンドイッチ): sandwich

san gatsu (三月): March

sango shō (珊瑚礁): coral reef

sangurasu (サングラス): sunglasses

san hatto (サンハット): sun hat

sanjū fun (三十分): half an hour

sankaku kei (三角形): triangle

sankusugibingu (サンクスギビング): Thanksgiving

sankyaku (三脚): tripod

Sanmarino (サンマリノ): San Marino

sanmyaku (山脈): mountain range

sansei desu (賛成です): I agree

sanso (酸素): oxygen

sansū (算数): arithmetic

Santomepurinshipe (サントメプリンシペ): São Tomé and Príncipe

sara (皿): plate

sarada (サラダ): salad

sarami (サラミ): salami

saru (猿): monkey

sarusa (サルサ): salsa

sasayaku (囁く): to whisper

sasori (サソリ): scorpion

satsuma imo (サツマイモ): sweet potato

satō (砂糖): sugar

satō kibi (サトウキビ): sugar cane

Saujiarabia (サウジアラビア): Saudi Arabia

sauna (サウナ): sauna

sawaru (触る): to touch

sawā kurīmu (サワークリーム): sour cream

sayōnara (さようなら): good bye

sebone (背骨): spine

se ga hikui (背が低い): short

se ga takai (背が高い): tall

seibetsu (性別): gender

seibi shi (整備士): mechanic

seibutsu gaku (生物学): biology

seichō suru (成長する): to grow

seifuku (制服): school uniform, uniform

seigen sokudo (制限速度): speed limit

seiji gaku (政治学): politics

seiji ka (政治家): politician

seika ten (青果店): fruit merchant

seikei geka (整形外科): orthopaedics

seiki (世紀): century

seikyū sho (請求書): bill

sei naru (聖なる): holy

seisetsu (正接): tangent

Seisheru (セイシェル): Seychelles

seishi (精子): sperm

sei shikaku kei (正四角形): square

seishin bunseki (精神分析): psychoanalysis

seishin ka (精神科): psychiatry

seisō in (清掃員): cleaner

seiuchi (セイウチ): walrus

seiyō eiga (西洋映画): western film

seiyō negi (西洋葱): leek

sekai kiroku (世界記録): world record

seki (咳): cough

sekidome (咳止め): cough syrup

sekidō (赤道): equator

Sekidōginia (赤道ギニア): Equatorial Guinea

sekiei (石英): quartz

sekitan (石炭): coal

sekizui (脊髄): spinal cord

sekkai gan (石灰岩): limestone

sekken (石鹸): soap

sekkusu (セックス): sex

sekushī (セクシー): sexy

semai (狭い): narrow

semento (セメント): cement

semento mikisā (セメントミキサー): cement mixer

semikoron (セミコロン): semicolon

senaka (背中): back

senchimētoru (センチメートル): centimeter

Senegaru (セネガル): Senegal

sengetsu (先月): last month

senmen ki (洗面器): basin

sen nenki (千年紀): millennium

sennuki (栓抜き): corkscrew

sensha (戦車): tank

sensha (洗車): car wash

senshū (先週): last week

sensui kan (潜水艦): submarine

sentaku basami (洗濯ばさみ): peg

sentaku butsu (洗濯物): laundry

sentaku kago (洗濯籠): laundry basket

sentaku ki (洗濯機): washing machine

sentaku yō senzai (洗濯用洗剤): washing powder

Sentobinsento Gurenadīn (セントビンセント・グレナディーン): Saint Vincent and the Grenadines

Sentokittsu Neibisu Renpō (セントキッツ・ネイビス連邦): Saint Kitts and Nevis

Sentorushia (セントルシア): Saint Lucia

seren (セレン): selenium

seriumu (セリウム): cerium

serori (セロリ): celery

serotēpu (セロテープ): adhesive tape

Serubia (セルビア): Serbia

seshiumu (セシウム): caesium

sesshi (摂氏): centigrade

shaberu (シャベル): shovel

shachi (シャチ): killer whale

shageki (射撃): shooting

shako (車庫): garage

shako no doa (車庫のドア): garage door

shakō dansu (社交ダンス): Ballroom dance

shamoji (しゃもじ): ladle, wooden spoon

shanpan (シャンパン): champagne

shanpū (シャンプー): shampoo

shashin (写真): picture

shashin ka (写真家): photographer

shashō (車掌): conductor

shatoru kokku (シャトルコック): shuttlecock

shatsu (シャツ): shirt

shawā (シャワー): shower

shawā jeru (シャワージェル): shower gel

shawā kyappu (シャワーキャップ): shower cap

shawā kāten (シャワーカーテン): shower curtain

shawā o abiru (シャワーを浴びる): to take a shower

shi (死): death

shibakari ki (芝刈り機): lawn mower

shichi gatsu (七月): July

shichimenchō (七面鳥): turkey

shichimenchō niku (七面鳥肉): turkey

shida (シダ): fern

Shierareone (シエラレオネ): Sierra Leone

shifuto rebā (シフトレバー): gear lever

shi gatsu (四月): April

shigoto (仕事): job

shigoto heya (仕事部屋): workroom

shiharau (支払う): to pay

shihei (紙幣): note

shika (鹿): deer

shikaniku (鹿肉): game

shiken (試験): exam

shikifuton (敷布団): mattress

shiki sha (指揮者): conductor

shikke (湿気): humidity

shikyū (子宮): uterus, womb

shima (島): island

shimauma (シマウマ): zebra

shimeru (閉める): to close

shimon (指紋): fingerprint

shinagōgu (シナゴーグ): synagogue

shinamon (シナモン): cinnamon

shinbaru (シンバル): cymbals

shinbun (新聞): newspaper

shinfonī (シンフォニー): symphony

Shingapōru (シンガポール): Singapore

shinguru rūmu (シングルルーム): single room

shingō (信号): traffic light, signal

shinkei (神経): nerve

shinkei ka (神経科): neurology

shinku (シンク): sink

shinkuronaizudo suimingu (シンクロナイズドスイミング): synchronized swimming

shinnen (新年): New Year

shinpai shite iru (心配している): worried

shinpan in (審判員): referee

shinpu (神父): priest

shinri ryōhō (心理療法): psychotherapy

shinshitsu (寝室): bedroom

shinsui kōen (親水公園): water park

shin taisō (新体操): rhythmic gymnastics

shinu (死ぬ): to die

shinzō (心臓): heart

shinzō byō gaku (心臓病学): cardiology

shinzō hossa (心臓発作): heart attack

shio (塩): salt

shiokarai (塩辛い): salty

shippai suru (失敗する): to fail

shirafu (しらふ): sober

shiri (尻): bottom

Shiria (シリア): Syria

shiriaru (シリアル): cereal

shirikon (シリコン): silicon

shirimasen (知りません): I don't know

shirinji (シリンジ): syringe

shiro (城): castle

shiro (白): white

shiroari (シロアリ): termite

shirokuma (シロクマ): polar bear

shiro wain (白ワイン): white wine

shiru (知る): to know

shiruku (シルク): silk

shisho (司書): librarian

shisshin (湿疹): rash

shita (下): below

shita (舌): tongue

shitagau (従う): to follow

shitai (死体): corpse

shitsumon suru (質問する): to ask

shitsū (歯痛): toothache

shitte imasu (知っています): I know

shitto appu (シットアップ): sit-ups

shiwa (皺): wrinkle
shiwa yō kurīmu (しわ用クリーム): antiwrinkle cream
shi yakusho (市役所): town hall
shizuka (静か): silent
shizuka na (静かな): quiet
shokki arai ki (食器洗い機): dishwasher
shokki tana (食器棚): cupboard
shokku abusōba (ショックアブソーバ): shock absorber
shokubutsu en (植物園): botanic garden
shokudō (食道): oesophagus
shokugyō kunren (職業訓練): vocational training
shokumin chi (植民地): colony
shomei (署名): signature
shoppingu basuketto (ショッピングバスケット): shopping basket
shoppingu kāto (ショッピングカート): shopping cart
shoppingu sentā (ショッピングセンター): shopping mall
shoten (書店): bookshop
shucchō (出張): business trip
shujutsu (手術): surgery
shujutsu shitsu (手術室): operating theatre
shukudai (宿題): homework
shuppan sha (出版社): publisher
shuppatsu (出発): departure
shussan (出産): delivery
shusshō shōmei sho (出生証明書): birth certificate
shuto (首都): capital
shuyō gaku (腫瘍学): oncology
shēbingu fōmu (シェービングフォーム): shaving foam
shībōgiumu (シーボーギウム): seaborgium
shīfūdo (シーフード): seafood
shīto (シート): seat
shīto beruto (シートベルト): seatbelt
shōbō gumi (消防組): firefighters
shōbō sha (消防車): fire truck
shōbō shi (消防士): firefighter
shōbō sho (消防署): fire station
shōchō (小腸): small intestine
shōdoku zai (消毒剤): antiseptic
shōga (生姜): ginger
shōgai tobikoshi kyōgi (障害飛越競技): show jumping
shō gakkō (小学校): primary school
shōgaku kin (奨学金): scholarship
shōgo (正午): noon
shōgyō chiku (商業地区): central business district (CBD)
shōhi kigen (消費期限): expiry date
shōka ki (消火器): fire extinguisher
shōka sen (消火栓): hydrant
shōken torihiki sho (証券取引所): stock exchange
shōko (証拠): evidence
shōmei suicchi (照明スイッチ): light switch
shōni ka (小児科): paediatrics

shōnin (証人): witness

shōsetsu (小説): novel

shōtaku (沼沢): marsh

shōto torakku (ショートトラック): short track

shō wakusei (小惑星): asteroid

shōzō ga (肖像画): portrait

shū (州): state, province

shū (週): week

shūchū chiryō shitsu (集中治療室): intensive care unit

shūdō onna (修道女): nun

shūki hyō (周期表): periodic table

shūsei suru (修正する): to fix

shūshi (修士): master

shūshuku suru (収縮する): to shrink

shūso (臭素): bromine

sobakasu (そばかす): freckles

sobo (祖母): grandmother

sofa (ソファ): sofa

sofu (祖父): grandfather

Somaria (ソマリア): Somalia

someta (染めた): dyed

sonshitsu (損失): loss

sore de mo (それでも): although

sori (そり): sledge

Soromon Shotō (ソロモン諸島): Solomon Islands

soshite (そして): then

soto (外): outside

sotsugyō (卒業): graduation

sotsugyō shiki (卒業式): graduation ceremony

su (酢): vinegar

suberidai (滑り台): slide

subete (全て): all

suchīru (スチール): steel

sudeni (既に): already

suetto bando (スエットバンド): sweatband

suetto pantsu (スエットパンツ): sweatpants

sugu ni (すぐに): immediately

suguri (スグリ): currant

suichi ryōhō (水治療法): hydrotherapy

suidō sui (水道水): tap water

suidō ya (水道屋): plumber

suiei (水泳): swimming

suiei bō (水泳帽): swim cap

suiei pantsu (水泳パンツ): swim trunks

suigin (水銀): mercury

suihan ki (炊飯器): rice cooker

suihei ki (水平器): spirit level

suijō sukī (水上スキー): waterskiing

suika (スイカ): water melon

suikyū (水球): water polo

suimingu pūru (スイミングプール): swimming pool

suimin yaku (睡眠薬): sleeping pill

suiryoku hatsuden sho (水力発電所): hydroelectric power station

suisei (彗星): comet

Sui sei (水星): Mercury

suisen (水仙): daffodil

suiso (水素): hydrogen

Suisu (スイス): Switzerland

suitō (水筒): water bottle

suiyōbi (水曜日): Wednesday

suizoku kan (水族館): aquarium

suizō (膵臓): pancreas

sukanjiumu (スカンジウム): scandium

sukeruton (スケルトン): skeleton

sukuea (スクエア): square

sukunai (少ない): few

sukuranburu eggu (スクランブルエッグ): scrambled eggs

sukuryū doraibā (スクリュードライバー): screwdriver

sukurīn (スクリーン): screen

sukurōru bā (スクロールバー): scrollbar

sukuwatto (スクワット): squat

sukyan suru (スキャンする): to scan

sukyanā (スキャナー): scanner

sukāfu (スカーフ): scarf

sukāto (スカート): skirt

sukēto (スケート): skates

sukēto bōdingu (スケートボーディング): skateboarding

sukī (スキー): skiing, ski

sukī ba (スキー場): ski resort

sukī janpu (スキージャンプ): ski jumping

sukī sutokku (スキーストック): ski pole

sukī wea (スキーウェア): ski suit

sukū (救う): to rescue

sukūru basu (スクールバス): school bus

sukūtā (スクーター): motor scooter

sumimasen (すみません): excuse me

sumāto fon (スマートフォン): smartphone

sumūjī (スムージー): smoothie

suna (砂): sand

sunaba (砂場): sandbox

sunakku (スナック): snack

sunea doramu (スネアドラム): snare drum

suneate (すね当て): shinpad

sunīkā (スニーカー): trainers

sunō bōdingu (スノーボーディング): snowboarding

sunō mōbiru (スノーモービル): snowmobile

sunūkā (スヌーカー): snooker

supageti (スパゲティ): spaghetti

supaiku (スパイク): football boots

supana (スパナ): screw wrench

Supein (スペイン): Spain

Supein go (スペイン語): Spanish

suponji (スポンジ): sponge

suppai (酸っぱい): sour

supurinto (スプリント): sprint

supurē (スプレー): spray

supākuringu wain (スパークリングワイン): sparkling wine

supēsu (スペース): space

supēsu shatoru (スペースシャトル): space shuttle

supīdo sukēto (スピードスケート): speed skating

supīkā (スピーカー): loudspeaker

supōtsu burajā (スポーツブラジャー): jogging bra

supōtsu jimu (スポーツジム): gym

supōtsu yōhin ten (スポーツ用品店): sports shop

supūn (スプーン): spoon

surimu (スリム): slim

Surinamu (スリナム): Suriname

surippa (スリッパ): slippers

Suriranka (スリランカ): Sri Lanka

surirā (スリラー): thriller

Surobakia (スロバキア): Slovakia

Surobenia (スロベニア): Slovenia

surību (スリーブ): sleeve

sushi (寿司): sushi

sutaffu (スタッフ): staff

sutanpu (スタンプ): rubber stamp

sutokkingu (ストッキング): stocking

sutoppuuocchi (ストップウオッチ): stopwatch

sutorecchi (ストレッチ): stretching

sutoresu (ストレス): stress

sutoronchiumu (ストロンチウム): strontium

sutorēto (ストレート): straight

sutorēto hea airon (ストレートヘアアイロン): hair straightener

sutorīto fūdo (ストリートフード): street food

sutsūru (スツール): stool

sutēji (ステージ): stage

sutēki (ステーキ): steak

Suwajirando (スワジランド): Swaziland

suwaru (座る): to sit

Suwēden (スウェーデン): Sweden

suzu (錫): tin

suzumebachi (スズメバチ): wasp

sābā (サーバー): server

sāfin (サーフィン): surfing

sāfubōdo (サーフボード): surfboard

sākitto torēningu (サーキットトレーニング): circuit training

sēringu (セーリング): sailing

sētā (セーター): sweater

sōda (ソーダ): soda

sōji ki (掃除機): vacuum cleaner

sōji ki o kakeru (掃除機をかける): to vacuum

sōji suru (掃除する): to clean

sōko (倉庫): warehouse

sōri daijin (総理大臣): prime minister

sōru (ソール): sole

sōryo (僧侶): monk

sōrā paneru (ソーラーパネル): solar panel

sōsharu media (ソーシャルメディア): social media

sō shihai nin (総支配人): general manager

sōshiki (葬式): funeral

sōsēji (ソーセージ): sausage

sōtai sei riron (相対性理論): theory of relativity

sū (吸う): to smoke

Sūdan (スーダン): Sudan

sūdoku (数独): Sudoku

sūgaku (数学): mathematics

sūpa māketto (スーパマーケット): supermarket

sūpu (スープ): soup

sūtsu (スーツ): suit

T

tabako (たばこ): cigarette

tabako (タバコ): tobacco

taberu (食べる): to eat

tabesaseru (食べさせる): to feed

tadashī (正しい): correct

Tai (タイ): Thailand

taida na (怠惰な): lazy

taifū (台風): typhoon

Taihei yō (太平洋): Pacific Ocean

taiiku (体育): physical education

taiji (胎児): foetus, embryo

taijū kei (体重計): scale

taikaku sen (対角線): diagonal

taiki (大気): atmosphere

taimu (タイム): thyme

taion kei (体温計): fever thermometer

taira na (平らな): flat

tairiku (大陸): continent

tairu (タイル): tile

Taisei yō (大西洋): Atlantic Ocean

taiseki (体積): volume

taishi kan (大使館): embassy

taishoku (退職): retirement

taisō (体操): gymnastics

taitei (たいてい): often

Taiwan (台湾): Taiwan

taiya (タイヤ): tyre

taiya ponpu (タイヤポンプ): air pump

taiyō (太陽): sun

Tajikisutan (タジキスタン): Tajikistan

takai (高い): high, expensive

taka sa (高さ): height

takatobi (高跳び): high jump

take (竹): bamboo

taki (滝): waterfall

takkyū (卓球): table tennis

takkyū dai (卓球台): table tennis table

tako (たこ): octopus

takushī (タクシー): taxi

takushī no unten shu (タクシーの運転手 　): taxi driver

tamago (卵): egg

tamanegi (タマネギ): onion

tana (棚): shelf

tanbarin (タンバリン): tambourine

tandemu (タンデム): tandem

tane (種): pit, seed

tango (タンゴ): tango

tangusuten (タングステン): tungsten

tani (谷): valley

tanin (他人): other

tanjō (誕生): birth

tanjōbi (誕生日): birthday

tanjōbikai (誕生日会): birthday party

tannō (胆嚢): gall bladder

tanoshimu (楽しむ): to enjoy

tanpan (短パン): shorts

tanpon (タンポン): tampon

tanpopo (タンポポ): dandelion

tanso (炭素): carbon

tantaru (タンタル): tantalum

tantei (探偵): detective

Tanzania (タンザニア): Tanzania

taoru (タオル): towel

taranchura (タランチュラ): tarantula

tariumu (タリウム): thallium

tashizan (足し算): addition

tasukeru (助ける): to help

tatakau (戦う): to fight

tataku (叩く): to hit

tatsu (立つ): to stand

tatsumaki (竜巻): tornado

tatsunootoshigo (タツノオトシゴ): sea horse

T bakku (Tバック): thong

te (手): hand

tebukuro (手袋): glove

tegami (手紙): letter

teiō sekkai (帝王切開): cesarean

tejō (手錠): handcuff

tekisuto (テキスト): text

tekisuto messēji (テキストメッセージ): text message

tekondō (テコンドー): taekwondo

tekubi (手首): wrist

tekunechiumu (テクネチウム): technetium

tekīra (テキーラ): tequila

te nimotsu (手荷物): carry-on luggage

ten in (店員): shop assistant

tenisu (テニス): tennis

tenisu bōru (テニスボール): tennis ball

tenisu kōto (テニスコート): tennis court

tenisu raketto (テニスラケット): tennis racket

tenjō (天井): ceiling

tenkan (癲癇): epilepsy

Tennō sei (天王星): Uranus

tenohira (手のひら): palm

te nokogiri (手のこぎり): handsaw

tensai (甜菜): sugar beet

tenshi (天使): angel

tenshin (点心): dim sum

tenteki (点滴): infusion

tento (テント): tent

tentō mushi (てんとうむし): ladybird

teoshi sha (手押し車): wheelbarrow

terasu (テラス): terrace

terebi (テレビ): TV

terebi jushin yō antena (テレビ受信用アンテナ): satellite dish

terebi setto (テレビセット): TV set

terubiumu (テルビウム): terbium

teruru (テルル): tellurium

tetorisu (テトリス): Tetris

tetsu (鉄): iron

tetsudatte kuremasu ka (手伝ってくれますか？): Can you help me?

tetsugaku (哲学): philosophy

tisshu pēpā (ティッシュペーパー): tissue

to (と): and

tobikomi kyōgi (飛込競技): diving

tobu (跳ぶ): to jump

tobu (飛ぶ): to fly

todokeru (届ける): to deliver

toire (トイレ): toilet

toire burashi (トイレブラシ): toilet brush

toirettopēpā (トイレットペーパー): toilet paper

toire wa doko desu ka (トイレはどこですか？): Where is the toilet?

toire yō surippa (トイレ用スリッパ): bathroom slippers

tokage (トカゲ): lizard

tokei (時計): clock

tomato (トマト): tomato

tomato sōsu (トマトソース): tomato sauce

tomodachi (友達): friend

ton (トン): ton

tonbo (とんぼ): dragonfly

Tonga (トンガ): Tonga

tora (虎): tiger

toraianguru (トライアングル): triangle

toraiasuron (トライアスロン): triathlon

torakku (トラック): lorry

torakku no unten shu (トラックの運転手): lorry driver

torakku rēsu (トラックレース): track cycling

torakutā (トラクター): tractor

toranku (トランク): rear trunk

toranpetto (トランペット): trumpet

toranporin (トランポリン): trampoline

toranshībā (トランシーバー): walkie-talkie

toreddomiru (トレッドミル): treadmill

Torinidādotobago (トリニダードトバゴ): Trinidad and Tobago

toriumu (トリウム): thorium

toronbōn (トロンボーン): trombone

toru (取る): to take

Toruko (トルコ): Turkey

Torukumenisutan (トルクメニスタン): Turkmenistan

toryufu (トリュフ): truffle

torērā (トレーラー): trailer

toshi (年): year

toshiyori (年寄り): old

tosho kan (図書館): library

totsuzen (突然): suddenly

tottemo (とっても): very

tozan (登山): mountaineering

tsuba o haku (唾を吐く): to spit

Tsubaru (ツバル): Tuvalu

tsuchi (土): soil

tsuchi de utsu (槌で打つ): to hammer

tsuikotsu (椎骨): vertebra

tsukareta (疲れた): tired

tsukeru (つける): to turn on

tsuki (月): month, moon

tsukue (机): desk

tsuma (妻): wife

tsumaranai (つまらない): boring

tsumasaki (つま先): toe

tsume (爪): fingernail

tsumekire hasami (爪切ハサミ): nail scissors

tsumekiri (爪切り): nail clipper

tsumemono (詰め物): dental filling

tsumeyasuri (爪やすり): nail file

tsumitate (積み立て): savings

tsunami (津波): tidal wave

tsurai (辛い): hot

tsuriumu (ツリウム): thulium

tsuru (釣る): to fish

tsurī hausu (ツリーハウス): tree house

tsuyoi (強い): strong

tsuā gaido (ツアーガイド): tour guide

tsūgaku kaban (通学鞄): schoolbag

tsūkō ryōkin (通行料金): toll

tsūro gawa (通路側): aisle

tāru (タール): tar
tēburu (テーブル): table
tēburukurosu (テーブルクロス): tablecloth
tēma pāku (テーマパーク): theme park
tēruraito (テールライト): rear light
tērā (テーラー): tailor
tīpotto (ティーポット): teapot
tī shatsu (Tシャツ): T-shirt
tōbu (頭部): head
tōbu gaishō (頭部外傷): head injury
tōchaku (到着): arrival
tōdai (灯台): lighthouse
tōfu (豆腐): tofu
tōgarashi (唐辛子): chili
Tōgo (トーゴ): Togo
tōhyō suru (投票する): to vote
tōi (遠い): far
tōki (陶器): pottery
tōmorokoshi (トウモロコシ): corn
tōnyō byō (糖尿病): diabetes
tōnyū (豆乳): soy milk
tōshi (投資): investment
tōsutā (トースター): toaster
tōten (読点): comma
tōyaku ryō (投薬量): dosage

U

uchū fuku (宇宙服): space suit
uchū sutēshon (宇宙ステーション): space station
ude (腕): arm
udetate fuse (腕立て伏せ): push-up
ude tokei (腕時計): watch
ue (上): above
uedingu doresu (ウエディングドレス): wedding dress
uedingu kēki (ウエディングケーキ): wedding cake
uesuto (ウエスト): waist
uetto sūtsu (ウエットスーツ): wetsuit
Uganda (ウガンダ): Uganda
uindosāfin (ウインドサーフィン): windsurfing
uingu (ウイング): wing
uisukī (ウイスキー): whiskey
uketsuke kakari (受付係): receptionist
Ukuraina (ウクライナ): Ukraine
ukurere (ウクレレ): ukulele
uma (馬): horse
ume (梅): plum
umi (海): sea
unchin (運賃): fare
undō gi (運動着): tracksuit
undō jō (運動場): sports ground

uoichiba (魚市場): fish market

uran (ウラン): uranium

ureshī (嬉しい): happy

urin (雨林): rainforest

URL (URL): url

uru (売る): to sell

uru/eru (得る): to earn

Uruguai (ウルグアイ): Uruguay

urusai (うるさい): loud

usagi (うさぎ): rabbit

USB memorī (USBメモリー): USB stick

ushi (牛): cow

ushiro (後ろ): back

usugata terebi (薄型テレビ): flat screen

utau (歌う): to sing

utsu (撃つ): to shoot

utsukushī (美しい): beautiful

Uzubekisutan (ウズベキスタン): Uzbekistan

uōmu appu (ウオームアップ): warm-up

W

waffuru (ワッフル): waffle

wa gomu (輪ゴム): rubber band

wain (ワイン): wine

waipā (ワイパー): windscreen wiper

waiyā (ワイヤー): wire

wakai (若い): young

wakarimasen (分かりません): I don't understand

wakeau (分け合う): to share

wakusei (惑星): planet

wani (ワニ): crocodile

warau (笑う): to laugh

warizan (割り算): division

warui (悪い): bad

warutsu (ワルツ): waltz

washi (鷲): eagle

watagashi (綿菓子): candy floss

watakushi no koto ga suki desu ka (私のことが好きですか？): Do you love me?

watashi (私): I

watashi no inu (私の犬): my dog

watashi tachi (私達): we

watashitachi no ie (私達の家): our home

watto (ワット): watt

webu kamu (ウェブカム): webcam

webusaito (ウェブサイト): website

weitā (ウェイター): waiter

Werinton būtsu (ウェリントンブーツ): wellington boots

winna warutsu (ウィンナワルツ): Viennese waltz

wirusu (ウィルス): virus

wokka (ウォッカ): vodka

wōtā suraidā (ウォータースライダー): water slide

Y

yagi (ヤギ): goat

yakan (やかん): kettle

yakedo (火傷): burn

yakisoba (焼きそば): fried noodles

yakkyoku (薬局): pharmacy

yaku (焼く): to burn, to bake

yakuzai shi (薬剤師): pharmacist

yakyū (野球): baseball

yama (山): mountain

yamome (やもめ): widower

yamori (やもり): gecko

yanagi (柳): willow

yane (屋根): roof

yanegawara (屋根瓦): roof tile

yaneura heya (屋根裏部屋): attic

yarinage (槍投げ): javelin throw

yaseru (痩せる): to lose weight

yashi (椰子): palm tree

yasui (安い): cheap

yasuri (やすり): file

yawarakai (柔らかい): soft

yobirin (呼び鈴): bell

yodare kake (よだれ掛け): bib

yoga (ヨガ): yoga

yoi (良い): good

yoko (横): beside

yokohaba (横幅): width

yoko ni naru (横になる): to lie

yokubukai (欲深い): greedy

yokusō (浴槽): bathtub

yome (嫁): daughter-in-law

yomu (読む): to read

yonjū go fun (四十五分): three quarters of an hour

yopparatte iru (酔っぱらっている): drunk

yori mo sukunai (よりも少ない): less

yoru (夜): night

Yorudan (ヨルダン): Jordan

yotto (ヨット): yacht

yowai (弱い): weak

yoyaku (予約): reservation, booking, appointment

yubi (指): finger

yubiwa (指輪): ring

yuderu (茹でる): to boil

yudeta (ゆでた): boiled

yudetamago (ゆで卵): boiled egg

yuigon sho (遺言書): testament

yuka (床): floor

yuki (雪): snow

yume o miru (夢をみる): to dream

yusei toryō (油性塗料): oil paint

yu tanpo (湯たんぽ): hot-water bottle

yā (やあ): hi

yādo (ヤード): yard

yōchi en (幼稚園): kindergarten

yōfuku saizu (洋服サイズ): dress size

yōgan (溶岩): lava

yōgi sha (容疑者): suspect

yōguruto (ヨーグルト): yoghurt

yōji (幼児): infant

yō koso (ようこそ): welcome

yōniku (羊肉): lamb

yōso (ヨウ素): iodine

yūbin bangō (郵便番号): zip code

yūbin haitatsu nin (郵便配達人): postman

yūbin kyoku (郵便局): post office

yūen chi (遊園地): fairground

yūgata (夕方): evening

yūkan na (勇敢な): brave

yūkari (ユーカリ): eucalyptus

yūro (ユーロ): euro

yūropiumu (ユーロピウム): europium

yūzai na (有罪な): guilty

Z

Zanbia (ザンビア): Zambia

zasshi (雑誌): magazine

zassō (雑草): weed

zeikin (税金): tax

zenritsu sen (前立腺): prostate

zensai (前菜): starter

zensoku (喘息): asthma

zetsuen tēpu (絶縁テープ): insulating tape

zubon (ズボン): trousers

zugaikotsu (頭蓋骨): skull

zukkīni (ズッキーニ): courgette

zutsū (頭痛): migraine, headache

zō (象): elephant

@

ācherī (アーチェリー): archery

āmondo (アーモンド): almond

ātichōku (アーティチョーク): artichoke

ātisuto (アーティスト): artist

īsuto (イースト): yeast

īsutā (イースター): Easter

Ōsutoraria (オーストラリア): Australia

Ōsutoria (オーストリア): Austria

ōboe (オーボエ): oboe

ōbun (オーブン): oven

ōdan hodō (横断歩道): pedestrian crossing

ōdōri (大通り): avenue

ōi (多い): many

ōkakumaku (横隔膜): diaphragm

ōkami (狼): wolf

ōkesutora (オーケストラ): orchestra

ōkina (大きな): big

ōmu (オウム): parrot

ōrora (オーロラ): aurora

ōsutorarian futtobōru (オーストラリアンフットボール): Australian football

ōtobai rēsu (オートバイレース): motorcycle racing

ōtomachikku (オートマチック): automatic

ōto mugi (オート麦): oat

ōtomīru (オートミール): oatmeal

ūru (ウール): wool

Printed in Great Britain
by Amazon

74500292R00139